'A detailed, deeply disturbing look at how the Bush administration makes policy . . . The main virtue of *The Price of Loyalty* is what it tells us about the administration's values and mode of operation . . . What emerges from Suskind's book is a picture of an entirely cynical administration – much more cynical than Nixon's'
The New York Review of Books

'The most explosive book of the year'
Esquire

'Compelling . . . Disturbing . . . Revelatory . . .
[An] extraordinary inside account'
Los Angeles Times

'Offers enough inside information to be a damning read'
The New Yorker

'An invaluable contribution both to the historical record and to the fierce public debate over the nature of the Bush administration's true views and motivations on issues of war and peace . . . What is most devastating is the textured insider portrait of the top Bush players bringing their ideological and partisan agenda to every issue of public policy'
The New York Times

'Paints a devastatingly detailed picture of an ideological president whose extreme tendencies are exacerbated by the group of yes-men advisers who surround him . . . A valuable and rare glimpse into how the country is run'
Seattle Times

'In a nutshell, Pulitzer Prize-winning journalist Ron Suskind has written an invaluable history . . . *The Price of Loyalty* is closing in on the Bible as a font of familiar sayings'
Boston Globe

ALSO BY RON SUSKIND

A Hope in the Unseen:
An American Odyssey from the Inner City
to the Ivy League

THE PRICE OF LOYALTY

RON SUSKIND

FREE PRESS

First published in the United States by Simon & Schuster Inc, 2004
First published in Great Britain by Simon & Schuster UK Ltd, 2004
This edition published by The Free Press, 2004
An imprint of Simon & Schuster UK Ltd
A Viacom Company

Designed by Ellen Sasahara

1 3 5 7 9 10 8 6 4 2

Simon & Schuster UK Ltd
Africa House
64–78 Kingsway
London WC2B 6AH

www.simonsays.co.uk

Simon & Schuster Australia
Sydney

A CIP catalogue record for this book is available from the British Library

ISBN 0-7434-9555-1

Printed and bound in Great Britain by
Bookmarque Ltd, Croydon, Surrey

AUTHOR'S NOTE

This is a work of narrative nonfiction, a form of writing about real events and people that relies on the power of story. The idea is that the telling of stories—now, just as ten thousand years ago around the fire—helps us make sense of ourselves and our world.

In this case, however, I think it is important for readers to be offered a glimpse of the machinery at work beneath the flow of episode, incident, and dialogue.

When this project officially began in February 2003, I was heartened, though not surprised, to find that Paul O'Neill had a striking view of the value of secrecy—*that it had almost no value*. We both happened to have read a 1998 book by Daniel Patrick Moynihan, a friend and mentor to O'Neill, who wrote that twenty years on the Senate Select Committee on Intelligence had taught him a single, sterling lesson: The threat to our national security is not from secrets revealed, it's from bad analysis. O'Neill, with his affinity for assessing how process leads to outcome, often cited the separation of information into silos—guarded as core assets by self-interested players—as one of the great obstacles to managing the huge, unwieldy American government. It has created an acute need for particularly skillful integrators—those who can move freely among silos, pick and choose, and form connections to create a fabric of shared purpose.

With his extraordinary access to the President and so many silos of both domestic and foreign affairs, O'Neill was a well-positioned integrator—one of the few in this administration. It was an involvement that, in the end, nourished his insights and conclusions about the larger struggles—of policy versus politics and ideology versus analysis—that define this presidency and its role in the world.

The founding idea of this book is to grant readers a similar vantage point so they, too, can draw their own conclusions. O'Neill agreed to this experiment in transparency and carried it through with his usual ardor. In February, he answered my request for his schedule with an extraordinary document. From the moment he was sworn into office to the final hour when he drove his car past the line of applauding staffers, each day is cataloged. There are 7,630 entries in the schedule, collected at the end of each day, including each meeting, those in attendance, the location, and the time—and a listing of every phone call, including who called whom and the length of the conversation.

That was just the start. In March, O'Neill approached his former colleagues at the Treasury Department for what he insisted was his due: copies of every document that had crossed his desk. One day, as he was leaving Washington for Pittsburgh, he passed me a few unopened CD-ROMs. "This is what they gave me," he said. When I started to open the disks, I wondered if there was an error on my hard drive: nineteen thousand documents were listed. They are image files, meaning that every document sent to O'Neill was xeroxed. Those images—an essential rendering of his two years as secretary—capture the activities of the full breadth of the U.S. government. They stretch from memoranda to the President to hand-scribbled thank-you notes, from minutes of meetings to hundred-page reports.

In March, I hired Alan Wirzbicki, a 2002 graduate of Harvard University and the former president of the *Harvard Crimson* as my assistant. He is a young man of capacious intellectual gifts and true grit. He dove into the documents—reading, categorizing, and filing each document in a retrievable format—and then began the process of assessing the worth of each. He also reported scenes for the book, analyzed a sweeping array of domestic and foreign issues, and worked, often, around the clock. His discretion, expertly honed, somehow, at the tender age of twenty-three, was invaluable. I could not have done this book without him.

I also benefitted from the assistance of countless people in the administration, from cabinet-level officials to executive assistants, who were cooperative. Many spoke off the record—this was not a project, God knows, that was sanctioned by the administration. Others, however, spoke openly, encouraged, in many instances, by O'Neill's example. As Bono said in a chat we had in November, "O'Neill is amazingly loyal—an old-fashioned thing, really—and he inspires great loyalty in others. That's because he looks at you as an equal; there's no arrogance there. He just wants to know what you're thinking—and he really listens." The people who are loyal to O'Neill or to the ideal of transparency—and its corollary, informed consent of the governed—granted hundreds of hours of their precious time for interviews, offered notes from meetings, and unearthed illuminating recollections. Scenes were checked from many viewpoints. Dialogue was vetted by all sides. Documents, in an administration that has worked so fiercely to control what information becomes public, speak volumes.

Finally, there is O'Neill himself. He has a stunning capacity to remember fine detail and broad stroke. He kept pads of personal notes, written in his speedy script, along with his own special files of papers and letters. And, as important as any document, any scrap of paper, is something that readers will notice on countless pages—his openness to describe what he felt day by day, moment by moment, including his doubts and frustrations and fears. This trust in honesty and disclosure is a virtue that animates every page of the book.

Which is why I let him read the finished manuscript to check for strictly factual errors. The few he spotted were corrected. His commitment to the accuracy of this book matches my own.

For Walter and Owen, my inspiration

Contents

Total loyalty is possible only when fidelity is emptied of all concrete content, from which changes of mind might naturally arise.

—HANNAH ARENDT

The PRICE of LOYALTY

CHAPTER 1

FIRST APPOINTMENT

PAUL O'NEILL LOOKED UP from his legal pad and out the window of USAir Flight 991 from Pittsburgh as it made a panoramic descent into Washington's Reagan National Airport.

God knows how many times he'd traveled this northwesterly arc high across the Potomac, an ideal angle to glimpse the Mall's Elysian symmetry of white marble and green expanse from the Capitol dome to Lincoln's Memorial. It still thrilled him, this confected balance, as it had when he arrived as a young, working-class kid, with a wife, two babies, an economics degree from unremarkable Fresno State College, and a few years working as a self-taught engineer. He'd landed a job working in the Veterans Administration by filling out an application for federal internships he'd picked up at the post office. Three hundred thousand applicants went on to take a federal standardized test. Three thousand were summoned for an oral review, where they were interviewed in groups of ten. Three hundred were offered jobs. It was 1961. Kennedy was President. The start of everything, really.

Now, thirty-nine years later, he had reasons, good ones, why he shouldn't come back. They were on the yellow legal pad, neatly lined and spaced, resting on the tray table. He checked it one last time, a list that covered three handwritten pages, then considered what had been said thus far and what would be expected of him in a few hours at his first meeting with the President-elect.

His old friend Richard Cheney—quiet, poker-faced Dick—had done almost all the talking thus far, starting with a mid-November call to Paul's cubicle at Alcoa's headquarters in Pittsburgh. The call was courteous and cool, like Dick. Always holding something back, making you wonder about the interior workings. He'd known the in-scrutable westerner since the Nixon days, when O'Neill was assistant director of the newly created Office of Management and Budget (OMB)—a senior management team, of sorts, that Richard Nixon created to solve a growing crisis of scale: the increasing inability of one elected man to make so many complex decisions in a responsible way.

OMB became the stop-and-think shop, where all major issues were studied and distilled into briefs about choices and conse-quences for the President. It was the spot to be, and O'Neill—nearly a decade in the government at that point—was a rising young man of his day, a budget wizard who became a deep driller on what was known and knowable in a wide array of policies. Dick Cheney was a twenty-eight-year-old Ph.D. student brought into the Office of Economic Opportunity—a policy sidecar headed by an ambitious ex-congressman named Donald Rumsfeld—which was charged with carrying forward Lyndon Johnson's War on Poverty. Rumsfeld, as a department head, was someone an OMB honcho like O'Neill regu-larly dealt with, and Dick was always at Don's side. A few years later, when everyone had moved up—Rumsfeld to chief of staff under Gerald Ford, with Dick as his deputy (Cheney took the top staff job when Rumsfeld became Secretary of Defense)—Dick started intro-ducing Paul, then OMB's deputy director, as "the smartest guy I know." Still did, or at least so Paul had heard from a few of their mu-tual friends—they had about a thousand of those.

That first call was just a "heads-up." Speculation had swirled in the press about O'Neill being tapped for OMB director, for Commerce Secretary, or—in a late October column by *The New York Times*'s William Safire—for Secretary of Defense. As someone who'd met George W. Bush—although only in passing, and although he'd never contributed to the campaign—O'Neill had managed to surface on plenty of lists. He was viewed as a favorite of the former President Bush, as a serious policy innovator among traditional Republicans, and as someone George W. Bush would need at his side, in some capacity, if he were to become President. That last issue was very much in question in mid-November 2000, as the Florida election results were still in dispute, but Dick wanted to lay down a marker.

"I don't know how this all will sort out, Paul, but you're at the top of our list," Dick had said on the phone.

"That's very flattering, Dick, but I don't think I want to go back to the government."

Dick pressed on, talking in general terms about Commerce or OMB and the challenge of getting talented people to serve. Paul let that sink in for moment and then said, "No, I don't think so, Dick. But thanks."

Three weeks later, the Supreme Court granted certiorari in the case of *Bush* v. *Gore*. The justices announced on Saturday, December 9, that they would examine the previous day's ruling by the Florida Supreme Court, which had mandated a manual recount of all ballots cast in the state. The Florida ruling had been a reprieve for the Democrats, the restart of a process that they were sure would level the playing field, with oral arguments on recount procedures scheduled for Monday. But the Supreme Court's Saturday halt to the recount—essentially taking the issue away from Florida's courts—shifted the betting line from even money to advantage Bush.

The next afternoon, Sunday, Paul was watching his beloved Pittsburgh Steelers lose 30–10 to the New York Giants, effectively knocking the hometown team out of the playoffs. The phone rang. He jumped up, grabbed it in the kitchen. Dick again.

"Soon I may have to call you Mr. Vice President."

"Maybe so, Paul. We've got our fingers crossed."

Fine, on to business.

"We really need you here in Washington."

"Dick, I'm really not interested."

Then he heard what he thought was Dick's suppressed, Sydney Greenstreet snigger. "You need to let me tell you it's Treasury."

Paul smiled. He could hear Dick smiling on the other end of the phone line. Yes, Treasury is the oldest—the first appointment made by George Washington himself—and the most venerable of the cabinet offices. It was and is a public trust, literally. Alexander Hamilton, one of the great geniuses of his era, sat in the chair first, a special chair.

"Well, yes, I suppose Treasury is a little different. I'll concede that." He paused a moment. "Okay, I suppose we can at least talk about Treasury."

"We'll be in touch," Dick said.

Paul hung up the phone and walked back into the living room. His wife, Nancy—levelheaded, resilient Nancy—was on the couch, looking hard at him. The novel she'd been engrossed in was closed on her lap.

"My God, Paul. We are not really going to do this!" she said. "You always said you're not going back there."

"Don't worry, we're not," O'Neill said, and sat back down in the lounge chair. "Don't worry." He flipped to CNBC. He could feel Nancy still staring at him. He had been excited to hear Dick's voice—he was sure she could pick that up, even from a room away. It was flattering, after all, to be asked. Especially about something as august as Treasury.

"Right," she said more softly, after a moment. "Hurry up and get down here so everyone can kick you around. Everything has become so nasty down there now. Come on, honey. You're not a politician. You know what it'd be like."

After forty-five years of marriage, they both knew everything. They'd been together, after all, since they were eighteen. Grew up together. A pair of small-town kids, made good. Paul was never the kind of American achiever who believed he was evolving, anxious thereby to match each success with *fresh start* accoutrements like new wives and dazzling possessions. Neither of them, in fact, felt they'd changed all that much since she saw him walk into her English class senior year at Anchorage High School in Alaska, the new boy who lived out on the military base. Yes, she'd since read press clippings that said he was God's gift to corporate America, or a messiah of good government, but to her he was just Paul, gentle, quirky, polite, loyal to a fault when that loyalty is earned, and if he were a garbage collector or doing construction in Alaska—his career choice before he chanced into the Claremont, California, Post Office—she'd still be at his side.

Not that there hadn't been struggles, as in any marriage, and, God knows, sacrifices. Plenty on Nancy's end. During the sixteen years in Washington—most of their first two decades together—she raised their three daughters and son by herself. Paul worked nearly seven days a week, seventeen hours a day, at a salary that went from subsistence to barely adequate. At the beginning, they couldn't even afford a phone. She made the kids' clothing herself. He loved to work; some men do. As he hit his stride in those seven years at OMB, he worked every day but Christmas and a short summer vacation. Things changed a bit after Gerald Ford lost and Paul took an executive job in 1977 at International Paper Company in New York City—at least there was money. That helped some; they started to enjoy a few of the rewards. Pittsburgh, though, had been their best stop: thirteen years at Alcoa, where Nancy built a life around Paul's blossoming success—scores of friends, leading roles in the community for them both—even while his days were still long, scheduled to the minute, and took him out of town, on average, once or twice a week. It was an extraordinary run, a legendary turnaround: a battered and beaten Aluminum Company of America went from $1.1 million in earnings, on sales of $8 billion, when Paul took over in 1987, to $1.5 billion in earnings, on sales of $23 billion in 2000, a year when Alcoa—now the world's largest aluminum producer—was the New York Stock Exchange's best-performing stock. Clean victories on every front. And soon, he'd go out on top. He had passed the CEO's job on to his handpicked successor in 1999. As for the chairmanship, he was due to retire at the end of this very month.

Just twenty-one days! There were already plans galore, curtain-raisers on a long-awaited valedictory chapter of their lives, with $60 million in the bank and, soon, all the time in the world. In an office nook off the kitchen, Nancy had a folder with maps and brochures for a once-in-a-lifetime journey across America, just the two of them. They were going to spend months driving across America's back roads. Paul had even picked out the car. They'd drive the blue highways in a Bentley.

Nancy turned back to her novel. Paul switched to football highlights. He's not going to do it, she thought to herself. *He just wouldn't.*

A week later, Paul silently gathered papers and his briefcase and slipped into his black cashmere overcoat on a snowy, dark Monday morning. He's an early riser, up at 5 a.m. most days and gone by 6. Nancy will usually sleep to a sane hour, seven o'clock or so. But not this morning.

She appeared in her pink satin bathrobe, her bare feet lightly clapping across the kitchen's Italian tile floor.

He turned, surprised.

"You're up early."

"I wanted to see you off."

Of course, Paul could figure out why she was padding about in darkness. "Listen, I'm just going down there to talk about it. It's a joint decision. We'll decide together."

She knew this was trouble. He was going to see Dick and the President-elect. They'd be persuasive. They'd say whatever he wanted to hear.

"Don't you go down there and tell them you're going to do it."

"Don't worry." He kissed her. "You know me better than that."

. . .

A LIGHT RAIN fell in Washington on December 18, 2000, President-elect George W. Bush's first morning in Washington. The dam of Florida press conferences and hanging chads, a prim, pained Supreme Court ruling, and an Al Gore concession of unexpected grace was beginning to recede beneath a quotidian tide of news cycles.

Every hour was being covered as an event, as an onrushing measure of forward motion. The President-elect's first date, at 8 a.m., was an hour-long breakfast meeting with Federal Reserve chairman Alan Greenspan at the Madison Hotel—about five blocks from the White House—where Bush was staying in a suite and holding court. It was followed by a brief press advisory at the hotel, where he said, "I talked with a good man right here." He then turned to Mr. Greenspan and patted him on the shoulder. "We had a very strong discussion about my confidence in his abilities."

Next stop, Capitol Hill, for a two-and-a-half-hour meeting with congressional leaders from each party, followed by a press availability in a chandeliered, wood-paneled, squash court–size room on the second floor of the Capitol. The President-elect stood on a threadbare Oriental rug beneath a life-size painting of George Washington and spoke like a therapist after a successful session.

"I made my rounds to the leaders here on the Hill," Bush said, standing shoulder to shoulder with his four conferees of midmorning: Senate Majority Leader Trent Lott and Senate Minority Leader Tom Daschle; House Speaker Dennis Hastert and House Minority Leader Richard Gephardt, a barbershop quartet of bipartisanship. "I want to thank all four for their hospitality and their gracious reception of the newly elected President. I made it clear to each that I come to Washington with the intention of doing the people's business, that I look forward to listening and occasionally talking, to work with both the Republicans and the Democrats."

Bush paused and looked side to side, as though he might call for a group hug.

"I told all four that I felt like this election happened for a reason"—reporters hung on the word "reason," a natural segue to the thing they were waiting for: an assessment of how the brokered, litigated presidential election would now define the act of governing—"that it pointed out the delay in the outcome. It should make it clear to all of us that we can come together to heal whatever wounds may exist, whatever residuals there may be."

Bush dodged it—the what-exactly-*is*-my-mandate-now issue—but this "heal whatever wounds may exist" line, it was instantly clear, would be the day's lead quotation on television and radio and in tomorrow's newspapers.

"I told all four that there are going to be some times where we don't agree with each other, but that's okay. If this were a dictatorship, it would be a heck of a lot easier, just so long as I'm the dictator."

That capped it: a startling turn of self-deprecation and bluster from a man who shrugged at questions of his legitimacy. The disputed, dead-heat election of 2000—concluding a presidential contest in which both candidates sanded off their sharp edges in a race for the political center—had finally delivered a historically half-hearted mandate: a charge that solutions in the coming months, of whatever shape or color, were expected to be unearthed from middle ground. A fifty-fifty split in the Senate, a modest, nine-vote Republican advantage in the House, and a President who assumed office after losing the popular vote meant that the public's grant of power was almost legally conditioned on the centrist ideal. The President, after all, is the principal elected representative of all the people. The vox populi, in sum, spelled middle.

The only dissonant chord was at that point barely audible, a comment the day before by Dick Cheney on CBS's *Face the Nation:* "As President-elect Bush has made very clear, he ran on a particular platform that was very carefully developed; it's his program and it's his agenda and we have no intention at all of backing off of it. . . . The suggestion that somehow, because this was a close election, we should fundamentally change our beliefs I just think is silly."

To be sure, that was a kind of pregame interview, the day before George W. Bush arrived in town. When the President-elect spoke this morning, backed by congressional leaders of both parties, it carried the weight of authority. A commitment to the humble search for common ground.

After fielding a few questions from reporters, Bush gazed at the bipartisan assemblage and said, somewhat dreamily, "It's amazing what happens when you listen to the other person's opinion. And we began the process of doing that today."

· · ·

THIS ECUMENICAL IDEAL—as of this morning, duly noted across America by mildly engaged voters, seasoned talk-show pundits, and dispirited ideologues of both parties—informed O'Neill's midmorning cab ride into the buzzing Capitol. It gave him confidence that it was worth seriously investigating whether the rest of his life ought to start with a return to Washington.

O'Neill was a believer in the middle ground. Not in compromise, so much. Or horse trading. He was never much on any of that. It was the fresh, unaffiliated idea that enlivened him. Across four decades of search and study in and near government, he was sure he'd spotted a staid, stoic truth beneath the heat lightning of political rhetoric: that on matters of policy there are answers—right answers—that eventually assert their primacy over political posturing. These right answers fall indiscriminately, here and there, along the left/right political axis, or create new territory not yet charted. An idea's first conceptual mold tends to form through plodding rigor, from a clear-eyed examination of available evidence and an open-minded—and sometimes humbling—assessment of opposing views. Fierce, frank dialogue commences; choices and consequences take shape. And, if everyone is honest about what they all know—and about what they've learned in this roiling process—an answer, a best remedy, emerges. Illusion will have its moment, but there is, in fact, a discernible underlying reality. It may take a while, but in the end that reality becomes visible and undeniable. In the end, it's all about process, O'Neill believed. Trust process and the ends take care of themselves.

Washington was ruled at this moment by a pragmatic, multi-sectarian community. Among the array of denominations—from battle-fatigued former radicals to fresh-faced seekers of "third way" innovations to tough-minded brokers who believed in cutting "a fair deal for all" and then breaking for cocktails—a true believer in the old church orthodoxy of *good process* would be viewed with a wary good humor, like a circuit-riding preacher who'd stir things up but be gone by morning. Mostly, though, O'Neill was granted that funny-hat catchall "maverick"—for someone who has a passport to various camps but doesn't neatly fit anywhere.

The pragmatists had been in charge, for the most part, since the end of Ronald Reagan's first term, when the reality of deficits began to temper Reagan's ideological zeal on tax cuts. Reagan—like the liberal Democrat Senator Paul Wellstone or the conservative Speaker of the House Newt Gingrich or the anti-tax activist Grover Norquist—was widely considered to be part of a surrounding army: the ideologues, animated by a sweeping philosophy and the ideas that happen to support it. Such men are not inclined to seek a middle ground so much as build a fortress at one pole or the other, hoping to create a place that will attract adherents until the midpoint, wherever it came to rest, ended up in their front yard. Only they, the ideologues attest, are truly driven by ideas. Big ideas that tend to explain history and human behavior and the way things are. They tend to stick with their own, find information that supports a wider view. As for their view of pragmatists, a succinct summation was first uttered in frustration by Representative Dick Armey of Texas in the late eighties, when Republicans were the long-standing minority in Congress. Fatigued from being enticed into conference, time and again, by the Democratic majority and leaving with little to show, Armey murmured that such encounters were not love, not sex, and not natural. "Bipartisanship," he was overheard saying, "is another name for date rape." Now, the same "date rape" line had been embraced by ideologues-in-waiting, like Norquist, in a boast about how the new one-party government would be able to have its way. The consensus, though, was that neither party would have a clear advantage. And, in the central focus of O'Neill's coming engagement—economic policy—a sanctuary had been well mapped. Fiscal prudence, once the province of Republicans, had been thoroughly colonized in the 1990s by Clinton Democrats. Now, everyone stood, somewhat uncomfortably, on this slender territory.

It was a peace won through sacrifice, starting with the price paid by George H. W. Bush, who had grown larger over the last decade in the eyes of the pragmatists. O'Neill had been a friend of the senior Bush since they had spent significant time together in the Ford administration. Bush was director of the Central Intelligence Agency, and O'Neill worked with him to implement harsh, post-Watergate sanctions recommended by the commission chaired by Nelson Rockefeller—and still preserve the agency's effectiveness. It was a tough task, and largely unsuccessful. But O'Neill was impressed by Bush. He was just back from being head of the U.S. Liaison Office to China, where he "dove completely into the task of understanding China, of mastering the intricacies of this new relationship . . . he was, fairly quickly, a top-drawer internationalist," O'Neill said, looking back. "He was more inquisitive than he at first appeared. He not only wanted to know what you thought, he needed to know how you got there." They instantly clicked: two men who share a thoroughgoing, set-your-course-and-follow-through style, both note writers. They stayed in touch from that point forward.

Just after Bush was elected in 1988, the new administration approached O'Neill to consider the job of Secretary of Defense. O'Neill had just started at Alcoa—he said he couldn't leave so soon—and recommended his old friend Cheney, who ended up with the job. President Bush soon convinced O'Neill to chair an advisory group on education that included Lamar Alexander and Bill Brock, moderate Republican heavyweights of that era, and Richard Riley, who would eventually be Clinton's Education Secretary. In large measure, though, it was an excuse to get O'Neill to Washington to talk about a wider array of issues. They met several times to discuss foreign affairs, military preparedness, health care, and the economy. O'Neill was part of the group of pragmatists, including domestic policy chief Roger Porter and OMB director Richard Darman, who believed the President should break his "Read my lips" pledge against raising taxes and halt the growth of deficits. He did, of course, suffering what may have been a fatal political wound.

The ideologues' view was that Bush should have tried harder to trim spending and shrink deficits. They say he was timid, when he needed to be firm, that he second-guessed himself after listening to the counsel of "honorable men," like those Mark Antony mocked at Caesar's funeral. Bush broke with Reagan's bold, winning mandate, they said, and got little in return. He received no credit from the Democrats for this step in their direction and drew the ire of core Republican constituencies, who felt abandoned by this shift and stayed home on election day. Their case lacked evidence, moderate Republicans countered, asserting that Bush would have prospered in the 1992 election by moving even more forcefully, and candidly, toward the political center. The former President, confusing the issue further, said in his convention speech in 1992 that he regretted breaking his pledge, but then, in interviews after he left office, appeared to backtrack from that apology.

An array of mavericks and hard-nut pragmatists—such as O'Neill, Greenspan, former senators Sam Nunn of Georgia and Warren Rudman of New Hampshire, members of the centrist Concord Coalition, and most of the men around the first Bush—saw the broken pledge and its aftermath as vindication: proof positive of how "right answers" can germinate and grow, even on a dry, partisan terrain. They said that by repealing a portion of Reagan's tax reductions, President Bush saved his predecessor's core principle and made it work effectively, much as Nixon—another hero of the policy pragmatists—is credited for smartly honing and targeting some of Johnson's liberal initiatives. More important, Bush started the government on a path of fiscal prudence. That meant not just talking about the virtues of a balanced budget but taking a courageous, *rather-right-than-reelected* stand, especially after the irresistible promise of supply-side economics—that tax cuts would create economic growth that would boost tax revenues and eventually shrink deficits—was shown to be hollow.

Because Bush acted against type by not defending the ideology of tax cuts, he gave Bill Clinton an opportunity (or "permission," Republicans like to say) to do the same with his mirror-image dilemma.

Rather than carrying on as a so-called tax-and-spend Democrat, President Clinton became a fiscal hawk, often suffering the ire of the left. In the late nineties, the federal budgets came into balance and then showed surplus. Interest rates dropped and it became clear, year by year, that receding federal deficits were a prime reason. Income that once went to interest payments became found money in countless kitchens and corporate suites. Debt became cheap. The equities markets surged, lifted on the clasped hands of productivity gains from technological innovation and a historically low cost of capital. The economy grew an average of 3.8 percent a year between 1996 and 2000.

To be sure, some of this might have happened no matter who was in the White House. But, across a decade of often angry partisanship, an *answer* somehow took shape: Fiscal prudence works. A balanced budget means that the government won't be out borrowing billions and, thereby, driving up interest rates. What's more, long-term rates started to be reined downward toward short-term rates, which the Federal Reserve controls with the discount rate and federal funds rate that it charges banks.

As Greenspan advised, and Clinton acknowledged, as far back as 1992, sellers of long-term debt tucked a significant premium, a safety cushion, of several points into interest rates, because of their bleak certainty that ongoing budget deficits and inflation would make tomorrow's dollar less valuable than today's. Balance the budget, while keeping inflation in check, and that premium will all but vanish. They were right. Long-term rates dropped to 7.6 percent by 2000, falling closer in line with short-term rates. In a nation with so much household and corporate debt—where children grow up fluent in the lexicon of interest versus principal—low rates have been embraced as an American version of virtue.

. . .

As THE CAB made its way along the Potomac toward Washington, O'Neill took a last run through his three beloved morning reads— *The New York Times, The Wall Street Journal,* and *The Washington Post*—a forty-year-long, phone-book-size addiction.

Along with a story about weakening Christmas sales, the *Times* front page was dominated by stories about the President-elect's early appointments—most notably Colin Powell as Secretary of State designee and Condoleezza Rice as national security adviser—together with a lead news story in column 6, datelined yesterday from Austin, about all the appointments. It was the largest mention yet of O'Neill.

> Mr. Bush is expected to move swiftly on the appointments to top economic slots, but his lunch with Mr. O'Neill was said to be an opportunity to get to know the aluminum executive, who has a master's degree in public administration from Indiana University and has also done graduate-level work in economics.
>
> Although there are other candidates, Mr. O'Neill "ended up ahead of the pack because the more traditional Wall Street candidates lacked a strong public-policy background," a Bush adviser said.
>
> "He has the right combination of skills, experience and personality to navigate the rough political waters of an aggressive tax-cutting proposal and the vagaries of the international financial market," this adviser said.

Not bad, O'Neill thought, figuring that the "adviser" must be Cheney—sounded like Dick, though Dick hated to talk to the press. The front-page story jumped to A21, the *Times*'s National page, alongside a news story about the administration's policy plan that began: "The incoming Bush administration signaled today that it would make education its first legislative priority after taking office next month, and pledged to move rapidly on the other main pieces of its campaign platform, including a big tax cut and overhauls of Social Security and Medicare."

These issues represented core competencies for O'Neill. He'd headed councils on education reform both nationally and in Pennsylvania since the late 1980s. He helped design the basic architecture for Medicare financing in the 1970s and then pioneered innovations for corporate health care financing while at Alcoa. And overhauling Social Security? He was early—maybe first—into that tent, ever since his friend George Shultz, former Secretary of State, had testified before Congress in 1973 that the aging baby boom generation would eventually bankrupt the system. Paul had briefed Shultz for that testimony.

Suddenly, it felt like familiar terrain under his feet, a continuation rather than a Rip Van Winkle return. The President-elect, who seemed to work well with a Democratic legislature in Texas, must be seeking top officials who can navigate the middle ground, who can ask the hard questions of both sides. After all, he, Powell, and New Jersey Governor Christine Todd Whitman—who news media said was being considered for EPA—were all known as centrists, arbiters of fractious debates, closely aligned with the first President Bush.

O'Neill wondered if the President-elect's father would come up in today's lunch. Clearly, he figured, it was part of the mix of reasons that he'd been summoned. He was uniquely qualified to finesse this delicate and defining relationship—an occurrence with only one precedent, in John Adams and John Quincy Adams—where you have a President whose dad was President, too. If he were Treasury Secretary, the top domestic official of the government—with the ecumenical Powell as the top official in foreign policy—the President's seniormost appointees would both be centrists who remained integral to his dad's wise, pragmatic crowd. That gang—Brent Scowcroft, Jim Baker, Larry Eagleburger, and Roger Porter—included some of O'Neill's closest friends.

On the plane, O'Neill had fussed over whether to include his advice to break the no-tax pledge—and his public efforts to lead CEOs in a ringing endorsement of Bush Senior's tough-on-deficits stand—on his list of *why not*s. He had decided against it, realizing that he was uncertain where the son actually stood on deficits. The matter hadn't come up much in the campaign. In fact, as the cab snaked through downtown, O'Neill realized he wasn't sure where the President-elect stood on a wide array of issues. He knew most of the one-line policy positions. But he didn't know the way the man thought.

. . .

THE CAB PULLED UP to 19th and K, the office tower address of Alcoa's Government Affairs Office. O'Neill had dropped in to Government Affairs from time to time over the past thirteen years in a halfhearted way. As one of the country's most Washington-savvy CEOs, he was bored by the process of influence peddling that keeps the lights on in this town. He went so far as kill off the Alcoa political action committee shortly after he took over as CEO in 1987. The whole process stinks, he'd said in a few CEO speeches that no one covered, even if working the political edges sometimes accrued well to a company's bottom line.

"Hey, Mr. Chairman." It was Russ Wisor, vice president of government affairs, twenty-three years in Alcoa's Washington office. "I guess I can call you that for another few weeks."

"After that, who knows?" Paul said. "You might not be able to call me at all."

Russ laughed. He knew why O'Neill was in town and that—if he were to take the plunge—Russ wouldn't even be able to get in line in front of the Treasury Department like all the other lobbyists. Appearance of impropriety and all. O'Neill was a stickler on that sort of thing.

They went to Russ's office, a spare, postmodern box, with a glass wall onto the hallway and a window overlooking K Street. Russ, who at six feet one and 230 pounds dwarfed Paul, raced off to get them coffee. Alcoa had just moved into this building, a smaller, less opulent office than the one Russ had spent much of the past two decades manning. The only remnant: a large bone china bowl that Russ now used as an outbox. Paul settled into a ladderback chair with aluminum cross slats—an emblem, like everything around him, of rectitude and transparency. O'Neill, who had long studied how environment guides attitude, nodded approval. He liked the new, frugal look. Russ returned with two steaming glass Alcoa mugs. O'Neill pulled out his pad and explained to Russ that he had made a list of good reasons why he shouldn't take the job.

"I think I should add what they ought to know about my time at Alcoa. I got into a few scrapes."

That was a prompt to run through a few war stories, battles that might have created enemies, starting with a skirmish in 1990 that first displayed for Russ and all the Alcoans their CEO's taste for a type of public improvisation usually reserved for performance artists.

The incident began in an unremarkable way. Jay Hair, head of the National Wildlife Federation—an umbrella for a wide array of environmental groups—announced that he was holding a press conference in Washington to cite the nation's worst industrial polluter. Word got out the next day that it would be Alcoa. This, of course, is part of a conventional public dialogue. An environmental group identifies an industrial polluter and heaps on criticism. The corporate offender is hauled to the town square for a day in the stocks, quibbles over details, says it is doing all it can and, maybe, that it will try to do more. If the "green" group is skilled, credible, or lucky, the exchange might rate a news story in *The New York Times* or a mention on a network news broadcast. It's part of a shadow dance that heavy industry lobbyists like Russ know by rote.

O'Neill, CEO at that point for just over two years, had created management havoc inside Alcoa—firing many of the top executives and rethinking the company's operations in a fashion soon to be included in Harvard Business School case studies. But the sleepy, century-old company was drawing little public attention.

Hearing of the imminent attack, O'Neill jumped aboard a morning flight to Washington, swung by Alcoa's Government Affairs Office to pick up Frank Jones—Russ's friend and predecessor as chief lobbyist—and off the duo marched to a nearby office building for the midmorning conference. O'Neill sat in the center of the front row. Five feet away, at the podium, Hair made his statement as reporters scribbled and cameras rolled. Hair didn't know what O'Neill looked like. He opened it up for questions. A white-haired man leapt up, approached the podium, all but elbowed Hair aside, and said, "I'm Paul O'Neill, CEO of Alcoa. The charges just leveled at Alcoa are not true, and I believe Mr. Hair knew they were not true." He explained that the powdery substance Alcoa was releasing—aluminum oxide—had been taken off the Environmental Protection Agency's toxic chemicals lists in 1988 because of doubts about whether it was at all dangerous, a material point that Hair knew but failed to mention. Before relinquishing the microphone, O'Neill called the comments by Hair—upright, but in state of shock—a "scurrilous attack on our integrity." Then he turned and walked out of the hotel. Of course, the incident was prominently featured on several news broadcasts that night. O'Neill seemed not to think that was a problem.

"You know what Frank said when we were walking back to the office?" he now asked Russ, egging him on.

Of course Russ knew. This story had long ago been burnished into myth. But he also knew that O'Neill, nearly at the end of his astonishing run at Alcoa—and on his way to meet the President-elect—might like to deliver the punch line himself.

No, no. What did Frank say?

"He said, 'Paul, you have the balls of a daylight burglar.' "

Russ suggested merrily that he put that line on his list of *why not*s.

So the morning passed. They sat and talked in a rambling, discursive way, a luxury the hyperefficient O'Neill almost never indulged in. Paul jotted a few notes on his pad. But, mostly, this was a chance to talk about what was ending, an era soon to close. O'Neill's reign at Alcoa was defined by a series of intensely personal campaigns—on worker safety, making Alcoa the safest major industrial company in America; on process innovations that dramatically boosted productivity; on an ideal of open space architecture (years before it became fashionable in high-tech companies) in which everyone, O'Neill included, left their offices for egalitarian cubicles, and staff meetings were held in the lunchroom; and a kind of "best ideas win" transparency—all executives had to post their weekly schedules publicly, and most interoffice memos were available to everyone.

Each campaign was a mission. Each one the result of years, or sometimes decades, of heated study and trial and error by O'Neill that, at some point, hardened into a conviction about the right path—the only path. After that, you wouldn't want to get in his way. Over those thirteen years, though, almost all those "right paths" turned out to be right paths, rewarding investors, infusing many of Alcoa's one-hundred-thousand-plus workers with a heightened sense of purpose, and inviting celebration in Pittsburgh and beyond. Along the way, O'Neill's natural gift for deconstructing and then creatively reassembling complex issues—the knack that first drew Nixon's attention and Cheney's admiration—transmogrified into something approaching a system of thought, a philosophy for processing almost everything that caught his eye. He became a neatly coiffed, buttoned-down Martin Luther, embracing the faith of independent thinking, self-examination, calling things by their proper names. On that last score, he might be called something of a zealot.

Russ and other lobbyists had watched in horror and fascination as O'Neill began to cast his gaze beyond the ken of almost any CEO in the country. A month after elbowing Jay Hair, O'Neill was running President Bush's Education Advisory Group—making headlines over his support of unified testing standards. Then he was in the thick of controversy over encouraging his friend, the President, to break his no-tax pledge. When the U.S. Chamber of Commerce was critical of Bush's move on taxes, O'Neill summarily pulled Alcoa out of the chamber. O'Neill's positions, whether his stance against the chamber and much of corporate America on the breaking of the no-tax pledge or a public position he'd taken in support of a gasoline tax to lower our foreign dependency and create funds for environmental repair, meant the phones at Alcoa's Government Affairs Office rang to meltdown, mostly local calls from K Street's corridor of corporate lobbyists: "What the hell is your guy doing to us!" Frank Jones and Russ would just shrug. "All we can recommend is you talk to him yourself." They themselves were flummoxed. On any issue, even those near and dear to Alcoa, it became impossible to predict where O'Neill might venture . . . or to know which map he might need to keep from leading his company into enemy territory.

O'Neill had come up in the sixties and seventies, an era in Washington where the topography of special interests was not so neatly ordained. He nosed about in the early 1990s like a man returning home after a long absence, seeing open spaces where condos had since been built—that was once a field, a stream runs under there—and ended up wandering into territory foreign for any Republican CEO. He asked impertinent questions and explained himself with philosophies about process that lacked known coordinates.

The result: a visit to the international trade wars, where countries would give incentive to homegrown industries by dumping products onto world markets, depressing prices, and driving foreign competitors out of business. The countermoves, of course, are tariffs or sanctions. In 1993, when Russia was dumping aluminum and U.S. producers were screaming for sanctions, O'Neill brokered an agreement for Russian and U.S. producers—led by Alcoa—to cut back production and shutter facilities so a price-depressing worldwide aluminum glut could be sold off gradually.

"It's typical that the industry people come in foaming at the mouth about the need for sanctions," W. Bowman Cutter, a deputy director of Clinton's National Economic Council under Robert Rubin, said about that deal in *The New York Times*. "Paul was totally balanced. He saw both sides and worked for a principled solution that made sense for everybody."

O'Neill had ended Alcoa's long-standing battle with its union, the United Steelworkers of America, by devising a new model for collective bargaining and striking up an unlikely friendship with the steelworkers' union hierarchy, including its then number two, George Becker. Becker ended up an ardent O'Neill supporter, and Alcoa ended up with a six-year contract with United Steelworkers, avoiding the annual, revenue-slowing pain of negotiations. O'Neill then wrote a research paper on the subject. Becker circulated it to almost all the corporate executives with whom he negotiated, creating improved union-management relations industrywide.

What took hold by the mid-1990s was a self-reinforcing process, as Alcoa's success both freed and encouraged the company's CEO to be a free-ranger, to challenge whatever convention he could seize.

In an era when a chief executive's public posture is as carefully managed as a company's subordinated debt, O'Neill wrote all his own speeches. That is, when he wrote them at all. Increasingly, giving a speech was simply a matter of turning on his thought process in public. During an Alcoa annual meeting in 1994, he called President Clinton's proposal for universal health care an "empty box" that would do "irreparable harm" to the nation, then offered quizzical shareholders a dissertation on what ailed the American health care system—and what Alcoa had done to refashion its huge corporate health insurance coverage. More headlines. More phone calls to Alcoa's K Street offices, this time from enraged White House officials.

Meanwhile, O'Neill was hungering for fresh turf—marshaling top Alcoa staffers and tapping leading scientists to know all that was knowable on global warming. By 1996, environmentalists noticed that the leader of an industry that produced significant greenhouse gases was setting up shop in their territory. Borders were blurring. In the front of most annual reports, there are two or three pages for a letter to shareholders from the CEO. There is no more precious real estate in the expository life of a chief executive. In Alcoa's 1997 annual report, issued in early '98, O'Neill devoted one of his three allotted pages to global warming. "We are environmentalists first and industrialists second," he wrote, and delved into discussions of science versus politics, the nature of the world climate change conference in Kyoto, Japan, and what Alcoa was committed to do. More calls to the Governmental Affairs Office, this time from befuddled Republicans, corporate lobbyists . . . and the White House.

By the late nineties, O'Neill's far-flung interests and endeavors were moving from avocation to a second full-time job—one that cried out for structure. That's when his friends at the RAND Corporation, the nonpartisan think tank, jumped in. They made O'Neill the chairman of RAND, which has offices in Santa Monica, California, and in Washington. At least now, the agitated and outraged wouldn't have to call Alcoa's office to complain. They could reach Paul at the ideas shop at RAND. Someone there would always have a way to reach him.

. . .

ALMOST TWO HOURS had passed in Russ's office; they'd swapped stories, downed coffee, and run through most of the thirteen-year timeline. Paul had a few more good reasons listed and, with lunch approaching, a clarity about what had brought him to this point.

They paused. Just sat.

"What do you think, Russ? Think I ought to take it?"

Russ thought it over for a minute.

"The town's changed, Paul. It's not like the place you left in 1977. I know you've been back from time to time, but it's very different now. It's just so much more partisan, more hard-charged. Either kill or be killed."

Paul nodded, leaving Russ the latitude to close it out.

"I can't tell you what to do. If it were me, I wouldn't do it. But it's hard to say no to the President."

"No doubt there," Paul said. Like the few others he had consulted, Russ seemed unconcerned about whether the President-elect was O'Neill's type of centrist/pragmatist. It was the tactics, the rules of engagement, that worried them.

"One more thing, Paul," Russ said. "One thing I'd ask you to keep in mind."

Paul nodded, all attentiveness. Russ seemed solemn.

"Those guys on the right wing of the party will watch everything you do. Be careful."

A few minutes later, a secretary ducked her head into Russ's office. Someone was here to see Mr. O'Neill. Two men, she said. They wouldn't say where they were from or why they'd come.

. . .

IN THE RECEPTION AREA, two tall, nondescript men—smiling, thirtyish, dark suits—were waiting to escort O'Neill out. A black Chevy van stood outside. The Alcoa office on K Street and 19th is about six blocks from the Madison Hotel, a five-minute walk. But this was not about what's doable. It was about what Dick wanted, and he had decided Paul would be spirited into the hotel, so as not to alert the media and create a lot of unwanted speculation. Dick had always been an adherent of secrecy.

The black Chevy pulled past the entrance of the Madison Hotel, made two quick rights into an alley behind the hotel, into the garage, and stopped at the service entrance. Good God, Paul thought, it wasn't as if people didn't know he was being considered for Treasury. It was on the front page of this morning's *New York Times*. He went into the service elevator, with its sour milk, service elevator smell, watched as the floors—6, 7, and 8—passed by, and emerged into a carpeted hallway, like Frank Sinatra being sneaked into the Palladium. Up ahead, he saw a security detail of Secret Service men around the door of a center suite.

O'Neill was ushered through several doors and into a sitting room. It was dark. The heavy floral curtains were closed. Dick entered and they shook hands. It took a moment to see that behind Dick was the President-elect. He and O'Neill were strangers. Their only encounter had been cursory and long ago, at President Clinton's 1996 education summit. O'Neill had made headlines when he stood from the floor, waved away shushing from the summit's moderator, IBM chairman Lou Gerstner, and endorsed the creation of national standards with the line "We can know by age nine if a youngster has the ability to become a self-learner. Then don't let that kid turn ten without remediation if it's needed." Hunting for a conversational opener for today's meeting, O'Neill had strained over the past few days to recall anything from that conference that Governor George W. Bush had said or done, and had come up dry. He didn't think Bush had said anything.

O'Neill clasped the hand of the President-elect. Seemed like a nice enough guy, solid and athletic. Better-looking than on TV.

They stood around for a second. There was little small talk. They sat down at a table in the center of the room.

Three men in blue suits, two older—both in their mid-sixties— and a younger man. They all took their jackets off and slung them over the chairbacks. A working lunch. The President-elect asked Paul what he thought about being Treasury Secretary. Paul reached into the briefcase leaning against his chair leg and pulled out his pad.

"I have a list with reasons why I'm not right for the job." Bush and Cheney laughed, in a tentative, prospective way, in case it was a joke.

Paul smiled and started in. "All right, if I were to do this, the media will dig into everything I've said in the last twenty-five years, and that will cause some problems.

"Let me run some down for you. In 1986, I gave a speech that was reported in the *Atlanta Journal-Constitution* where I called for a fifty-cent-a-gallon tax on gasoline. The idea was that we need to reduce our dependency on oil and develop alternative fuel sources, and this is a way to do that while raising revenues."

The President-elect just listened. Dick Cheney nodded.

Paul pushed forward, not wanting to offer any opportunity for comment until he had read to the end.

"Also, I'm deeply involved in global climate change, and that might upset some of your supporters. . . .

"I've had some famous engagements in the media over environmental issues, like this time where I publicly challenged the head of a large environmental group . . ." and he ran through the story, leaving out Frank's testicular punch line.

Bush listened, then held up his hand.

"Where's lunch?"

They'd ordered cheeseburgers, but after fifteen minutes, they had not arrived.

"Go get me Andy Card," Bush said to one of the Secret Service agents. Card, the designee as chief of staff, entered from an adjoining room. Along with Cheney, Card was running the transition, and he had a long history, having served every Republican president since Ronald Reagan took office. He is stolid and jovial, a man of solid, loyal character.

Bush looked impatiently at Card, hard-eyed. "You're the chief of staff. You think you're up to getting us some cheeseburgers?"

Card nodded. No one laughed. He all but raced out of the room.

O'Neill watched it all, not sure if he was seeing correctly. When he ran Alcoa, he had a rule if he was considering buying a company, and he bought many: See how the CEO interacts with the receptionist, the secretary, with whoever is at the very bottom. It's a sign of how a boss values the people around him. It's a character issue.

Bush's gaze was back on him. "All right, Paul. Keep going," he said with a tight smile. O'Neill snapped to attention.

"The key thing . . . is that I've been the boss for thirteen years. I like to come up with my own data and my own decisions. I like that, and I'm quite good at it. I think it might be hard to take a staff job. To be just another bird in the nest."

O'Neill thought he needed to reinforce the point.

"I like to say what I think, especially on subjects I've spent a few decades thinking through. In Washington, these days, that might make me a dangerous man."

Bush laughed. Dick laughed.

"We know all that stuff," Bush said. "Doesn't matter. We want you to take the job."

Dick, silent throughout the lunch, added, "I had a list just like yours, except I had three heart attacks on mine."

More laughter, and this second round sealed it. O'Neill felt his "concerns were registered, noted, and dispensed with."

The conversation began to range, this way and that, about Bush's campaign promise to cut taxes by $1.6 trillion over ten years. "You've got to pursue what you said you're going to pursue," the President-elect said. "And I'm not going to negotiate with myself. I don't do that."

O'Neill saw that supporting the tax cut was a non-negotiable item, part of the package. He mentioned that the surplus had been estimated at nearly $5 trillion over the next ten years, but Bush didn't engage. After a few minutes, O'Neill found he was doing most of the talking, holding forth that "the tax system is a complete mess. I think that's something we might really dive into."

Bush agreed. "Major tax reform is a priority."

Then they moved on to Social Security and how it could be fixed with "wealth accumulation accounts," as opposed to private accounts, one of O'Neill's favorite ideas. Bush was noncommittal. There were many proposals for creating a private option.

The burgers were gone, and Bush seemed to want to sum up. "Everything you said we already knew, and it makes no difference to us," he said. "We decided we want you. What do you think?"

O'Neill said he'd like to think it over for a day. Everyone nodded, stood up. O'Neill grabbed his jacket.

"There's one more thing on my list," he said.

Bush looked at him quizzically.

"My wife thinks this is a really bad idea."

"Would it help if I called her?"

O'Neill paused, as though he were thinking over this offer, but it was just for effect.

"No, sir. I don't think that would be helpful."

. . .

IT WAS NEARLY nine o'clock at night when O'Neill opened the door to his room at the Grand Hyatt in Manhattan. The price of being a predawn riser is a sudden, one-hoss-shay collapse at some modest hour of mid-evening—in O'Neill's case, usually about 10 p.m.—which would give him about an hour to unwind and collect his thoughts. Since the moment he had slipped out of the Madison for a shuttle to La Guardia, then a late afternoon meeting and a dinner with Alain Belda, his successor as Alcoa's CEO, he'd had little chance to stop and think about the day's lunch.

He'd need to make a decision in the next day, for sure. He'd need to talk to Nancy. But first, he needed to figure out his own mind. He hung his suit jacket up and flipped on CNBC.

The phone rang. It was a familiar voice.

"Alan?"

"So, I hear you had an interesting day."

"News travels fast."

It was Greenspan. Paul had tried to stay in touch with people who had served under Gerald Ford, and he'd been reasonably conscientious about it. Alan Greenspan was the exception. In his case, the effort was constant and purposeful. When Greenspan was the chairman of Ford's Council of Economic Advisers, and Paul was number two at OMB, they had become a kind of team. Never social, so much. They never talked about families or outside interests. It was all about ideas: Medicare financing or block grants—a concept that O'Neill basically invented to balance federal power and local autonomy—or what was really happening in the economy. It became clear that they thought well *together*. Ford used to have them talk about various issues while he listened. After a while, each knew how the other's mind worked, the way married couples do.

Alan, it so happened, was on the Alcoa board of directors in the mid-1980s. He championed the idea that Paul, then the president of International Paper, be made a director. Then he promoted Paul as a candidate for CEO of Alcoa.

In the past fifteen years, they'd made a point of meeting every few months. It could be in New York, or Washington, or Pittsburgh. They talked about everything, just as always. Alan, O'Neill told a friend, "doesn't have many people who don't want something from him, who will talk straight to him. So that's what we do together—straight talk."

O'Neill felt some straight talk coming on.

"Paul, I'll be blunt. We really need you down here," Greenspan said. "There is a real chance to make some lasting changes. We could be a team at the key moment, to do the things we've always talked about."

The jocular tone was gone. This was a serious discussion. They digressed into some things they'd "always talked about," especially reforming Medicare and Social Security. For Paul and Alan, the possibility of such bold reinventions bordered on fantasy, but fantasy made real.

"We have an extraordinary opportunity," Alan said. Paul noticed that he seemed oddly anxious. "Paul, your presence will be an enormous asset in the creation of sensible policy."

Sensible policy. This was akin to prayer from Greenspan. O'Neill, not expecting such conviction from his old friend, said little. After a while, he just thanked Alan. He said he always respected his counsel. He said he was thinking hard about it, and he'd call as soon as he decided what to do.

The receiver returned to its cradle. He thought about Greenspan. They were once young men together in the capital. Alan stayed, became the most noteworthy Federal Reserve Bank chairman in modern history and, arguably, the most powerful public official of the past two decades. Paul left, led a corporate army, made a fortune, and learned lessons—about how to think and act, about the importance of outcomes—that you can't ever learn in government.

But, he supposed, he'd missed some things. There were always trade-offs. Talking to Alan reminded him of that. Alan and his wife, Andrea Mitchell, White House correspondent for NBC News, lived a fine life. They weren't wealthy like Paul and Nancy. But Alan led a life of highest purpose, a life guided by inquiry.

He picked up the receiver, punched the keypad.

"Hi, babe, how was your day?" he said, always his opening.

"You at the hotel?"

"Yeah, it was a long day."

He started going into the details of his trip to New York from Washington, but he's not much of a phone talker—Nancy knew that—and the small talk trailed off.

"I think I'm going to have to do this."

She was quiet. "You know what I think," she said, surprisingly cool.

She knew him too well, maybe. How bullheaded he can be, once he decides what's right. How he had loved these last few years as a sovereign, his own man. How badly he was suited to politics, as it was being played. And then there was that other problem: she'd almost always been right about what was best for him.

"Whatever, Paul. I'm behind you. If you don't do this, I guess you'll always regret it."

But it was clearly about what *he* wanted, what *he* needed.

Paul thanked her. Though somehow a thank-you didn't seem appropriate.

And then he realized she was crying.

. . .

On December 30, the Associated Press ran a story that Bush would hold a two-day economic forum with business leaders and economists the following week to discuss his view that "the economy is in serious trouble." The AP reported that the meeting, to be held at the Governor's Mansion in Austin, would include Paul O'Neill, Commerce Secretary–designate Donald Evans, and Bush economic adviser Lawrence Lindsey.

O'Neill was in Pittsburgh, at the neighborhood diner he'd arrived at for coffee at 5:45 most mornings for the past thirteen years, when he read the item in *The New York Times*.

A short while later, he was back at the tasteful, sprawling colonial in Pittsburgh's stately Shadyside section, with Karl Rove on the phone.

"I think it would be better, Karl, if someone had bothered to first ask me whether I thought this was a good idea and then whether I thought it would be a good idea for me to attend," O'Neill said impatiently. "My answer to both questions is no."

A penitent Rove talked for a moment about who else was coming, mostly CEOs who'd been supportive of the President, along with a few selected economists, led by Larry Lindsey.

O'Neill told Rove that if they really wanted to discuss what was right or wrong with the economy—and "build a genuine consensus" behind some of Bush's proposals—they "were going about this all wrong. You should get a group that represents a diversity of opinions, including labor and various schools of economic thinking. And then have a real discussion."

Rove was deferential. The two men had never met. "Karl said that this was, in fact, 'mostly an event to give airtime to businessmen who had supported Bush in the campaign,' " O'Neill recalled later.

Fine. O'Neill said he certainly had better things to do. He remembers that his "tone was impatient, a sort of 'Who the hell is Karl Rove?' I was accustomed to the prevailing view that political people in a White House are, well, political people. There to shape a message, but not at the center of key decisions."

He hung up, reached for the legal pad, and scribbled:

Get KR and others in the press/media operation to agree we're going to coordinate our outside face and that the outside face will be driven by substance, not by the need to have a line of the day. We need to give the media what we want, not what they want, and we should run a strict system that does not permit free-lance leaks and backgrounders.

But discussion of the Austin conference—and especially the mention of Larry Lindsey—spurred a more consequential analysis. There was a central question: How, exactly, would economic policy be created?

O'Neill knew Lindsey—everyone knew Larry, an engaging, political fellow who had moved around a bit in the academic, political, and policy worlds but never created much traction in any one realm. He was a junior professor at Harvard in the 1980s but never tenured. He was always political, though, and allied himself with the supply-side thinkers, a group led by Harvard professor Martin Feldstein, a leading economist who was a chairman of the Council of Economic Advisers under Reagan. Lindsey followed his mentor's path to Washington. He got a job in George H. W. Bush's administration as a staff analyst in domestic policy, working under Bush's domestic policy chief, Harvard government professor Roger Porter. Porter knew Lindsey from Harvard and never gave him any core tasks of policy analysis. Lindsey was stalled.

In 1991, though, a deadlock over whom to name vice chairman of the Fed unexpectedly left open a seat on the Board of Governors. In the scramble to fill the slot, Lindsey's name came up. Even his friends were surprised. During Lindsey's confirmation hearings before the Senate, he was asked about what experience he had in business. Lindsey said he'd run a hot dog stand in college. Some senators snickered. They thought he was joking.

Greenspan gave him several tasks, seemed reasonably pleased, and Lindsey used this professional break to fullest effect: he traveled and spoke often, building a profile in the Fed regions. He was comfortable in front of a crowd. His layman's explanations of economic theories were appealing to audiences.

Shortly after he left the Fed in late 1997, Lindsey showed up in the orbit of Texas governor George Bush. A resident scholar at the American Enterprise Institute, in 1998 he became an informal adviser to Bush, visiting Austin for three long sessions to instruct him about the workings of the U.S. economy and to advocate major tax cuts. In December 1998, Lindsey argued in a *Wall Street Journal* op-ed for a 10 percent across-the-board tax cut; a few months later, in an issue of *The American Enterprise*, he suggested that a two- or three-year temporary tax cut might help extend the economic expansion. That summer, after being named officially to the Bush economic team, Lindsey attacked the Clinton administration's plans to use the budget surplus to "save" Social Security, calling instead for the money to be given back to the people via tax cuts.

By the time the governor announced his candidacy in the winter of 1999, Lindsey had risen to head Bush's economics brain trust, which consisted of several like-minded Hoover Institution economists, including John Cogan, Michael Boskin (who served as chief White House economist for the first President Bush), Martin Anderson (a policy adviser to Reagan and Nixon), Stanford's John Taylor, and Glenn Hubbard, a rising economist from Columbia University. The group was technically managed by Hubbard—who acted as the honest broker of competing views—so that Lindsey would be free to advocate positions. There was a ready consensus: the group started advocating significant tax cuts in its first public pronouncements. The size of the tax cut rose during the campaign season as the projections of budget surpluses grew. In 1999, it was a $468 billion cut. In the summer of 2000, the Clinton administration announced that the surplus would be $5 trillion over ten years. By the fall of 2000, Bush's tax cut proposal had reached $1.6 trillion.

. . .

AFTER THE CALL to Rove, O'Neill retreated to the high-ceilinged library in his home, surrounded by nearly two thousand books, and thought about Lindsey, slated to head the National Economic Council (NEC). The NEC was created under Clinton to act, specifically, as a broker between competing views from the Treasury Department and the President's Council of Economic Advisers, both of which have large staffs to investigate policy choices. Robert Rubin had briliantly handled that role of consensus builder in the first two years of the Clinton presidency, while Lloyd Bentsen was Treasury Secretary. He was seen by many competing camps as someone who could ably articulate to the President both sides of any issue.

Lindsey had wanted the job of Treasury Secretary and had been mentioned several times in media reports during the campaign as a possible choice. But once Bush was elected, Cheney and others made it clear that they felt that Lindsey didn't have enough gravity for the job. The chairmanship of the Council of Economic Advisers, meanwhile, was a job traditionally held by a leading, respected economist. Lindsey was simply not in that category, O'Neill thought.

Lindsey was already in Washington, busily preparing to head the NEC, while O'Neill was at home thinking about process. Lindsey's status would need to be articulated. Having him in the honest broker's chair—and being a partisan rather than a broker—could be disastrous, especially for a President who had little experience in economic analysis. It couldn't be clearer. He grabbed the pad and wrote.

> Get an Agreement for LL to be the honest broker not the unilateral adviser to the P. or get him out of the broker role.

. . .

NANCY WAS STAYING in Pittsburgh. This was their home. She was not selling the house. They'd think about buying an apartment in Washington in the spring. It was a four-hour drive, and O'Neill loved to drive, so that's what he'd do: drive home on Friday nights and then back on Sunday.

He got a room at the J. W. Marriott on 13th and Pennsylvania Avenue, a seven-block stroll to the marble fortress of the Federal Reserve, where he arrived for breakfast at 8:30 sharp on January 5. He settled into the chairman's private dining room, newspapers under his arm. He'd been here two dozen times, maybe more, during Greenspan's thirteen years as Fed chairman. O'Neill's *always* on time. Always. And he loved it when Alan was a little late, which he was every once in a while.

After a few moments, Greenspan poked his head in, sheepishly.

"Jesus, Alan, I read all the papers already and, you know, there's really not a *whole lot* to do around here. . . ."

Greenspan shrugged. They'd done this routine before. "Traffic was miserable . . . *like you wouldn't believe.*" This was one of Alan's standards, along with, "Andrea and I were out late last night and it was impossible to get up this morning. . . ."

These are men of ritual and precision—not easy men to meet, unless you know their daily organization chart. But when they lock into a relationship, they lock in tight. After thirty years of breakfasts, they slipped easily into step, knowing each other's routines as a postman knows his route.

A waiter appeared, and Paul, who had already eaten his small daily breakfast at 5:45 a.m., ordered another—English muffin, grapefruit slices, and coffee, regular. For Greenspan, oatmeal with raisins, grapefruit slices, and coffee, decaf. Like always.

"So, what do you think about the current state of play?" Paul said, in one of his traditional openings. "Got any new numbers we ought to roll around in?"

Greenspan started to cite some "top line" numbers, unemployment, inflation, manufacturing inventories, money supply. It was a kind of limbering-up exercise for these two, starting with traditional trend analysis on unemployment and inflation, some predictions of generally unpredictable ups and downs, the where-are-we-now snapshot of the current economic metrics. They were akin to mariners discussing tides and winds. Context, mostly.

The December unemployment rate, just released, was only 4 percent but expected to creep northward. Employers announced 134,000 layoffs in the month, more than triple the number in November. Inflation, at an almost historic low of 2.2 percent, seemed to have been effectively tamed by a decade of Greenspan-led tight-fistedness in monetary policy and years of Clinton-Rubin prudence on the fiscal side.

But beneath the surface, there was cause for caution. The enveloping issue, both men agreed, was the struggle to keep productivity—the great engine of the nineties prosperity, in Greenspan's view—on the rise. Some sectors were driving these productivity gains—like manufacturing-intensive industries embracing automation, or computer makers, whose productivity had risen nearly 60 percent each year since 1995. It meant consumers got more for less. Meanwhile, sectors such as health care and services that rely on expert labor and are less directly impacted by technology showed almost no productivity gains. For them, revenue growth is mostly a matter of price hikes. It was a split, almost like two separate economies. But now, they were both being drawn toward a shared crucible: with consumer confidence, and spending, turning sluggish, managers in *both* economies would have to squeeze productivity gains from cost reduction. They'd have to cut workers, while holding off spending for infrastructure, information technology, equipment, and various capital investments that drive growth. This meant you could have flat or modest economic growth and still be losing jobs.

O'Neill and Greenspan started to look for where, and how dramatically, this was happening. The morning's financial papers were running the December figures on wholesale inventories, like paper, petroleum, food, electronic equipment. Inventories had been building up almost everywhere. But those were already "historicals" to these two—they were digging around two levels below that and a hundred yards ahead.

For years, they'd talked metals. Greenspan had been on Alcoa's board. Both knew how often such ubiquitous materials—steel, aluminum, lead—are leading indicators that cross business sectors. They tell you what next month's numbers will be.

"What do Alcoa's order rates look like?" Alan asked. Paul ticked off Alcoa's numbers (down), then ran through London Metal Exchange (LME) prices, mostly down. Alan noodled this. What fraction of replacement cost of capital do these prices represent? he asked. Paul said he'd get current inventories of the LME, then he and Alan discussed inventories that were not even being counted.

Breakfast was gone, second cups poured, and they branched out, doing granular analysis of the "customer side" (as in big buyers of commodities) in various sectors—talking fast in shorthand, finishing each other's coded sentences—about "forward orders" for airplanes and "days inventory" (means average number of days a product sits unsold) for autos. Sixty days, eighty-five days? At that rate, automakers were just producing cars for inventory, because it's too expensive to shut down plants. Both men had pads. They jotted down numbers. Telecommunications equipment was the area of greatest concern. There was no room for further downdrafts there—it was a crisis beckoning disaster.

Insofar as they shared a skepticism of economic theory, this was why: race across the country's top twenty industries in forty minutes, your bare feet pounding the cold earth, and it's almost possible *to feel* the American economy.

Pulling up after this sprint, they agreed that the ground felt, for the most part, solid, though in a few places it was softening rapidly.

So, what to do? Greenspan had a magazine of fresh powder in terms of monetary policy. On January 3, two days before this breakfast, the Fed had cut its target for the federal funds rate—the overnight lending rate to banks and financial institutions—by half a percent, or 50 basis points, to 6 percent. There was plenty of room to cut, in Greenspan's estimation, without stirring inflation. O'Neill focused on his realm: there was an extraordinary situation in fiscal policy. The first question: How big *was* the surplus? Second: How could a wide slice of this historic, maybe once-in-a-lifetime surplus be protected for the thing he and Alan had dreamed of for nearly three decades, saving Social Security? It was now or never.

"Five trillion over ten years?" O'Neill asked, trying to get a fix on the big number.

"It's certainly not money in the bank," Greenspan said.

But, of course, both saw the effect of the magic number, however speculative. It was like pumping ether into the executive and legislative branches. No hard choices would be required. Everything seemed possible. Already initiatives were being launched for boosts in education spending, defense spending, and prescription drug coverage for seniors. Republicans and Democrats were lining up: a party so good, everyone has to come.

This enthusiasm set off alarms for O'Neill and Greenspan. They needed a plan for fiscal management that would capture this moment and many to follow. First, O'Neill said, do the numbers. Take out the trust funds, the untouchables: nearly half of the total surplus would go to obligations for Social Security and Medicare. What was left—$2 trillion plus.

Then there was the President-elect's $1.6 trillion tax cut. Paul mentioned that Bush was unmovable on the tax cut—that he'd said over their cheeseburgers that it was important to do what he was elected to do and "not negotiate with myself." Though this was not news to Alan, it seemed worth saying out loud.

If the surplus held, there would be close to enough left over to save Social Security—which meant replacing it with a better system—without slipping deeply into deficit spending. Deficits were a dragon that Greenspan felt had finally been slain.

We're not going back into the red, Greenspan said. Paul nodded solemnly. For these two, it was a blood oath.

Greenspan felt the surplus needed to be cleared away. There was currently $3.2 billion in federal debt that required interest payments and created a drag on the economy. Add to that a large surplus locked in dusty, low-yielding vehicles, like government bonds, and there would be additional drag on the economy. On the other hand, if the surplus was left unattached, Congress and the President would find a way to spend it.

O'Neill—the budget hawk—already had a plan. Prior to this meeting, he had written on his pad:

> We can strengthen our own hand on what to do with the surplus by articulating the principle of a dedicated flow to continuing debt reduction.

He recited the line to Greenspan, who considered it for a moment. Fine—reduction of debt is a priority—but what happens to the big item, the tax cut, if the surpluses evaporate? he asked.

"Triggers," O'Neill said. "A good enough idea, if it can be sold."

It would be a statutory enforcement of fiscal prudence. Balance-sheet behavior common to most companies and households—whereby spending is linked to availability of funds—would continue to apply to the country's largest balance sheet. Moving into deficit would "trigger" a host of reactions. To wit: Fiscal policies based on the availability of a surplus would be altered if that surplus disappeared. Of course, as both Alan and Paul knew, that would include the President-elect's proposed tax cut—the largest ever in total dollars and only slightly less, as a percentage of gross domestic product, than the historic Reagan tax cut of 1982.

Neither man opposed a tax cut. Total federal revenues as a percentage of GDP—a key calculation that shows the level to which the U.S. government taxes its citizens—hit 20.8 percent in 2000, the highest percentage in the last forty years, during which time the average was 18.6 percent. Who makes those payments is another, more complex calculation, but that top line percentage was driven by a dropping share from corporate taxes—4.2 percent of GDP at its peak in 1967, down to 2.1 percent in 2000—and a rising portion from Social Security taxes from 3 percent of GDP in 1962 to 6.7 percent in 2000. It was a matter of what was affordable, across an unknowable arc of ten years. If a tax cut could be afforded, fine and good.

If, however, a combination of tax cuts and depressed tax receipts from an economic slowdown caused the surplus to evaporate—and if there were not spending cuts to avoid slipping into deficit—the tax cut would be reined in. O'Neill and Greenspan's view of history's "top line" was succinct: We went through this before, under Ronald Reagan, and it took nearly two decades to pay off the debts. Tax cuts are easy, spending cuts are hard. If you want one, you need to embrace the other. And if the political system is too dysfunctional to have that debate, you stay put and avoid dramatic action.

"Our political system is what needs fixing," O'Neill said in a moan that Greenspan had heard many times. "It needs to be based on reality. Not games."

And so it was hatched: a secret pact. What they were doing felt perfectly natural. Two men with nearly ninety years of experience in and around Washington, colluding to prevent an elected president—with virtually no experience in setting national economic policy—from acting in a way that they were convinced was ill-considered. He'd thank them later.

O'Neill smiled. "Think you could find a way to mention triggers in one of your upcoming pronouncements?"

Greenspan smirked. "Why me?"

"Because I thought of it," O'Neill said with a friendly gloat. "That means you have to sell it."

. . .

AT THE BUSH presidential transition office, a nondescript beige brick government building on 18th and G Streets, O'Neill and other senior officials settled into offices on the eighth floor, with Cheney presiding from the corner office. When compared with most transitions, this one was efficient and purposeful—every one of the hundreds of staffers knew his or her place and what he or she was expected to do. O'Neill was expected to start creating an economic policy, and for the first time, he had extended discussions with Lindsey.

He found Lindsey astonishingly bleak. "Larry was sure that we were on the brink of disaster—it seemed he'd believed that for a few years at that point—and was convinced that deep tax cuts were the cure," O'Neill recalled. "While Larry had grown up drinking the supply-side water, he never mentioned this philosophy to me. I figured it was out of his system, like most everyone else. He just seemed to feel that the economy needed stimulus and we had these surpluses, so full steam ahead."

The more they talked, the more they seemed to disagree. "The numbers, the real numbers, don't support a lot of what you're saying, Larry, about the sky falling, or the stimulative power of these tax cuts," O'Neill said in one meeting. He began to put Lindsey through an intellectual regimen, what Nixon and Ford colleagues called O'Neillian analysis. Lindsey was using a variety of economic models that provide only the most general, after-the-fact rendering of the U.S. economy. "You're looking through the rearview mirror, Larry, and you may be nearsighted," O'Neill would say in a tone of bonhomie. For him, this was pure joy, a kind of give-and-take you could "really sink your teeth into." For Lindsey, it may have felt like an affront, an attack on his credibility as a leading economist, always a sore point. But Lindsey wouldn't engage in the kinds of exchanges O'Neill had long enjoyed with Greenspan, or with several leading conservative economists, including some—like Stanford's John Cogan—who served on Lindsey's all-star group of campaign advisers. Cogan, who had flown in from California to help with economic planning during the transition, ducked into O'Neill's office in the transition building about this time and said, "It's an honor to finally meet the legend." In fact, O'Neill's reputation as one of the most original thinkers in the Republican camp also meant he would be difficult to control—a problem if economic prescriptions were already set and non-negotiable. So, in meetings that unfolded through January, Lindsey was polite, listening, often biting his tongue.

O'Neill grew concerned. More and more, he began to view Lindsey—who had long served as Bush's economics tutor—as an advocate, and an advocate who would soon sit about thirty feet from the Oval Office. Trouble.

It would be important to pick his moment carefully. It was late on a weekday night. Much of the staff was gone. Two lifelong workaholics were still at their posts: O'Neill and Dick Cheney.

He marched down the hall to Dick's office and closed the door.

"Dick, I think we need to talk," O'Neill said. These were things Dick understood: how setting sound process to manage the White

House and executive branch—entities that were truly beyond human scale—would determine outcomes. O'Neill said that he was concerned that Lindsey was masquerading as the honest broker and was anything but. O'Neill didn't have an immediate remedy—he had to run Treasury and might not have the time to entertain competing economic views, to be the broker, as someone inside the White House was better positioned to do. But his concern stretched across the entire realm of domestic affairs. Without a process that included strongly positioned honest brokers and a rigorous, disinterested vetting of various proposals, O'Neill said, "all you've got are kids rolling around on the lawn."

Cheney listened, nodded a few times, listened some more. As O'Neill spoke, he recalled more about his long history with Dick, under Gerald Ford, during Paul's visits to "41" and since. Dick was not a talker. His cards, held close, were virtually never shown. He could seem reassuring, even sympathetic, but you couldn't gauge depth. It was easy to paint what you hoped to see on Dick's concerned, pensive mien. But you could never be certain what he was thinking or what he would do.

O'Neill felt he had laid out his case. It couldn't have been clearer to him, and he was sure that it was equally clear to Cheney. The need to really "run the traps" on every potential presidential move was more important for this Bush than for his father or Gerald Ford, both of whom had vast experience in the federal government. God knows, Cheney would understand that as well as anyone. Then there was silence. Dick thanked Paul for his insights, and O'Neill left feeling that he had done his duty. Leave it to Dick. He'd know what to do.

. . .

A BLACK SUV wound down Chain Bridge Road, the area's old highway, and through the plush hills of McLean, Virginia. It passed the unmarked gates of the Saudi ambassador's residence, then, a mile along, a green highway sign—

**George Bush
Center for
Intelligence
CIA**

—before turning into the gated community where Dick Cheney lived.

O'Neill and Greenspan slid out of the high backseat, and in a moment, Cheney welcomed them into the foyer of his two-story brick town house, where boxes were already packed for the end-of-the-week move to the Vice President's official mansion. It was the late afternoon of January 14, the Sunday of the final week of the transition. They settled at the kitchen table, three men in ties, blazers, and slacks, CEO casual, making final preparations for the coming era.

They raced across topics, a kind of review of what had been decided. The President-elect had said little about foreign affairs during the campaign or since, and in any event, Powell and Rumsfeld, just now coming aboard, were working up some of their own ideas. Domestic issues were all anyone was focused on. The tax cut was the priority, they all agreed. After the close election, Cheney said, it was important that the new President score a clean victory on taxes. If it went the other way, opponents would feel empowered and all anyone would talk about was how he'd lost the popular vote.

But Cheney, speaking often to Lindsey, had been concerned that the economy was weakening fast—a central issue both materially and tactically to the tax cut—and asked both men to give their views.

O'Neill gave his "don't panic" rendition of what the numbers said and then added, "The best, first stimulus, truth be told, may be monetary policy."

It was important, Greenspan said, not to overreact. If people felt the underlying economy was essentially solid—and he suspected it was—they'd act accordingly. They'd get over mourning for lost stock values and begin to spend and invest. He talked broadly about monetary policy—that they were ready with more rate cuts if needed—but he didn't cross the barrier to tell what he was thinking of doing, and Cheney knew not to ask.

O'Neill then elaborated, trying to close the circle. The key, he said, was to match interest rate cuts with a sense "that we are continuing to act with real fiscal restraint and prudence." That, he said, would please the bond markets and, probably, boost stocks. "It's important we display our good sense in handling these surpluses, something we haven't had much experience doing."

Greenspan echoed that. Any tax cuts, he said, need to be seen as sober and very responsible.

Cheney mostly listened, not offering much. Earnest, opaque. The two leading players in economic policy had offered their opinions, and he had duly noted them. Then he moved the discussion to the economic fallout from what he saw as an energy crisis. In this, he took the helm. Years at Halliburton had granted him a sense of mastery of this area.

California was blowing up. Its power shortages were making headlines each day. Cheney said it was not a problem of supply. It was a "malfunctioned distribution system, not a fundamental inadequacy of capacity," O'Neill recalled. "His question was, what kind of regulatory intervention would be the right one, both in California and in similar situations that might occur elsewhere." Cheney mentioned how the crush of environmental regulations had slowed the building of new facilities—how those regulations might be eased—and talked through the possibility of creating a national energy grid. At present, the country is divided into three, bordered grids—East, West, and Texas. State regulations governing energy production, distribution, and use add another set of borders.

All three men had served in the White House under Richard Nixon and Gerald Ford when energy crises hit. Greenspan and O'Neill pressed the point about alternative sources. They all agreed that there was no way the country could really be energy-independent on hydrocarbons, O'Neill recalls, "and that our resources were being used up at an amazing rate. It's a matter of national security that we diversify."

Cheney took that cue to focus on nuclear power, citing France's reliance on nuclear for more than 60 percent of its electricity. "He said, 'We need to revive nuclear power,' " O'Neill recalled, "and that the President wanted him to head up a special task force on energy. It was clear that Dick would pretty much be in charge of the whole thing. It was his baby."

O'Neill and Greenspan responded with their proprietary desires: using the surplus to finally refashion Social Security. Then O'Neill talked about reforming Medicare and changing the tax system. Cheney nodded along, unreadable.

Two hours had passed. Cheney moved to close the big circle. The shape of things to come? Tax cut, Cheney said, front and center. A task force on energy, which he would run. And everyone stay in close touch about the condition of the economy. All other matters—like global warming or education reform—would move on a slower track.

The conversation was purposeful and focused and familiar. At least on the surface. Here were three friends who'd known one another for three decades, busily constructing the government on behalf of someone only Cheney really knew, and not as well as they knew each other.

But subtle divisions, barely discernible, were already taking shape around the kitchen table. Cheney had recommended O'Neill for the job in part because of his long bond with Greenspan. It may have been the uneven relationship between Greenspan and the first Bush

administration—friends of "41" complained—that freed the Fed
chairman to hold back on stimulating the economy in 1992. They
claimed it contributed to Bush's loss. Greenspan had said then, and
since, that fighting inflation was that moment's key issue. He'd pull
tight the reins on money supply, again, under similar circumstances.
His actions, moreover, were born of loyalty to a core principle: to
know all that can be known and then try, every day, to do what is
in the best *long-term* interest of the U.S. economy. The Bushes, of
course, have relied on a different oath: loyalty to a person, whether
"41" or "43," and to the family. There might be disagreements on
what position the best available facts or political calculations recommend. But you stick together, *no matter what.*

Cheney had long made peace with this notion of personal loyalty.
It was at the core of why men in power—including both Bushes—always felt comfortable investing their confidences, secrets, doubts,
delights, and very careers in the hands of this quiet man from
Wyoming. It was a quality that had propelled him to the office he
would take within the week.

Despite similarities in experience and outlook, O'Neill and
Greenspan were of a different cast. They relied on oaths of personal
conduct, bound up with their code of frankly discerning reality and
then acting on it. Each of them had been his own man for quite a
while. They stuck together, primarily, because each liked the way the
other made sense of the world. "I like the way he thinks," each would
say. It was a bond of loyalty that demanded performance and constant renewal; it was conditional and transparent.

Dick, following a different oath, was now unshakably loyal to
someone neither Paul nor Alan really knew . . . even if he was about
to become President. That, suddenly, made the political philosophy
and policy passions—the *mind* of Dick Cheney (a subject of some
mystery, even to close friends)—subordinate issues. Literally.

Greenspan's autonomy—his claim of loyalty to inquiry rather

than person—was a tailored suit he'd worn since being appointed Fed chairman. Until a month ago, it had also been an easy fit for O'Neill. But since he had signed on as Secretary of the Treasury, many of those around Bush expected O'Neill to be loyal, without question, to the President. The problem was that Bush hadn't earned his loyalty.

All this became clear to Paul O'Neill and Alan Greenspan at the same instant, midway through the waning afternoon. When the centerpiece of the President-elect's plan for America—the $1.6 trillion, ten-year tax cut—was discussed, neither man felt comfortable mentioning the secret "trigger" pact to Dick Cheney.

They couldn't be sure what Dick would think.

• • •

THE PRESIDENT would arrive this week to prepare for the inauguration. On Wednesday, January 17, at his confirmation hearings before the Senate Finance Committee, O'Neill had a chance to talk publicly about principle.

In his opening statement, he said that helping fix the crisis in Social Security was what "convinced me that it was appropriate for me to accept the challenge to return to public service."

To Frank Murkowski, Republican of Alaska, who asked about use of the tax code to stimulate investment—a trusted weapon in the federal policy arsenal—O'Neill testified, "I'm thinking about whether I can get away with still being a maverick for another couple of days"—a line that drew laughter—then stated that, as a CEO, "I never made an investment decision based on the tax code," and that "good business people don't do things" on the basis of tax code inducements.

Then to Louisiana Democrat John Breaux, who asked whether O'Neill would recommend "a monetary policy fix or . . . a broad-based tax cut fix" to boost a slowing economy, O'Neill said, "I think the first line of action is monetary policy. My point is this. If we're going to have a tax reduction, which I'm hearing more and more people say they're in favor of a tax reduction, then I don't know why we wouldn't want it now, not because it's a major component to drive the economy, but because it won't hurt."

The next day, the lead story in *The New York Times* was headlined:

TREASURY CHOICE VARIES FROM BUSH ON TAX OUTLOOK

In his first public comments since Mr. Bush selected him to head the Treasury Department and serve as the leader of the new administration's economic team, Mr. O'Neill supported tax cuts with words that were noticeably less rousing than Mr. Bush's. He said he favored tax relief because he did not see the harm in lowering the tax burden while the government had big surpluses.

But in a three-hour confirmation hearing in front of the Senate Finance Committee, he did not spell out the benefits of tax cuts in any detail. The former Alcoa executive and Nixon and Ford administration budget expert also cast a shadow of doubt on Mr. Bush's contention that tax cuts are the right antidote to the looming economic downturn.

He said the Federal Reserve, through its control of monetary policy, was the "first line of action" to fight a downturn and suggested that even cuts of the magnitude Mr. Bush has promised would likely have relatively little immediate impact on the nation's economy.

Karen Hughes, White House communications director, Karl Rove, and others close to the President read the story and boiled, especially about one particular paragraph:

Mr. O'Neill also praised the Clinton administration's record of fiscal discipline and economic stability as "wonderful." He said the Bush administration should aim to collect enough in taxes to pay for government operations each year without going into debt—even when the economy barely expands.

O'Neill read the *Times* at his desk in the transition building. He had known there'd be some stir, but he thought it was important to make clear where he stood. He and Greenspan had studied these issues longer—and together had more relevant practical experience—than almost any other pair in town. And they were in concert about everything he'd said at the hearings. The President's views were general and evolving. O'Neill felt his candor would nourish that evolution, or at least offer a counterweight to whatever Larry Lindsey might be saying.

The *Times* noted that O'Neill's position "differs in some respects from the view held by some supply-side economists, who steadfastly defend President Ronald Reagan's tax cuts of the early 1980's as having revolutionized the economy, even if they also contributed to giant budget deficits. Lawrence B. Lindsey, Mr. Bush's chief economic aide, is a leading proponent of Reagan-era tax cutting and the main architect of Mr. Bush's tax cut plan, which is estimated to cost $1.6 trillion over 10 years."

And then, the us-versus-them clincher: "His comments illustrate why some conservatives distrust Mr. O'Neill's economic instincts. As a budget official in the Nixon and Ford administrations, he developed a reputation as a pragmatic thinker on fiscal matters, inclined to run a lean and efficient government, but skeptical of ideological extremes."

O'Neill put the *Times* in his briefcase, emerged from his office, and saw Larry Lindsey in the hallway.

"Nice story, Paul," Larry said, seeming rather upbeat. "It's important people know where we stand."

"Absolutely," O'Neill responded. "That's the whole point. People need to know what we're thinking. Let's not be afraid to tell them."

CHAPTER 2

A WAY TO DO IT

P AUL O'NEILL ARRIVED at 6:15 a.m. on his first morning in office.

The President, he understood, was also an early riser—in his office by 7 a.m.—and O'Neill mused that maybe this would be part of what defined this administration: people of fortitude and clarity, always first to work. At the very least, this was one thing the President and he had in common.

His secretary, Annabella Mejia, was already there. "You're late," she chided. "Mr. Secretary, it's practically afternoon."

"Thanks, I'll get my own coffee," he said with a chuckle. "Can I get *you* anything, Annabella?"

Before almost anyone else had arrived, O'Neill had drafted a strategic memo to the President. By midmorning, it was ready. He had his secret pact with Greenspan. But the goal of pushing forward the President's plan was central to his job description. A core responsibility. O'Neill decided he could be a team player and still feel like himself. Good policy could make good politics—at least, it was possible. With a surplus number of $5 trillion—a number O'Neill understood from a friend at the Congressional Budget Office would soon rise to $5.6 trillion—he needed to help the President set the right priorities.

> Memorandum to the President
> *From:* Paul H. O'Neill
> *Subject:* Tax Reform
> *Date:* January 22, 2001
>
> I believe there is an opportunity to get quick action on your tax proposal if we move now.
> You have won the general argument on the desirability of a tax cut and the opposition has been cornered into arguing how large the cut should be, and, their numbers are moving toward your numbers and scope. . . .

O'Neill knew that special interests, with their congressional advocates, were already lined up at the White House door, pushing for midsize proposals—abolishing inheritance taxes or offering a tax credit for each legitimate child—along with perennials like tax incentives for ethanol production or inner-city fix-ups. Bundling everyone's favorite items would create "a working majority" and "a way to get a quick victory in the tax arena," O'Neill wrote, aware that this was something that the President's political team found attractive. Considering the election results, any show of strength, or weakness, would be read as a trend. A quick victory was crucial. The problem, he wrote the President, was that his proposed across-the-board reductions in marginal tax rates might be left behind.

O'Neill had made his own decision about priorities. The bundle of many targeted credits and exemptions, with their myriad schedules and provisions, would be difficult to rein in with a trigger. A broad tax rate reduction would have a kind of simple, manageable clarity. It would progress, year by year, on a schedule, depending on whether there was a surplus. If the excess were to be used up, the rate reductions would halt.

Now, he had to help the President see that this was also the strategically sound move. One of the keys was speed. "Growing agreement, even alarm in some quarters, with regard to the slowing economy," O'Neill wrote, could justify swift action on this one defining issue, provided they could get a proposal to Congress in a few weeks and push through marginal rate cuts—most likely through a tweak of withholding—retroactive to January 1.

The only congressional argument to counter this "insurance policy against the slowing economy," he noted, would be that "it doesn't fit their process." Failure to act, moreover, would expose members to blame if the economy slipped into recession.

Embrace reality, he suggested. This plan would take us out of the "morass about the theology of economics"—a shot at anyone who might be whispering about supply-side concepts—and stress that "we care about taking practical action right now." Meanwhile, it would leverage the current economic uncertainties. "We know the real economy has slowed and the official statistics will reflect the slowing over the next quarter, at least. If the current slowness starts moving toward re-acceleration late in the second quarter, it would weaken the argument for quick action."

After a few paragraphs about the need to stress how this rate reduction would benefit low- and middle-income Americans and "stop the drumbeat about a tax cut for the rich," O'Neill unsheathed the blade.

In order to stay within your total tax reduction numbers and provide early implementation for marginal rates we will have to stretch out implementation of some of the other initiatives. We should argue that we will revisit implementation dates for other features, if the economy permits us to do so.

He read it, satisfied—the meat of fiscal reality, with a dash of conditionality, between two slices of political strategy—and typed in, "cc: Vice President Cheney, Larry Lindsey." Of course, the current proposal—even if it were retroactive to January—wouldn't provide much actual stimulus. But if they hitched their wagon to the *need for stimulus*, they'd be obligated to actually create something that resembles a stimulus . . . at some point.

. . .

"PABLO?"

"Mr. President."

"Let's get comfortable," George Bush said as O'Neill entered the Oval Office.

The President moved toward the wing chair near the fireplace, tucked between one of two sofa-and-chair clusters in the thirty-nine-by-twenty-two-foot oval. Bush sat in the wing chair facing the clock, where presidents always sit—and O'Neill sat on the near end of the small adjacent mustard-colored couch, where someone sits if he or she is the only visitor. As O'Neill navigated all this—he'd been here many times and knew the complex seating rules—his mind raced back to a conversation with George W. Bush just before the mid-December press conference in Austin, where the President-elect had announced his nomination . . . yes, there may have been a "Pablo" thrown in among the "Paul"s. O'Neill didn't think anything of it. He didn't know, back then, about Bush's odd enthusiasm for nicknames.

He knew now and settled into the couch . . . and his new identity: a sixty-five-year-old man named Pablo.

"So, whatta ya got?" the President barked, all business.

It was the afternoon of Wednesday, January 24, the third day of the Bush administration. The President calls the meetings. It is traditional protocol. One might suggest the need for a meeting to an Andy Card or Cheney, who would then pass it along, but the President issues the summons.

Bush had O'Neill's memo—Paul figured they'd talk about that—and then they'd discuss whatever came up. Cheney had said to him at one point that it might be valuable for Bush at the start of his presidency to have these meetings. To range around a bit.

O'Neill, as Treasury Secretary, institutionally designated to be the President's leading voice on the economy, offered a fifteen-minute overview on what he considered the informed opinion (that is, his and Greenspan's) and said that they were in the early stages of either an apparently mild recession or a pronounced inventory correction. The key was to remain sober. To watch the numbers. If we look concerned and talk up recession too much, he said, it will depress spending and encourage a downturn. O'Neill explained that the major problem was not the "encumbrances on capital"—there was plenty of low-cost capital out there, unable to find a profitable home. The problem was on the consumption side. The real numbers, he assured the President, did not support the bleakness of some "economic theorists."

O'Neill referred to items of his memo. Marginal rate cuts, if they were affordable, should be the priority. He said the tax cut plan, under almost any permutation thus far proposed, wouldn't provide measurable stimulus in the short term; what would create positive economic effects is "a sense that fiscal discipline has been preserved"—something that should boost equities markets and keep long-term bond rates in check. All that left the economy well suited to respond to a rate cut from the Fed.

There were a dozen questions that O'Neill had expected Bush to ask. He was ready with the answers. How large did O'Neill consider the surplus, and how real? How might the tax cut be structured? What about reforming Social Security and Medicare, the budget busters? How will we know if the economy has turned?

Bush didn't ask anything. He looked at O'Neill, not changing his expression, not letting on that he had any reactions—either positive or negative.

O'Neill decided therefore to move from the economy to a related matter. Steel tariffs. It was a simmering issue—the U.S. steel industry was hurting and pushing for protections. He said to the President, "You were admirably clear during the campaign about your stance in support of free trade—it's the only stance to take—and there's no way it can be squared with tariffs." He suggested that, as Treasury Secretary, he round up all the world's major producers and create a structure of shared incentives and sacrifices that would avoid tariff wars. He'd already tried some of this to good effect with the aluminum industry in 1993.

The President said nothing. No change in expression. Next subject.

Certainly, each president's style is different. But O'Neill had a basis for comparison. Nixon, Ford, Bush 41, and Clinton, with whom he had visited four or five times during the nineties for long sessions on policy matters. In each case, he'd arrived prepared to mix it up, ready for engagement. You'd hash it out. That was what he was known for. It was the reason you got called to the office. You met with the President to answer questions.

"I wondered, from the first, if the President didn't know the questions to ask," O'Neill recalled, "or did he know and just not want to know the answers? Or did his strategy somehow involve never showing what he thought? But you can ask questions, gather information, and not necessarily show your hand. It was strange."

With steel tariffs left hanging, O'Neill shrugged—if this was to be a monologue, he'd better make it sing.

They'd both been at that education conference five years before, so he went with that. "No Child Left Behind, I like that," O'Neill said, "but the idea that really moves us forward—a real action plan— is One Child at a Time."

It was an idea he'd road-tested with educators for years—that we need "an individualized mandate, where children would be constantly be assessed, *one child at a time*, in order to help create a little strategic plan for each student," a personalized learning strategy to fill gaps and develop latent potential. "It's a rethinking of what's possible, Mr. President. There's nothing more important than nurturing our human potential as a nation—our future depends on it."

Bush shifted in the wing-back chair. "Right, that's the concept of disaggregation"—a term used by educational statisticians to break down test scores—"I have that covered."

O'Neill wondered if he should point out that the President might be misusing that term but thought again. Instead, he spoke of the need to rigorously assess how federal money is spent in key areas and how to get more value for each dollar and apply it "to the trillions we've spent in foreign aid over the years . . . what were the goals underlying those expenditures and what were the outcomes." Once that evidence is gathered, O'Neill said, it would be appropriate to examine whether institutions like the World Bank and the International Monetary Fund needed restructuring.

The President seemed to nod in affirmation. O'Neill couldn't be sure.

Using the same model, O'Neill proffered a structure to assess the value of America's role in international economic crises—such as Mexico in 1995 or Indonesia in 1997. O'Neill was no longer expecting a response. He discussed ways to apply "value analysis" to the reform of health care and shrink federal expenditures, an area where he is considered by many as one of the country's most original thinkers. Then he offered a similar analytical framework to approach Japan's economic woes and craft an appropriate role for the United States.

O'Neill took a breath. The Oval Office's eighteenth-century grandfather clock—eight feet ten inches of mahogany with satinwood inlays—was to his back. He glanced at his watch. He'd been talking for just over fifty minutes. The meeting was scheduled for an hour.

"All right, Mr. President, maybe to finish up we could talk about global climate change . . ." Along with his memo on the tax cut strategy, O'Neill had sent over a booklet Alcoa had produced in 1998 with the text of an extensive speech he had given—a thorough analysis of the issue, what was known and as yet unknown, and principles to guide future actions. Bush seemed to indicate with a tilt of his head that he'd read it. But, again, O'Neill wasn't certain.

He pushed forward, adding his current thoughts on what the President might do on the issue—a flash point for environmental policy. He assessed the flaws of the Kyoto treaty and offered thoughts about how they might be remedied.

Both men are precise. And the hour was up. They stood at the same moment to shake hands.

"Get me a plan on global warming."

O'Neill nodded, a bit surprised.

Bush said it again. "Get me a plan on it."

Yes, fine, he'd create a plan, O'Neill said. Then he slipped out of the Oval Office, wondering whether that meant he was supposed to call EPA administrator Christie Whitman—the person designated to handle that area—or to *not* call her.

. . .

ACROSS TOWN, Alan Greenspan walked through the high hallways of the Hart Senate Office Building and into the office of Senator Kent Conrad, the Budget Committee's senior Democrat. Greenspan had worried that his statement the next morning in front of the committee would be viewed as too complex at a moment of economic uncertainty. So he had done something he rarely does: sent out confidential advance copies of his testimony to members of the Budget Committee. That way they could parse it and prepare cogent questions.

Conrad had read the testimony and was not pleased. "If you endorse these tax cuts, Alan, you're going to unleash the deficit dogs. All bets are going to be off. Because all those who want more tax cuts will see this as confirmation that they're right everybody who wants more spending will see this as a green light to them. What you'll do is throw fiscal responsibility out the window."

Greenspan was sobered. Conrad, a mild-mannered North Dakotan, began complaining about how unreliable ten-year forecasts are, that there was no $5.6 trillion surplus, that half was Social Security, and "if the government would just engage in honest accounting and take appropriate notice of its long-term liabilities, there'd be no surplus . . . these surpluses are fictional!"

The Fed chairman interrupted. "There are a lot of caveats attached to my statement. I'm recommending real limitations, like triggers and making tax cuts conditional, in how they're phased in, on the availability of surplus."

Conrad seemed to calm down. "Look, I'm for tax cuts, but the tax cuts being proposed here are much too much over the ten-year period and they're too small on the front end to provide much stimulus. It's the worst of both worlds."

Greenspan shrugged. It wasn't *his* tax cut policy—he hadn't designed it. But distributing the surplus in a safe, economically sound fashion was his concern. "Senator, I'm deeply worried about too much accumulation of money in the hands of the federal government. To the extent that we run cash surpluses, the government will accumulate cash, and, to get some reasonable return on that money, will have to invest it in the markets. Investments of this size, by the government, will politicize the economy. Nothing could be worse."

The senator took Greenspan's measure. "Well, you have a lot of debt to pay down before you get there."

"The numbers show we'll be virtually out of debt, the held debt of the government, by 2008," Greenspan said.

"Let's worry about that, Mr. Chairman, when we get close to that point. We have plenty of time, if that develops."

Conrad knew Greenspan didn't believe in the idea that investment screens (mechanisms meant to disguise the identity of a large investor) could be effective or that investing the surplus in huge indexed funds could hide the government's hand. He had a point. There could be dangers of politicizing the markets. But, suddenly, the Fed chairman raised this problem to match the threat posed by his long-standing enemy—federal deficits.

Greenspan left. Conrad called Bob Rubin, imploring him to talk to the Fed chairman. Rubin, who had not read the testimony, called Greenspan. He suggested that the surpluses could be distributed, as they appeared each year, in the form of refundable tax credits. It was a variation on the kind of conditionality that Greenspan and O'Neill would strive for with their triggers. Rubin said it was all about perceptions and that Greenspan might be seen as endorsing Bush's tax cut.

"I can't be in charge of people's perceptions," Greenspan said. "I don't function that way. I can't function that way."

. . .

THE NEXT MORNING—January 25—the Fed chairman arrived in the hearing room of the Senate Budget Committee at his usual time for testimony, 10 a.m., so that the markets would have most of a full day to respond.

But he was too late—the markets were already responding. Sending out advance copies of his testimony had backfired. His testimony had been leaked. That morning's *USA Today* had a ten-point banner headline: GREENSPAN TO BACK TAX CUTS; FED CHIEF "APT TO CHANGE" STANCE ON HOW BEST TO USE SURPLUS.

Greenspan sat at the witness table and, in three thousand or so carefully chosen words, attempted a primer on budgetary reality. The surpluses, he began, were driven by gains in productivity, largely from a rising arc of technological advances, and it was anyone's guess where we now were on that long curve. "To be sure," he read, "these impressive upward revisions to the growth of structural productivity and economic potential are based on inferences drawn from economic relationships that are different from anything we have considered in recent decades. The resulting budget projections, therefore, are necessarily subject to a relatively wide range of error."

Noting the uncertainty of budget forecasts, he suggested that a future tax cut "could include provisions that, in some way, would limit surplus-reducing actions if specified targets for the budget surplus and federal debt were not satisfied. Only if the probability was very low that prospective tax cuts or new outlay initiatives would send the on-budget accounts into deficit, would unconditional initiatives appear prudent."

Now that the trigger proposal was unveiled, Greenspan ran through a wide array of cautions, from rising interest rates elevating the price of large deficits to his fear that large surpluses would create a drag on the economy. He ended with his main concern: that the government could dangerously alter financial markets by attempting to invest these excess funds.

"In today's context," he elaborated, "where tax reduction appears required in any event over the next several years to assist in forestalling the accumulation of private assets, starting that process sooner rather than later likely would help smooth the transition to longer-term fiscal balance. And should current economic weakness spread beyond what now appears likely, having a tax cut in place may, in fact, do noticeable good."

The news was delivered. Reporters in the room typed or jotted furiously; a few exited the hearing room to call in the confirmation of *USA Today*'s scoop. Kent Conrad watched them slip out and shook his head. People weren't even staying around for the end of the prepared testimony, much less the questioning by committee members.

A few moments later, Greenspan wrapped it up with his final cautionary note. "With today's euphoria surrounding the surpluses, it is not difficult to imagine the hard-earned fiscal restraint developed in recent years rapidly dissipating. We need to resist those policies that could readily resurrect the deficits of the past and the fiscal imbalances that followed in their wake."

At this point, it was an afterthought. The spotlight was elsewhere.

. . .

O'NEILL RUSHED from his first meeting with his department heads—commissioner of the IRS, head of Alcohol, Tobacco and Firearms, and the rest—to flip on the television in the walnut breakfront behind his desk. The Fed chairman, who was now well into his questioning by senators, was fencing with Ernest "Fritz" Hollings, South Carolina's silver-maned Democrat, about large and growing obligations for funding Social Security and whether surpluses—as the Fed and Treasury currently define them—really exist. "Where, Mr. Chairman, do you find a surplus?" chided the theatrical Hollings. "I find a deficit. I'm looking at the record here, but you correct me—"

The phone rang—Annabella said there was a call from Jim Lynn—and O'Neill turned away from the TV, always tuned to CNBC, to pick up the line.

"Hey, stranger," O'Neill said.

"Just wanted to tell you how proud the old gang is of you, Paul."

Lynn had been head of OMB under Ford; he was a numbers man with good political instincts, who had provided cover for O'Neill's fierce analytical crusades, which as often killed policies (and the armies manning them) as created new campaigns.

"So, how do you think Alan's doing?" Lynn asked. "Will people understand what he's saying?"

"I hope so," Paul said. "Alan and I have been working through these issues all month. People may just hear 'tax cut,' but I hope they hear 'prudence.' An awful lot is riding on it."

Both men—along with former chairs of congressional budget committees and retired officials from OMB and the Fed—had been members of the Committee for Responsible Budgets, a group that meets twice a year and circulates papers on fiscal management. There is general agreement in the committee that the budgeting process is under constant threat from political chicanery—and that caps, ceilings, and triggers, although imperfect, are a kind of methadone treatment for an addiction to partisan illusions.

Along those lines, Lynn—who left OMB eventually to head Aetna, the insurance company—offered an analogy, one retired CEO to another. "Think about the way we used to offer, say, a pre-ferred dividend, a special dividend, and everybody knows that you're going to look at it every year, and see if we can do the same as the previous year, or something more or something less," says Lynn. "Everyone understands the preferred dividend is conditional on how things went in that year, for the company, the economy."

O'Neill thought that the proper analogy was a dividend on common stock, to all shareholders, insofar as each citizen was a shareholder of sorts in the U.S. government. "The question, as it is with a dividend, is how do we give away our money but keep it, too," O'Neill said. "How do we give back to shareholders what is fiscally appropriate and not make an open-ended grant that eventually bankrupts the company?"

Having a carrot—with a tax cut of some size flowing from this surplus—might be the key. "We're giving them something, but it can't be something for nothing," he told Lynn. "The trade-off is accepting real principles for restraint going forward."

. . .

TWO HUNDRED YARDS due west, on the ground floor of the West Wing, Press Secretary Ari Fleischer stepped to the podium for his midday briefing. He was selling a different message: The President welcomes Chairman Greenspan's support.

Reporters asked about Greenspan's comment that a tax cut package like the one the President was proposing wouldn't provide any short-term stimulus to the economy.

"I think there's plenty of room for agreement among economists or slight disagreement among economists about the speed at which a tax cut could help the economy," Fleischer said. "But clearly Chairman Greenspan came out today and advocated that there is room for tax cuts and that Congress can cut taxes, given the budget restraints that we're all operating under, which are now an era of large surpluses."

As to some of Greenspan's suggestions of "triggers" or "conditionality," Fleischer stated the administration's response. "We need to make it [the tax cut] the *permanent* law of the land," he said tersely.

The White House's line of the day was now solidly rooted. It was the "golden trio" of message delivery: tell them what you're going to say; say it; then tell them what you just said. *USA Today* had handled the first part. Greenspan said, "Tax reduction appears required in any event," as expected. Fleischer had merely to close the circle.

Inside the West Wing, however, there was concern. Greenspan's exposition had shown his thinking on fiscal policy, including some things O'Neill had put forth in his confirmation testimony. No, the tax reduction wouldn't be particularly stimulative, contradicting what the President was advertising. And Greenspan wanted triggers, phasing in a tax cut over years, and rigorous conditionality based on availability of surpluses, especially for the out years of the proposal's ten-year arc. Even if these were to be noted only in subordinate paragraphs of the next day's news stories, it showed that Greenspan was anything but on the team.

Meanwhile, Larry Lindsey turned his attention to O'Neill. He and other adherents of the tax cut orthodoxy understood that O'Neill's close tie to Greenspan was considered a key asset by Bush. But since Greenspan had staked out an independent position, a question now took hold: Is the Treasury Secretary more in sync with his old friend the Fed chairman than with his new boss, the President?

That day, Lindsey wrote a memorandum to chief of staff Andy Card—a way of getting it to the President without listing Bush as a recipient.

The specific charge was that the Treasury's Office of Tax Analysis (OTA) was unable to provide "the revenue cost for the President's tax reform program before the beginning of next week," when Bush was slated to make some key decisions about tax and budget matters. That meant the White House would have to rely on Treasury baseline assumptions and revenue cost estimates of the Joint Committee on Taxation, a bipartisan congressional group—numbers that showed only modest economic growth from the tax cuts and a negligible impact on prospective tax revenues—rather than rely, as Lindsey wrote, "wholly on Administration estimates."

The estimates, Lindsey felt, should be judged based on "dynamic scoring"—a theory, embraced by some economists, that growth created by a tax cut had certain multiplicative effects, much like the compounding of interest, that weren't being fully factored into what they called the static scoring traditionally used by budget officials.

The staff at the Office of Tax Analysis, meanwhile, had barely been introduced to their new bosses. Mark Weinberger, O'Neill's designee for assistant secretary for tax policy, wasn't due to arrive until early February. Generating such revenue cost estimates takes about a week—a long process of feeding numbers through a complex computer model that shows how tax cuts wash through arteries of the U.S. economy—and career Treasury staffers are less than enthusiastic about working the model for a proposal that may soon change.

A rather conventional give-and-take between policy shops, an internecine matter, seemed to Lindsey an opportunity of sorts.

"I personally find this deplorable," he wrote. "I am puzzled that the OTA did not have a model of the President's tax proposal in an operable condition so that it could be combined with the latest economic assumptions. This must mean that not only was one not written since it was determined that the President would take office, but that none was written during the campaign either. As you know, the President has been steadfast in sticking to his tax proposal since he proposed it in December, 1999."

Lindsey sent copies of the memo to O'Neill and OMB director Mitch Daniels. Soon, it would be leaked to the press.

That afternoon, O'Neill fenced on the phone for an hour with Phil Gramm, the Republican senator from Texas who has long led the party's conservative wing on tax issues. Gramm talked about Greenspan's testimony and his distaste for any limits, including a ten-year time frame, on a proposed reduction in tax rates—"What's the point of that?" Gramm asked. "You reduce them or you don't"—and probed the Treasury Secretary for his view of what the Fed chairman had said. O'Neill was noncommittal. He knew Gramm talked to the President, Karl Rove, and Lindsey, so he moved the discussion to other issues.

Later, Greenspan stopped by O'Neill's office. He was aggrieved at the *USA Today* leak and felt that he would need to further build his case for conditionality and prudence in other congressional appearances slated for the coming weeks. "Got sideswiped a bit today," he said.

"At least the idea of caps or triggers is out there," O'Neill said. "It'll start a discussion. That's all we need."

The afternoon waned. Condoleezza Rice called about foreign debt issues, Karen Hughes about "message unity" in the tax battle ahead. Then O'Neill got his copy of Larry's memo.

He read it, half in disbelief. The criticisms of the tax office were absurd. His team wasn't even assembled—the office hadn't started officially working for this President until two days ago—and Treasury's assumptions, along with the joint committee's numbers, were sufficient to guide the President in these early discussions. If Larry wanted a set of numbers that supported his case, he'd have to get them somewhere else.

On a second read, he realized that the letter wasn't about any of that. It was a statement of loyalty. Lindsey was saying that he was a stalwart supporter of the President and that O'Neill was not. This was the breach O'Neill had feared: that the "honest broker" was an advocate. Hard-eyed analysis would be painted as disloyalty. He was clearly being characterized as contrarian.

He grabbed a printout of the memo and scribbled across the top:

> *Larry: This is bureaucratic chicken——.*
> *You must have something better to do with your time*
> *than send me memos such as this one.*

> *Paul O'Neill*

He jotted cc's to Andy Card and Mitch Daniels and threw it into the mail.

If they wanted a fight, he'd give them one.

. . .

ON THE AFTERNOON of January 30, ten days after his inauguration as the forty-third president, George W. Bush met with the principals of his National Security Council for the first time.

The innermost circle filed into the situation room downstairs from the Oval Office at 3:35 p.m. sharp, some of them surprised to see the President already there, all but checking his watch. Presidents are notorious for starting meetings like this a little late and letting them run longer than scheduled.

All assumed their seats around the table according to longstanding ritual: at the head, the President; to his right, the Vice President; then O'Neill, CIA director George Tenet, and Condoleezza Rice at the table's far end; to the President's left, Powell, Rumsfeld, and Joint Chiefs of Staff Chairman General Hugh Shelton. Andy Card was there, and each principal had brought a top deputy, a backbencher; these assumed seats directly behind their bosses.

Bush offered a few introductory remarks about "the structure of things in my NSC.

"Condi will run these meetings. I'll be seeing all of you regularly, but I want you to debate things out here and then Condi will report to me. She's my national security adviser."

The designated topic was "Mideast Policy," but the agendas that had been sent around over the preceding days had offered only thin details. O'Neill and the other principals had been briefed by their staffs about the only issue of recent consequence in the region, the Arab-Israeli conflict.

Through the fall and winter of 2000–2001, the Clinton administration had made a final desperate push for a settlement. Clinton had called together Palestinian leader Yasir Arafat and Israeli prime minister Ehud Barak. Earlier they had all but camped at Camp David. Clinton became deeply involved in the process, making it his personal mission. With Barak barely clinging to power and desperate for a settlement, and Clinton anxious, virtually all the Palestinian demands were met, including a separate state with UN-defended borders and $32 billion in aid.

But along the way, the Clinton team had isolated Arafat, figuring they could induce cooperation by separating him from more radical factions in the Palestinian camp. That move left Arafat disempowered, unable to represent the fractious array of Palestinian interests. As the agreement was all but inked in December, Arafat pulled away from the table, murmuring about two-thousand-year-old claims to religious rites on Jerusalem's Temple Mount. In retrospect, it was clear to many of those involved that he had been left with insufficient authority to sign any pact.

President Bush echoed this view: "We're going to correct the imbalances of the previous administration on the Mideast conflict. We're going to tilt it back toward Israel. And we're going to be consistent."

"Clinton overreached, and it all fell apart. That's why we're in trouble," Bush said. "If the two sides don't want peace, there's no way we can force them."

Then the President halted. "Anybody here ever met [Ariel] Sharon?"

After a moment, Powell sort of raised his hand. Yes, he had.

"I'm not going to go by past reputations when it comes to Sharon," Bush said. "I'm going to take him at face value. We'll work on a relationship based on how things go."

He'd met Sharon briefly, Bush said, when they had flown over Israel in a helicopter on a visit in December 1998. "Just saw him that one time. We flew over the Palestinian camps," Bush said sourly. "Looked real bad down there. I don't see much we can do over there at this point. I think it's time to pull out of that situation."

And that was it, according to O'Neill and several other people in the room. The Arab-Israeli conflict was a mess, and the United States would disengage. The combatants would have to work it out on their own.

Powell said such a move might be hasty. He remarked on the violence on the West Bank and Gaza and on its roots. He stressed that a pullback by the United States would unleash Sharon and the Israeli army. "The consequences of that could be dire," he said, "especially for the Palestinians."

Bush shrugged. "Maybe that's the best way to get things back in balance."

Powell seemed startled.

"Sometimes a show of strength by one side can really clarify things," Bush said.

He turned to Rice. "So, Condi, what are we going to talk about today? What's on the agenda?"

"How Iraq is destabilizing the region, Mr. President," Rice said, in what several observers understood was a scripted exchange. She noted that Iraq might be the key to reshaping the entire region.

Rice said that CIA director Tenet would offer a briefing on the latest intelligence on Iraq. Tenet pulled out a long scroll, the size of an architectural blueprint, and flattened it on the table.

It was a grainy photograph of a factory. Tenet said that surveillance planes had just taken this photo. The CIA believed the building might be "a plant that produces either chemical or biological materials for weapons manufacture."

Soon, everyone was leaning over the photo. Tenet had a pointer. "Here are the railroad tracks coming in . . . here are the trucks lined up over here. . . . They're bringing it in here and bringing it out there. . . . This is the water cooler."

Cheney motioned to the deputies, the backbenchers, lining the wall. "Come on up," he said with uncharacteristic excitement, waving his arm. "You have to take a look at this."

And they crowded around as well. Now, well over a dozen people, including the President, gazed intently at the tablecloth-size photograph.

After a moment, O'Neill interjected, "I've seen a lot of factories around the world that look a lot like this one. What makes us suspect that this one is producing chemical or biological agents for weapons?"

Tenet mentioned a few items of circumstantial evidence—such as the round-the-clock rhythm of shipments in and out of the plant—but said there was "no confirming intelligence" as to the materials being produced.

Then the CIA director rolled out more scrolls. One was an airstrip with an Iraqi plane that U.S. jets had destroyed. Another detailed the routes of U.S. surveillance planes. A third showed the dense antiaircraft fortifications Saddam Hussein had set up around Baghdad that stretched in a kind of funnel toward the south, where a no-fly zone was being enforced.

There had been a recent incident in which a U.S. surveillance plane was nearly shot down, and General Shelton said that U.S. reliance on aerial intelligence presented an acute risk that one of our planes might be hit and a pilot killed or captured.

O'Neill inquired about our ability to blast their antiaircraft batteries—"for every missile they fire we respond by destroying ten of their batteries"—and the talk turned technical. Rumsfeld chimed in about missile guidance systems. Tenet interjected that intelligence remained so poor that, in terms of targeting military installations or weapons factories, "we'd be going in there blind."

The President said little. He just nodded, with the same flat, unquestioning demeanor that O'Neill was familiar with. But a new direction having been set from the top, this policy change now guided the proceedings. The opening premise, that Saddam's regime was destabilizing the region, and the vivid possibility that he owned weapons of mass destruction—a grainy picture, perhaps misleading, but visceral—pushed analysis toward logistics: the need for better intelligence, for ways to tighten the net around the regime, for use of the U.S. military to support Iraqi insurgents in a coup.

A major shift in U.S. policy was under way. After more than thirty years of intense engagement—from Kissinger and Nixon to Clinton's last stand—America was washing its hands of the conflict in Israel. Now, we'd focus on Iraq.

Powell said the sanctions were ineffective, that "we were playing into Saddam's hands and losing support among the Iraqi people."

The sanctions needed to shift "from a list of what is allowed to a list of what is prohibited," to become, instead of a broad sanctions regime, an arms control regime. "We need to strictly control the import of materials that might be used for weapons construction and allow the import of goods that are not, now, getting through," the Secretary of State said. Saddam was manipulating the current situation. Needed medicines and other essentials were not reaching the Iraqi people, even though Saddam Hussein had nearly $3 billion in his oil-for-food accounts at the United Nations that he'd left unspent. Powell pointed out that the sanctions weren't shrewdly targeted, creating mishaps like a power plant failing because it couldn't get repair parts and Iraqis dying at a hospital that lost electricity. "This is not endearing us to the Iraqi people, whose support we're hoping to elicit—if I understand our position correctly—to help overthrow this regime."

"That's a problem. The people need to be with us," Bush said.

Tenet mentioned that the CIA had received intelligence assessments that Saddam was paying rewards to the families of some suicide bombers on the West Bank and Gaza. He was also selling underpriced oil to Jordan and Syria, creating a web of interdependency and support among neighboring countries.

"We need to know more about this," Bush said, "and also his destructive weapons."

Over the next minutes, speculative, nonspecific talk volleyed across the table about how to remedy inadequate intelligence, discover the nature of Saddam's weapons program, and bomb selected Iraqi targets.

Those present who had attended NSC meetings of the previous administration—and there were several—noticed a material shift. "In the Clinton administration, there was an enormous reluctance to use American forces on the ground; it was almost a prohibition," one of them recalled. "That prohibition was clearly gone, and that opened options, options that hadn't been opened before."

The hour almost up, Bush had assignments for everyone. Powell and his team would look to draw up a new sanctions regime. Rumsfeld and Shelton, he said, "should examine our military options." That included rebuilding the military coalition from the 1991 Gulf War, examining "how it might look" to use U.S. ground forces in the north and the south of Iraq and how the armed forces could support groups inside the country who could help challenge Saddam Hussein. Tenet would report on improving our current intelligence. O'Neill would investigate how to financially squeeze the regime.

Meeting adjourned. Ten days in, and it was about Iraq.

. . .

O'NEILL WALKED BACK to Treasury, running scenes from the situation room through his head. "Getting Hussein was now the administration's focus, that much was already clear," he recalled. He knew that Rumsfeld and some of the people he was lining up for deputies, like Deputy Secretary of Defense Paul Wolfowitz and Doug Feith—a longtime foreign policy analyst who was then managing a Washington law firm—felt it had been a mistake not to dispose of Saddam in 1991.

But, ten years later, Hussein seemed caged and defanged. Clearly, there were many forces destabilizing the region, most particularly the Arab-Israeli conflict itself, which we were now abandoning. Who, exactly, was pushing this foreign policy, and were they asking themselves hard questions about choices and consequences? The meeting had seemed scripted. Rumsfeld had said little, Cheney nothing at all, though both men had long entertained the idea of overthrowing Saddam. Rice orchestrated, and Tenet had a presentation ready. Powell seemed surprised that we were abandoning the Israeli-Palestinian dispute and making Iraq the focal point. General Shelton appeared concerned. Was there already an "in" group and an "out" group?

Was this a matter of simply completing what the first Bush administration had left undone? Was a multipronged assault on Saddam Hussein really a priority in early 2001? The dialogue today had been mostly about *hows*—how to weaken or end Saddam's regime. With the administration at the start of its second week, O'Neill wondered, when, exactly, the *whys*—why Saddam, why now, and why this was central to U.S. interests—were to be discussed.

. . .

SHORTLY AFTER he returned to his office, O'Neill opened a memo from Donald Rumsfeld.

It was titled "Talking Points, FY01 and FY02–07 Budget Issues."

For the most part, however, it was not a traditional budget document. In describing why the military budget was due for a dramatic increase, Rumsfeld articulated, with a five-point illustration of a dire global landscape, the underlying ideas that were now guiding foreign policy.

1. The collapse of the Soviet Union has produced centrifugal forces in the world that have created new regional powers. Several of these are intensely hostile to

the United States and are arming to deter us from bringing our conventional or nuclear power to bear in a regional crisis.

2. The post Cold War liberalization of trade in advanced technology goods and services has made it possible for the poorest nations on earth to rapidly acquire
the most destructive military technology ever devised
including nuclear, chemical, and biological weapons and
their means of delivery. We cannot prevent them from
doing so.

3. The civil sector, not the defense sector, now creates
the enabling technologies for advanced military capabilities. These universally available technologies can be
used to create "asymmetric" responses by small or
medium sized states to our conventional military power
that cannot defeat our forces, but can deny access to
critical areas of Europe, the Middle East and Asia. Conventional submarines, advanced air defense, attacks on
our C4ISR [Command, Control, Communication,
Computers, Intelligence, Surveillance, and Reconnais-
sance] infrastructure and similar "asymmetric" approaches can limit our ability to apply military power.

4. China, Russia, Iran, Iraq, North Korea and others are
investing in these capabilities that exploit provocative
lapses in US capabilities. Liberalized international trade
will propagate these capabilities to others.

5. The threats can emerge very rapidly and with little or
no warning.

NOTE: Observations of FMR SECDEF Bill Cohen—
missile threat to US could emerge in one year.
CONCLUSION: The risk to US and Alliance security is in-

creasing as the US fails to respond effectively and deci-
sively to asymmetric threats likely to characterize the
first quarter of the 21st century.

O'Neill had known Rumsfeld since the late 1960s. Their paths,
since then, often crossed. Their wives were friends. They had both
left government to become CEOs. Don was chairman of the RAND
Corporation. And then Paul was chairman.

In mid-December, when O'Neill had gone to Texas to be introduced as Bush's selection for Treasury, he spoke to Bush about
Rumsfeld. At that point, Indiana senator Dan Coats and Paul Wolfowitz were among the leading contenders for the Defense Secretary's job. In a meeting at the Governor's Mansion, Bush quipped
that Cheney was too close to Rumsfeld to be objective and asked
O'Neill for his opinion. "He'd be a great agent for change," O'Neill
said, endorsing Rumsfeld and advising Bush on "how to best utilize
Don's abilities."

O'Neill was one of the few people who spoke bluntly to the head-
strong Rumsfeld. He was someone who would tell Rummy when he
was dead wrong.

Now, O'Neill flipped through the six pages of the document, a
first rendering of what kind of Defense Secretary Rumsfeld would
be. Rumsfeld's stark view was followed by a long list of responses as
to how the military should change and what the cost would be.

The memo distilled ideas that had evolved since the first Bush administration. The collapse of the Soviet Union in 1991 meant that
nearly every principle underlying America's global posture was due
for reevaluation. A first glimpse of what top U.S. officials were
thinking in that regard emerged in 1992, when a classified Pentagon
draft report, entitled *Defense Policy Guidance*, was leaked to *The New
York Times*. The plan, written by Paul Wolfowitz, then the undersecretary for policy under Defense Secretary Dick Cheney, stressed

how new centers of power, some of them hostile to the United States, were growing. The draft report recommended the United States be forceful in deterring the growth of "competitors," which included China and Russia along with allies like Germany and Japan.

Meanwhile, a related dialogue was evolving about what kind of military could best project U.S. power in a technologically changed world. This line of discussion was driven by a soft-spoken defense analyst named Andy Marshall, who had been running the Pentagon's Office of Net Assessment, an in-house policy center, for nearly thirty years and frequently visited RAND, where he met with Rumsfeld and O'Neill. Marshall is considered the founder of a school of thought known as "Revolution in Military Affairs," which asserted that one of history's infrequent leaps in military tactics and technology was afoot. The two key features of the present leap were the development of precision long-range weapons, which make aircraft carriers, air bases, and other conspicuous platforms vulnerable to remote attacks; and advances in information technology—from satellite-based cameras to robot probes and global positioning systems—which allow commanders to see a shifting battlefield, stay in close touch and coordination, and respond to opportunities.

The military of the future, Marshall and his supporters asserted, would be a smaller, swifter, technologically augmented force on land and sea, supported by precision long-range weapons and a sophisticated, intelligence-driven air attack.

This so-called transformation theory didn't show many tangible results in the 1990s. President Clinton's relations with the armed forces started badly with his gays-in-the-military stance and never significantly improved, giving military traditionalists plenty of ammunition to halt initiatives by Marshall and the reform-minded Defense Secretary, William Perry. Despite much talk of a large "peace dividend," Clinton dropped defense spending only slightly in real, inflation-adjusted dollars in something of a negotiated truce.

Neither was there an embrace of bold doctrine under Clinton. Defense and foreign policy teams tended to approach geopolitical issues, such as the Bosnian conflict or relations with China, case by case. They improvised, pulling together international partners and trying, with some success, to carve out settlements and hold the middle ground. In fact, they felt that the end of the Cold War freed them from wide, organizing dogma such as "containment" or "détente."

In Kennebunkport in 1998, George H. W. Bush introduced his son to Condoleezza Rice, a political science professor at Stanford University and the school's provost. The governor was beginning to think about what it might mean to be President. He had insights into only one foreign country thanks to Texas's long shared border with Mexico. Rice teamed up with Paul Wolfowitz, and a tutorial commenced. Over the next year and a half, others were called in, almost all of whom were part of a small, neoconservative community.

Renditions of what went on in these sessions are sketchy. What the governor knew—what he learned and from whom—is mostly limited to comments about his having "good instincts." One exception is from the loquacious Richard Perle, a fellow at the American Enterprise Institute and former assistant secretary of defense in the Reagan administration, who commented publicly, "The first time I met Bush 43, I knew he was different. Two things became clear. One, he didn't know very much. The other was he had the confidence to ask questions that revealed he didn't know very much. Most people are reluctant to say when they don't know something, a word or a term they haven't heard before. Not him. You'd raise a point, and he'd say, 'I didn't realize that. Can you explain that?' He was eager to learn."

At this point, the end of January, those who had presided over the inception of many of the ideas that would form the foundation of the administration's foreign policy would preside over their execution.

Cheney would offer oversight and protection. Rumsfeld would be the point man. Wolfowitz would back Rumsfeld up from the inside. And from the outside, Richard Perle, heading a special civilian group called the Defense Policy Advisory Group, would counsel the Pentagon, the White House, and the CIA.

The premise of Rumsfeld's memo was that threats to U.S. security had taken root and grown quickly in the years since the globe's bipolar orderliness had dissolved. As new regional powers with intense hostility to the United States "are arming to deter us," Rumsfeld wrote, trade in advanced technologies has made it possible for even "the poorest nations on earth to rapidly acquire the most destructive military weapons ever devised." This dire prospect of a planet teeming with nuclear, biological, and chemical weapons—and, it was assumed, a desire to use them on the United States—is unavoidable, a fait accompli, the memo asserted. "We cannot prevent them from doing so."

A traditional counterpoint, that international organizations and a web of economic and cultural interdependencies—as well as protective alliances—could help to control such deadly proliferation, is not mentioned in the six-page memo. The neoconservative view places little faith in such arrangements or, for that matter, in diplomacy.

In the "asymmetric" case, there may not be a state with which to negotiate. The term—used of late by military strategists to encompass anything other than a conventional force-on-force engagement of heavy divisions—essentially refers to guerrilla warfare. Augmented by universally available weapons of mass destruction, such asymmetric approaches, Rumsfeld wrote, would be enough to deny the United States access to many regions of the world and "limit our ability to apply military power."

Rumsfeld listed Iraq, along with China, Russia, Iran, and North Korea, as moving down this path—and then noted an observation of former Defense Secretary William Cohen, in the Clinton administration, that a missile threat to the United States could emerge in one year.

O'Neill flipped to the last part of Rumsfeld's memo, to the statement of principles. He had heard much of this before, in meetings he'd attended in the late 1990s at the American Enterprise Institute, where all the leading neoconservatives were present: a statement of enveloping peril and no hypothesis for any real solution.

The next pages highlighted the deterioration in conventional U.S. forces—the effect of Clinton's "procurement holiday" on transport and weapons systems—and recommended an increase in defense spending of between $255 billion and $842 billion over the next five years. The application of this money would be to preserve the current forces while building tomorrow's military.

In a concluding section, "What Are We Trying to Achieve?," there were general recommendations to "sustain our ability to deter the use of WMD and long-range missiles against the US"—a play for more money for missile defense systems—and then to use our "existing force structure to dissuade nations abroad from challenging our interests while we transform our armed forces to meet 21st Century conditions."

The key word was "dissuade." Rumsfeld's use of it made clear that he had started to plot coordinates for a global response, if not necessarily a solution.

But how, O'Neill wondered, could the United States dissuade other sovereign countries from being guided by a natural, inexorable growth in their own technological capabilities?

· · ·

THE NEXT MEETING of the NSC principals was called for 3 p.m. on Thursday, February 1, in the White House Situation Room.

O'Neill arrived a few minutes early and read the cover sheet of his briefing materials.

Purpose: To review the current state-of-play (including CIA briefing on Iraq) and to examine policy questions on how to proceed.

Attachments:

Tab A: Agenda and Policy Questions (from NSC)— SECRET
Tab B: Economic Background on Iraq (from Deutsche Bank)
Tab C: Executive Summary: Political-Military Plan for Post-Saddam Iraq Crisis (interagency working paper)—SECRET
Tab D: Summary of United States Sanctions on Iraq
Tab E: "Iraq Sanctions Regime," State Department, for use in public statements

Sitting across from O'Neill was Colin Powell. They chatted amiably as they waited for Rice to start the meeting. Whereas his old friends Cheney and Rumsfeld had seemed circumspect in the first meeting—as though they felt comfortable talking candidly only in private meetings with the President—Powell was clearly trying to ask the kinds of hard, fundamental questions that O'Neill most appreciated. What's more, he was doing it with all the principals present, trying to make the decision-making process more inclusive and transparent.

Powell's report for today's meeting was to do with altering the sanctions regime. Yet the briefing materials provided by the State Department served as an apt catchall, touching upon specific goals of Defense, Treasury, and other departments in tracing the wide arc of the new initiative against Saddam Hussein.

"This outline," read the State Department's summary,

> deals with the issues that need to be resolved in order to
> re-energize sanctions against Iraq, rebuild the coalition
> and deal with Iraqi WMD programs. It is not a complete
> discussion of Iraq policy which would also need to cover
> approaches to a possible regime change, war crimes initia-
> tives, dealings with the Kurds, coalition military posture
> and redlines [key aspects of policy not up for negotiation or
> compromise]. Our overall objective would be to prevent
> Iraq from threatening its neighbors or the national security
> more broadly on the basis of continued control of Iraqi rev-
> enues, [a] ban on military and WMD related imports and
> weapons inspections. This approach has two tracks which
> are mutually reinforcing and which we would pursue con-
> currently; one track is to intensify sanctions enforcement
> and the other is to implement UN Security Council resolu-
> tion 1284.

The Security Council resolution, passed in December 1999, was the last in a series of modifications of the sanctions regime that had been in place since Iraq invaded Kuwait in 1990. This alteration lifted many of the remaining constraints from the Iraqi economy so there would be no reason for Iraqis to suffer malnutrition or a short-age of medicine—a move that was part of an attempt by the United States to give ground on the sanctions side in exchange for more in-ternational support for weapons inspections. The State Department believed that its new plan to target the sanctions toward arms control would be covered by 1284. O'Neill and Treasury assessed ways to convince banks in Turkey, Jordan, Syria, and other Arab states to halt transactions with Iraq's banks, cutting the flow of capital to Hussein. Defense and CIA, meanwhile, were busy handling, in State Depart-ment parlance, "possible regime change, war crimes initiatives, deal-ings with the Kurds, coalition military posture and redlines."

Rice, presiding, outlined the agenda and what was expected of each presenter.

Powell began by discussing the new strategy for "targeted sanctions." But, after a moment, Rumsfeld interrupted.

"Sanctions are fine," he said. "But what we really want to think about is going after Saddam."

He then launched into an assessment of the broader U.S. goal of getting rid of Saddam and replacing the current regime with one more inclined toward cooperative relations with the United States and its Western allies.

"Imagine what the region would look like without Saddam and with a regime that's aligned with U.S. interests," Rumsfeld said. "It would change everything in the region and beyond it. It would demonstrate what U.S. policy is all about."

Rumsfeld began to talk in general terms about post-Saddam Iraq, dealing with the Kurds in the north, the oil fields, the reconstruction of the country's economy, and the "freeing of the Iraqi people."

The hanging question was how to arrive at this desired goal. Rice, Rumsfeld, and General Shelton talked generally about rebuilding the military coalition from the 1991 Gulf War—though an invasion was never specifically mentioned. Tenet talked about a coup and said the prospects for success were not particularly good. Powell said we "don't just want to replace one bad guy with another bad guy." Rumsfeld added that we might use the no-fly zone operations tactically to help some of the opposition groups as they moved militarily.

Rumsfeld hedged, however. "It's not my specific objective to get rid of Saddam Hussein," he said. "I'm after the weapons of mass destruction. Regime change isn't my prime concern."

Everyone noted this statement, and then the discussion of options and tactics commenced.

O'Neill thought about Rumsfeld's memo. It described how everything fit together. The sudden focus on Saddam Hussein made sense only if the broader ideology—of a need to "dissuade" others from creating asymmetric threats—were to be embraced. That was the *why*.

A weak but increasingly obstreperous Saddam might be useful as a demonstration model of America's new, unilateral resolve. If it could effectively be shown that he possessed, or was trying to build, weapons of mass destruction—creating an "asymmetric threat," in the neoconservative parlance, to U.S. power in the region—his overthrow would help "dissuade" other countries from doing the same. At least, that seemed to be the idea.

"There was never any rigorous talk about this sweeping idea that seemed to be driving all the specific actions," O'Neill said, echoing the comments of several other participants in NSC discussions. "From the start, we were building the case against Hussein and looking at how we could take him out and change Iraq into a new country. And, if we did that, it would solve everything. It was all about finding *a way to do it*. That was the tone of it. The President saying, 'Fine. Go find me a way to do this.' "

CHAPTER 3

NO FINGERPRINTS

THE ADMINISTRATION burst into its first, frenetic month—
the initial strides so telling of the character of a presidency,
from campaign promises to policies.

An economic plan of deep tax cuts was unfurling, even as O'Neill and Greenspan were quietly working to trim the administration's policy. In foreign policy, demonstrating a policy that would soon be called "preemption" with the overthrow of Saddam—despite Bush's campaign pronouncements that the United States would be "humble" in its global posture and never engage in "nation-building"— was already a central mission.

Cabinet secretaries were invited into the Oval Office for initial sit-downs with the new President. Andy Card gathered White House staffers for an introductory meeting and told them to look left, look right, and recognize that "one of you will be gone in eighteen months." Karen Hughes took the corner suite with the best views—north toward Pennsylvania Avenue and east overlooking the first family's residence—while Karl Rove settled around the horseshoe of the West Wing's second floor in an understated warren of offices.

O'Neill's portfolio, meanwhile, was wider than he could have imagined. Across his desk were passing all pertinent documents of the U.S. government's engagements here and abroad, from Labor Department statistics to CIA briefings. Everyone at the helm of the administration was regularly soliciting his advice, from Rumsfeld to Karen Hughes.

And, of course, the President. The sessions with Bush were now called "standing meeting with POTUS" on O'Neill's schedule, a weekly session to cover the countless policies a president—any president—needs to master. Bush, O'Neill recalled, had "seemed to be limited in his knowledge of most domestic issues," but he continued to listen intently, in his expressionless way.

O'Neill was not sure how to read these encounters—perhaps the President was just collecting input for decisions to come; maybe he hadn't thought very much about certain domestic issues; maybe this was part of some innovation in strategy, of a president knowing that even a show of interest in this area could end up guiding policy. Maybe it was all of the above.

In any event, the regular meetings were provoking O'Neill's assessment of the value of *his own* thought process—to mixed effect. He had said in December that he might find it difficult being "just another bird in the nest."

In most of his early engagements, he was anything but. In the first cabinet meeting on January 31, he had passed out copies of his Alcoa booklet on global climate change to a half-dozen cabinet members, including Christie Whitman, who seemed surprised and a bit wary that O'Neill was encroaching on her turf. In the February 1 NSC meeting on Iraq, O'Neill had questioned Rumsfeld about the ability of the United States to attack Iraqi batteries that were firing at American military planes patrolling the no-fly zone. He requested a meeting with Education Secretary Rod Paige to discuss ways to energize the education debate. Paige wondered what O'Neill wanted to talk about. "Everything," O'Neill said.

The first working meeting of the Vice President's energy task force, called the National Energy Policy Development Group, or NEPD, was on February 9. As elsewhere, O'Neill jumped fully and energetically into the proceedings—he knew energy, he knew business, he knew about deregulating markets—but he was struck by how artfully, how productively, Cheney fenced with his challenges. The Vice President controlled the proceedings, stuck to his agenda, and moved debate forward in a large room of heavyweights, including EPA administrator Whitman, Energy Secretary Spencer Abraham, Transportation's Norman Mineta, Agriculture's Ann Veneman, Commerce's Donald Evans, Interior's Gale Norton, and himself— each of them with a few top aides—as well as Karen Hughes, Karl Rove, and the political staff lining the back wall. O'Neill had yet to see Bush command such a room.

Cheney, it was clear, was quietly developing national energy policy. And O'Neill felt ready to do the same on the economic front. The difference was that the Treasury Secretary felt no hesitation in talking about what might constitute an economic policy in plain view.

The long dissertations during his confirmation hearings—which had drawn generally favorable reviews—were now matched by long, on-the-record discussions with reporters. His new press secretary, Michele Davis, who had been a top aide to House Majority Leader Dick Armey, said he should craft a few things he wanted to say in interviews, say them, and make the rest off the record. "That way," she told him, "you can edify them about the broader issues, but be quoted in areas where you want to be heard."

O'Neill ignored her advice. After years writing his own speeches, and thinking aloud in public, he stuck with what he knew. "People will appreciate the truth," he told her. That was especially true, he felt, at *The Wall Street Journal*, a paper that he—like CEOs across the country—had long relied on for its probity and consistency, like a trusted friend.

At a meeting with *Journal* reporters in late January, O'Neill spoke on a sweeping array of issues pertaining to fiscal policy, international financial institutions, and U.S. tax policy. He also said, "Go talk to people who make practical business decisions about how much [research and development] tax credits influence the level of R&D that they invest in. You find somebody who says, 'I do more R&D because I get a tax credit for it,' you'll find a fool."

Then, in discussing the public's fixation on the daily ups and downs of the equities markets, he said that Wall Street traders are "people who sit in front of a flickering giant screen, and they make decisions on a carefully constructed, but nevertheless speculative basis. I don't know how to do that [but] I probably could learn in about a couple of weeks."

The *Journal* reporters were stunned and giddy. "Both things may be true," said one *Journal* reporter who was at the meeting. "But those are two significant constituencies you just offended—a few million folks in the financial services industry and anyone who works on directing the tax system to help business, which is about half of Washington."

A week or so later, in a similar meeting with a team of reporters at *The Washington Post*, O'Neill challenged criticism of the President's tax cut as a giveaway to the wealthy. Democrats and their allies, he said, play to the populist instinct "to get those rich, dirty SOBs, and the way we're going to do it is to tax them. I think we've demonstrated as a people that we don't think some form of socialism is the way to run a society."

Reaction was quizzical, if muted. Some Democratic congressmen complained. The quotations, after their first run in the *Journal* and the *Post*, became fodder for a few columnists and TV pundits. But it was still within the realm of expectation: O'Neill spoke his mind. That, after all, is what mavericks do.

. . .

THE UNITED AIRLINES flight landed at Milan's Malpensa International Airport at 7:16 a.m. on February 16, and the chief financial officials of the United States lumbered down the ramp, half-asleep after an all-night flight from Washington. It would be a few hours before the connection to Palermo, Sicily, and the meeting of the G-7—the confederation of seven leading industrial powers that would discuss concert and competition on financial matters—so the delegation from the world's premier economic power wandered into an airline passenger lounge in desperate search of fresh coffee.

Michele Davis and O'Neill's new chief of staff, Tim Adams, who had formerly been the managing director of the G-7 Group, a global economics advisory service, sank into cushioned chairs beneath a television set with their steaming cups and the day's itinerary.

In a moment, they jumped up in horror. "The dollar is dropping quickly in today's trading based on the comments of Treasury Secretary Paul O'Neill to a German newspaper that the U.S. is no longer following a strong dollar policy . . . ," a news anchor reported. Then the newscast went to a taped report on the roiling markets.

Davis gasped. Two days before, in Washington, O'Neill had been interviewed in his office by a young reporter with *Frankfurter Allgemeine Zeitung*, the German daily. O'Neill had rambled a bit, become professorial, and explained his view of how the price of the dollar is set. Gleaned from O'Neill's exposition was a quote that was shooting across the globe: "We are not pursuing, as it is often said, a policy of a strong dollar. In my opinion, a strong dollar is the result of a strong economy."

The strong-dollar policy had been formulated by Robert Rubin, and "the United States supports a strong dollar" was the continuous, one-line pronouncement of Treasury officials between 1995 and the end of the Clinton administration. What did it mean? Many things and nothing in particular. An appreciating U.S. currency played an important role in the country's unprecedented growth in the 1990s— helping suppress inflation when domestic demand rose precipitously. It was something the United States "supported," but not with any specific action. There really wasn't any action to take. Truth be told, the strength of the dollar versus another currency is determined by the relative strengths of those two economies. "We support" means something akin to "we appreciate." And also enjoy the benefits extended to consumers—whose dollar buys more value in the purchase of foreign-made goods—and to most businesses. An exception would be major U.S. exporters of raw materials such as steel or aluminum, whose goods are more expensive to overseas manufacturers.

With an aluminum executive running Treasury, and the formerly strong U.S. economy in a slowdown, O'Neill's comment sounded anything but academic. Times change; so do administrations. Traders worldwide wondered whether this could be a historic change in U.S. policy.

Davis burst through the doors of the club and into the airport concourse. Seven reporters traveling with the delegation were already crowded onto two kiosks of phones, talking excitedly to editors. She broke in: *"Everybody!* I have a statement: There's no change in U.S. policy—we continue to support a strong dollar." The reporters looked at her with blank, "duly noted" stares and turned back to the phones.

In the passenger members club, O'Neill was chatting with Alan Greenspan, who attended G-7 meetings infrequently but was part of this delegation. O'Neill knew there was a mess brewing with the dollar, but communing with Greenspan after the long flight helped redirect him to what he considered the "essentials": the economy's gentle sag—which they talked about between sips of coffee in their usual investigatory fashion—and then the way "triggers" had managed to get a foothold in Congress despite the fact that everything in Alan's January testimony had been eclipsed by his recommendation for tax cuts. O'Neill tried to assure Greenspan that he was overly concerned about the investing of surpluses, that it would be possible without altering the equities markets; the Fed chairman felt the issue had not been sufficiently studied.

Then a noisy alternative reality encroached. Michele Davis—five feet eight, in a black pants suit, hands on hips—was standing over them, catching her breath.

"This is a disaster," she said.

O'Neill looked sheepishly at her. He excused himself, and the two slipped down a nearby hallway out of Greenspan's earshot.

"It's irresponsible for the reporter not to ask if an offhand statement means a shift in our policy," O'Neill said, summoning righteous rage. "It's unconscionable!"

"Mr. Secretary. It was a young reporter who doesn't need to worry about having a relationship with you. He did what a lot of reporters would do—he took the quote and ran. I know it's wrong but this is the way the world works."

Five hours later, O'Neill entered the lobby of the Villa Igea Hotel in Palermo and a G-7 staffer handed him a sheet showing that day's trading of the dollar. When the plane had left Washington, the euro bought 90.42 U.S. cents. Now, the euro bought 91.32 cents, with the dollar still falling. "My God," O'Neill gasped. He knew this market intimately—he frequently checked it on his Bloomberg screen—and realized it was the largest movement of the dollar in some time.

"These sons of bitches are making millions off of my screw-up," he shouted, and threw the sheets in the trash.

. . .

ON FEBRUARY 27, O'Neill awoke in his hotel room with hours of darkness still ahead. Though he and Nancy had just bought a $1.2 million apartment at the Watergate—tenth floor, overlooking the Potomac—it would take months for her to remodel and decorate it, so he was now on his own, having moved from the Marriott to the Hotel Washington and a slightly threadbare suite they gave him for a thousand a month. O'Neill, poor kid still, felt a swell of satisfaction at this discount, an unbeatable rate, each night as he locked out the world.

At times of crisis, or rapid change, at Alcoa or, before that, at OMB, he would often scrap his beloved rituals, get home after midnight, and be back at his desk at Treasury before the sun was up. Now, he was under attack. He could feel it all around. It was a self-inflicted wound, and despite his attempted recovery on the second day of the G-7—saying that "he'd rent Yankee Stadium" for the announcement if, indeed, the United States had changed its currency policies—he knew the line between maverick and loose cannon was a fine one that was easily crossed.

He arrived at his desk before the night security shift had changed and read a *USA Today* feature story:

> After just one month on the job, Treasury Secretary Paul O'Neill has roiled international currency markets, all but called Democrats socialists, insulted Wall Street traders and disparaged business lobbyists for seeking a tax credit that even President Bush supports.
>
> To some in the nation's capital, the new Treasury secretary's candor is delightfully refreshing. To others, including some White House officials, it is unnerving, even politically and economically dangerous.
>
> To O'Neill, 65, the only thing remarkable is that his pro-

nouncements are considered so remarkable. "I just find it astounding that people find it unusual that I tell the truth," he said Tuesday in an hour-long interview with *USA Today*.

After nearly a decade of circumspect comments from the Treasury Department, straight talk has returned to the corner office overlooking the White House. The question is, how long can it—or O'Neill—last?

His press secretary, Michele Davis, was right. John McCain could be a maverick—he was just one of a hundred senators. But when you sign the dollar bill, you've got to watch everything you say. O'Neill just wasn't sure he could do it.

Some politicians have what might be called a long-shot personality; they're at their best when the odds are longest. O'Neill, possessing few of the qualities common to a winning politician, had that one—with its mix of denial and resolve.

He'd *last* as long as he damn well pleased. Or, rather, as long as the President pleased. That was the key difference—after years of sovereignty, he was not now the top man, and that was turning out to be harder to swallow than he'd expected. Holding forth on every subject under the sun—for so many unscripted hours, he rationalized, that the occasional gaffe was unavoidable—might well be a practice born of frustration, of a yearning for the primacy of inquiry and analysis that the President didn't seem to embrace. In any event, he needed to think not about himself but about what was best for the boss, the Leader of the Free World, even if Bush had done little, at this point, to earn his confidence. No matter. Paul H. O'Neill had succeeded at everything he'd tried for as long as he could remember. He just had to find a way to make this work.

He turned to the morning's papers. He wasn't the only one making headlines. A variety of cabinet members seemed to be leading the news.

The first column in *The New York Times* was a story about Colin

Powell winning an agreement from Arab nations to modify the Iraqi sanctions by more sharply controlling cash and strategic items sought by Hussein while easing the strictures on civilian supplies.

Beneath the surface was a battle O'Neill had seen brewing since the NSC meeting on January 30. It was Powell and his moderates at the State Department versus hard-liners like Rumsfeld, Cheney, and Wolfowitz, who were already planning the next war in Iraq and the shape of a post-Saddam country.

Documents were being prepared by the Defense Intelligence Agency, Rumsfeld's intelligence arm, mapping Iraq's oil fields and exploration areas and listing companies that might be interested in leveraging the precious asset.

One document, headed "Foreign Suitors for Iraqi Oilfield Contracts," lists companies from thirty countries—including France, Germany, Russia, and the United Kingdom—their specialties, bidding histories, and in some cases their particular areas of interest. An attached document maps Iraq with markings for "supergiant oilfield," "other oilfield," and "earmarked for production sharing," while demarking the largely undeveloped southwest of the country into nine "blocks" to designate areas for future exploration. The desire to "dissuade" countries from engaging in "asymmetrical challenges" to the United States—as Rumsfeld said in his January articulation of the demonstrative value of a preemptive attack—matched with plans for how the world's second largest oil reserve might be divided among the world's contractors made for an irresistible combination, O'Neill later said.

Already by February, the talk was mostly about logistics. Not the *why*, but the *how* and *how quickly*. Rumsfeld, O'Neill recalled, was focused on how an incident might cause escalated tensions—like the shooting down of an American plane in the regular engagements between U.S. fighters and Iraqi antiaircraft batteries—and what U.S. responses to such an occurrence might be. Wolfowitz was pushing for the arming of Iraqi opposition groups and sending in U.S. troops to support and defend their insurgency. He had written in *Foreign Affairs* magazine in 1999 that "the United States should be prepared to commit ground forces to protect a sanctuary in southern Iraq where the opposition could safely mobilize."

During his confirmation hearings, Powell had said that arming the Iraqi opposition would be logistically difficult and ultimately unsuccessful in toppling Saddam. Since then, Powell had discovered that he was outnumbered.

So, O'Neill marveled as he read the *New York Times* story, Powell had taken the battle public—using the issue of sanctions. "The message I've consistently heard is that overdoing it with the sanctions gives [Saddam] a tool that he is using against us—and really is not weakening him," Powell told the *Times*. But he said his outline of a plan for narrowing the sanctions would be criticized in Washington. "The charges will come that it is weakening," he said. "There will be a lot of people who will want to hear more."

O'Neill had witnessed many State-versus-Pentagon struggles over the years, often among his own friends—Henry Kissinger versus James Schlesinger during Ford's administration, George Shultz versus Caspar Weinberger during Reagan's. But it was rare to have pitched combat of the sort launched in the first month of an administration.

The cause, in this case, would be visible only to someone at the very top of this administration—in short, someone like O'Neill, with regular access to the President. George W. Bush was just learning the issues. Surround a president like that with one of the most experience-heavy teams of any recent administration, and you have senior officials both formulating and, in some cases, conducting U.S. policy.

It was a broken process, O'Neill thought, or rather no process at all; there seemed to be no apparatus to assess policy and deliberate effectively, to create coherent governance.

That night, Bush would deliver his first State of the Union

speech. There was going to be a reception for senior officials at the Vice President's Congressional Office in the Capitol before Bush's nine o'clock address to the joint session. O'Neill decided to try to get Cheney alone and talk, again, about creating a structure for generating and vetting policies in a responsible, reality-based way—a process that would suit the particular needs of this President. A month ago, when he had said to Cheney that without a good policy process, all you had was "kids rolling around on the lawn," he couldn't have foreseen that some of those "kids" would be experienced, ambitious men and women atop vast federal agencies, acting, in many cases, on little more than hunches about what the President might think—what he might have suggested with a nod or wink during some presentation of options—or what he might, someday, be convinced was the right path, long after the U.S. government had already embarked on it.

The sun was fully up on an unseasonably warm day for late February. O'Neill had breakfast with Ohio senator George Voinovich, a moderate Republican and key swing vote on the tax bill. After that, Hawaii governor Benjamin Cayetano was coming by, and he had to read briefing materials to know about issues pertinent to Hawaii and what the devil its governor was interested in discussing.

. . .

ACROSS TOWN, EPA administrator Christine Todd Whitman testified before a congressional committee about the administration's "brownfields" policy for cleaning up thousands of abandoned toxic waste sites. But her plan was to hold forth after her testimony was concluded.

In the hallway, after the hearing, a group of reporters huddled around her. This was a ritualized, planned encounter—an "availability" for environmental reporters—and Whitman used it to full effect. "There's no question but that global warming is a real phenomenon that it is occurring," she said emphatically. "And while scientists can't predict where the droughts will occur, where the flooding will occur precisely, or when, we know those things will occur."

This was several articulations further than Bush had ventured during the campaign. He had asserted in one of the presidential debates that "global warming needs to be taken very seriously," but then had asked Gore whether "some of the scientists" were not "changing their opinion a little bit on global warming." Bush's proposed energy policy, issued shortly before the debates, proposed mandatory reduction targets for "four main pollutants: sulfur dioxide, nitrogen oxide, mercury and carbon dioxide." Conservatives and energy executives were outraged. The *Oil & Gas Journal* declared that "regulation of CO_2 as an air pollutant is a bad idea that belongs on the outer fringes of environmental extremism." But it allowed Bush to seize some political capital among independents and suburban voters, who viewed the environment as a central issue—an area in which Gore had staked much.

As for the 1997 Kyoto Protocol on controlling greenhouse gas emissions, Bush said he had problems with the treaty as it now stood—implying that he would be willing to return to the negotiating table. At the administration's behest, the United Nations delayed the next round of Kyoto treaty negotiations from May until the summer of 2001. But Bush had never publicly endorsed the science that underlay Kyoto. Now, his EPA administrator had done so.

· · ·

WHITMAN'S DEFINITIVENESS was part of her unfolding strategy to clarify U.S. environmental policy before she attended her first major international meeting: a summit on environmental issues of the leading eight industrialized nations that was to commence three days later, on March 2, in Trieste, Italy, on the Adriatic coast.

At fifty-four, Whitman had arrived in Washington from the New Jersey Governor's Mansion with an attractive independent profile. Among cabinet officials, her national standing and name recognition were, arguably, second only to Colin Powell's. She also had the confidence born of privilege and success at virtually everything she had tried. The child of a wealthy, politically connected judge, she graduated from Wheaton College in 1968 and went to work for Nelson Rockefeller's campaign for the GOP nomination. From there, she went to Nixon's Office of Economic Opportunity, a catchall to handle many of Johnson's Great Society programs, which was run by Donald Rumsfeld. She stayed in close touch with nationally prominent Republicans, married a prosperous Wall Street banker—whose father was once New Jersey's governor—dabbled in civic affairs as a young mother, and then decided in 1990 to challenge Democratic U.S. senator Bill Bradley. At the height of his popularity, Bradley was considered unbeatable. Whitman was the nominee by default: the sacrificial opponent. She lost by less than three percentage points. In 1993, she all but marched into the Governor's Mansion. Her profile—pro-choice, fiscally conservative, and socially moderate—gave her cross-party appeal and clout with independents. Instantly, she was being touted as a possible vice-presidential choice and she won reelection in 1997.

Whitman had conversed with George W. Bush at various meetings they'd attended as fellow Republican governors. She and the Texas governor were often placed side by side, as Republican centrists who worked well with Democrats and had national name recognition. At several conferences they'd discussed the environment, a focus of governors in that pollution crosses state borders, toxic waste is often a not-in-my-state issue, and, over the past decade, concern had grown about Washington's intentions on Kyoto, global warming, and regulating carbon dioxide in the United States. Whitman felt that, in general, she was aligned with Governor Bush on most of these issues, and she was heartened by candidate Bush's few pronouncements about Kyoto and regulating carbon dioxide emissions in the United States.

But, after a full month as EPA administrator, Whitman found that was all she had to work with: inference. Neither during her interview for the EPA job at the Madison Hotel (she arrived a few minutes after O'Neill left), nor during a brief, perfunctory welcome-to-office meeting she had with the President in January, had relevant issues of environmental regulation been discussed.

On one hand, Whitman assumed nothing had changed since the campaign. Why would it? There had been no significant events on the environmental front in the past few months. But, as late February approached, the lack of direction was unsettling. The tone of the first meeting of the Vice President's energy task force had been decidedly anti-regulatory, and foreign leaders were pressing her about the specifics of U.S. policy on global warming.

At the meeting in Trieste, environmental officials from around the world would gather for three days in a warm-up for the official Kyoto Protocol meetings in the summer. They would press her. What was the official U.S. policy? She couldn't arrive empty-handed.

In mid-February, Whitman scheduled meetings with Andy Card and Condoleezza Rice. They had regular access to the President. Maybe they knew his mind on carbon regulation and Kyoto.

Whitman presented a sensible hedge to Rice and Card: stress in Trieste that the administration was preparing to list carbon dioxide as a toxic substance; that would allow for emissions to be regulated in the United States, which was responsible for more carbon dioxide emissions than any other country in the world. With that forward motion as her lead, Whitman would win the latitude to be non-committal as to what changes the United States would suggest to the Kyoto Protocol.

Both Card and Rice told Whitman that that strategy squared with the President's position. It sounded, to both, like a sensible tactic. Whitman left the White House relieved.

A few days later, she offered a glimpse of this new, more fully realized posture. On CNN's *Crossfire* on Monday night, February 26, conservative commentator Robert Novak pressed Whitman about global warming. Feeling empowered by the meetings with Rice and Card—and by her distaste for the combative, ideological Novak—she launched forward. "George Bush was very clear during the course of the campaign that he believes in a multipollutant strategy, and that includes CO_2," she said. Novak was obviously surprised. Whitman elaborated. Like O'Neill, she felt there should be some articulation of the administration's position. "He has also been very clear that the science is good on global warming," she added, noting that "introducing CO_2 to the discussion" is a crucial step in attacking a genuine problem.

The next morning, after her brownfields testimony, Whitman improvised her final, creative step, a sort of icing on this confection. She told the reporters clustered in the hallway that there had been recent "discussions inside the administration" about how to add carbon dioxide to the existing regulatory mix. It sounded like logistics, as if the issue had been settled and they were just working on the fine points. Of course, the "discussions" were mostly her blind stabs at deducing the mind of the President. When the reporters pressed her for more details—who said what, when, and at what level—she could offer none. But heading back to her EPA office, Whitman was confident that even her speculative pronouncement would create headlines and an impression, when read by those coming to Trieste, that the United States had a policy on global warming.

. . .

O'NEILL RETURNED to his office at midday. Michele Davis handed him a report about Whitman's hallway statements. Really? he thought. The President had never embraced the science of climate change or the jeremiads about impending environmental disaster. He sensed that Whitman's tactic was similar to the one employed by Powell: a cabinet member trying to formulate policy in a high-stakes game of blindman's bluff, calling out ideas and recommendations in an effort to locate the mind-set of the President, or create a mind-set . . . or simply proceed, even if blindfolded, without Bush's guidance.

Now, it was O'Neill's turn. He turned to formulating his own global warming strategy and having Bush sign on. His staff had been working on its analysis steadily since early February.

John Hambor, director of Treasury's Office of Microeconomic Analysis, in a memo dated February 6, said it was crucial that "an interagency process be established soon" to ensure that "policy positions developed are efficient, effective, pragmatic and integrated effectively with the administration's overall energy strategy." Indeed, energy policy and climate change policy—two key concerns for the administration and for the American public—were moving on separate paths and at varied speeds. An energy plan, under Cheney's direction and executive authority, had begun to race forward; global warming languished, undirected.

Aware that EPA had a similar process under way, O'Neill directed Hambor to help create an interagency process from departments other than EPA. On February 21, there was the first such meeting, chaired by the State Department's assistant secretary for oceans, environment, and science and including officials from Treasury, State, and the White House Office of Science and Technology Policy. The process seemed to be started appropriately: first, create a model to put a price on carbon emissions, then apply that model to countries around the globe based on their obligations under the Kyoto Protocol. This sort of follow-the-facts analysis—a theology for O'Neill—was inherently unwieldy in a political context. Generating fresh analysis may undercut various ideological positions.

One of the members of the interagency group—the State Department's Daniel Bodansky—was already in the crosshairs of conservative opponents of action, any action, on climate change. An anonymous memo sent in mid-February on State Department letterhead to five conservative Republican senators, including Chuck Hagel of Nebraska and Jesse Helms of North Carolina, attacked Bodansky and the NSC's Ian Bowles—both of whom had served under Clinton—as "Gore supporters who are seeking to box the Bush Administration into a corner where it will have to choose between a bad deal and international embarrassment." The memo alleged that the two were resuming international negotiations on climate change "without specific political guidance from the new administration." Hagel circulated the anonymous memo widely—including to Deputy Secretary of State Richard Armitage and Donald Evans at Commerce.

Though O'Neill's access to both camps made him suspect that there were some ideologues among them, his advice to Bush was sober, including some lines that even Hagel might have embraced. It noted that "if the Kyoto treaty were fully implemented as agreed, it would push out the atmospheric accumulation of greenhouse gases by eleven years. In other words, the currently projected accumulation for 2050 would occur in 2061. (This is a trivial impact if the problem is real. As you know, I think this could be a very big problem.) For the U.S., full implementation of Kyoto," O'Neill summed up, connecting this modest impact with cost, "would mean reducing our energy consumption from its projected level by more than 30% in the 2008–2012 time period."

His ecumenical access to a spectrum of opinions meant that O'Neill could tell the President that despite these limited impacts, environmental groups "supported Kyoto anyway, believing it to 'be a nose under the tent' and 'the only game in town.' " His suggestion was to widen and deepen what had become an increasingly partisan debate, with industry lined up against environmentalists, and the United States taking on the world. He offered an action plan—starting with a document stamped by the President, for broad public use, spelling out what is known and knowable about the science of the issue.

Then, he said, change the focus to concentrations of greenhouse gases, which are now measurable, rather than the old method of tracking emissions—a material shift that many environmentalists think is sensible but hesitate to embrace for fear of losing the modest gains from Kyoto.

He suggested creating "comprehensive catalogs" of information—on what is known about where greenhouse gases come from and on the costs and benefits of various actions—to attempt to find a single set of blended, shared facts (rather than an array of competing sets that gridlock debate).

With all this at the ready, O'Neill wrote to Bush, they would be in a strong position to prepare an analysis of how to amend or replace Kyoto. "Hopefully, the major work needed to stake out the U.S. position can be completed in time for the continuing Kyoto treaty talks scheduled for this summer."

Under a final section, "How to Get Started," he suggested the President form an interdepartmental group, possibly in conjunction with the Vice President's energy task force—"since energy and the environment are in many ways the same problem." Then the President should solicit involvement from wise outsiders. Among them, he listed George Shultz—"the best convener of experts, developer of policy positions I have ever known"; Jared Cohen, president of

Carnegie-Mellon University, who is also an environmental scientist; and Michael Oppenheimer. A Princeton professor, who was once chief scientist at Environmental Defense, a nongovernmental environmental organization that helped develop much of the scientific case for global warming, Oppenheimer is a pariah to the many industries and conservative advocates who dismiss the very idea that human activity is altering the global climate.

O'Neill, of course, knew this. Oppenheimer, he felt, should be on any presidential commission—not in spite of these controversial facts, but because of them. Conservatives were attacking Bodansky because he didn't buy their worldview, because he was being guided, instead, by something O'Neill considered real, nuanced, and tangible: the preponderance of evidence. Yes, O'Neill knew, "Michael's a pain in the ass, smarter than hell, and he's really done his homework—that's why I put him on my list." And there was another point—beyond O'Neill's delighted anticipation of the look on Hagel's face when the President mentioned Oppenheimer—involving credibility. "You only have that when you bring together the strongest voices from opposite poles," O'Neill said later, reflecting on this memo. "Otherwise, the outcomes are suspect. If you want to be seen as open and honest, you've got to do the hard work of bringing combatants together, and then just see how things sort out. What does the data say? That last part is not something you can control."

. . .

AFTER SENDING OFF the memo to the President, O'Neill checked with his chief of staff to get updated on the day's events.

He soon found himself in a cluster of irate, flustered senior staffers.

A crisis. Michele Davis grabbed a copy of *The New York Times*. While O'Neill had focused on Powell's gambit, another of the front-page stories had started a stir that had grown through the morning into midday storm.

Richard Stevenson's *Times* story revealed one item the President would be addressing that night in his State of the Union: over the next ten years the United States could pay down only $2 trillion of the $3.2 trillion of debt—once the $2.4 trillion of Social Security surplus was set aside. Specifically, the White House would contend that $1.2 trillion of the debt would not be able to be paid down largely because it matured after the ten-year period.

There was a clear inference: if we can't use $1.2 trillion of the surplus to do what both Democrats and Republicans have been advocating for much of the 1990s—pay down the federal debt—we might as well give it back in the form of a tax cut.

The story's key quote came from Gary Gensler, the undersecretary for domestic finance under Clinton—and the official who had so ably handled O'Neill's debriefing during the transition. Gensler, a former investment banker and head of bond trading at Goldman Sachs, said there were a variety of ways to replace the long bonds—mostly thirty-year Treasury notes—with rolling buybacks and purchase replacements. The amount that would be difficult to buy back would be a maximum of $500 billion, not $1.2 trillion.

O'Neill quickly huddled in a conference room with assistant undersecretaries. "Gensler's right, isn't he?" Nods all around. None of them had been consulted. It was a mistake of nearly $700 billion. "What do you mean, no one was consulted?" O'Neill moaned.

Over the next hour, the path of this gremlin was revealed. A midrung career analyst at OMB had worked up a paper on the so-called payback problem—extrapolating from a more general, academic footnote in the final budget submitted by Clinton upon his exit—and then passed it north to his bosses at OMB. Delighted at what seemed to be added justification for the tax cut, they passed it over to the President's speechwriting team and political staff—led by Karl Rove and Karen Hughes—which had lately been asserting its centrality in the Bush orbit. Fearful of leaks, and distrustful of the agendas of expert staffers in the various departments, they had circulated final drafts of the State of the Union to almost no one outside the West Wing.

The phones at Treasury were ringing. New York investment houses were calling to make sure they had read the story correctly. If the President was stating that the United States would always leave untouched the $1.2 trillion, that would imply certain Treasury policies for how bonds, notes, and bills of various maturities would be issued. It would also imply that the bond buyback that had been successful would be diminished, slowed, or discontinued. All of these issues significantly affect markets by both adding uncertainty and altering rates.

Michael Paulus, deputy assistant secretary for federal finance, told O'Neill that the pricing on bond futures was already shifting. "Trading desks are calling in a panic. What the hell do we tell them?" he implored O'Neill.

Tell them it's not our policy, O'Neill said. "Tell them that the Treasury Department, which handles the bonds, was not consulted. Tell them that it's an OMB number. That Treasury will decide how to handle the long bonds at a later date, and *we* will announce it."

Paulus ran to the phones. But, after a moment, he let his staff handle the calls. The President's budget was to be released in the next few days. Paulus checked the final draft. OMB had slipped in the $1.2 trillion calculus and incorrect definitive language about penalties for buying back bonds prior to maturity. He called an official at OMB. She told him the budget was at the printers. There might still be time to cut, paste, and water down the language of that section. "Meet me at the printer!" he yelled into the phone, and ran out the door.

Treasury staffers called the White House. Excerpts of the State of the Union, which included the flawed calculus, had already been disclosed to the press. It was too late.

O'Neill was incensed. How could the White House political staff "decide to do things like this and not even consult with people in the government who know what's true or not? Who the hell is in charge here?" he ranted. "This is complete bullshit!"

That night, Bush stood before the nation, described the state of the Union in the most important speech a president gives, in any given year, and said something that knowledgeable people in the U.S. government knew to be false.

. . .

ON TUESDAY, March 6, O'Neill interrupted a meeting with his senior staff at 11:10 a.m. to take a call. It was Christie Whitman. "How was your trip?" he said, and waved everyone out of his office.

Wonderful, Whitman said. She was exhausted, having just returned from Italy, but feeling ebullient. The ministers from the countries present had poked at her to gauge the solidity of the U.S. position and seemed to come away from the three-day conference, she said, "looking to us for leadership."

It certainly seemed that way from what O'Neill had read. He mentioned a story in the *Financial Times* from the day before, which noted that delegates were "pleasantly surprised" and "impressed by the stance taken by Christie Whitman, head of the US delegation, who calmed fears that the US would ignore the problem of global warming." Prominently featured in that story, as in all the coverage, was Whitman's statement: "The president has said global climate change is the greatest environmental challenge that we face and that we must recognize that and take steps to move forward."

Just as long as the President believes that, O'Neill said. They discussed ways to get him to be more specific and emphatic, to let the world community know his mind on this issue. Whitman had done what she could. One pronouncement she endorsed was that the G-8 nations would "strive to reach agreement" in July in Bonn at the next set of talks on the Kyoto Protocol. That was only five months away. Countries were already beginning preliminary discussions in preparation for Bonn, Whitman said. If the United States didn't join in that process, its absence would be conspicuous.

Whitman said she was drafting a note to Bush, a short memo that would report on progress from Trieste and encourage the President to be forceful on his key stances. She knew O'Neill had already spent a good deal of time with the President. She asked if he would give it a read and said she'd fax it over in a few hours.

"The President needs to be clear about what he believes and why," O'Neill said at the end of the twenty-minute call. "We have to help him do that."

. . .

MIDDAY ARRIVED on the first Tuesday in March—time for the standing weekly lunch of the economic policy group, which included Larry Lindsey, Mitch Daniels, deputy chief of staff Josh Bolten, Commerce Secretary Don Evans, and a new arrival, the chairman of the President's Council of Economic Advisers, Glenn Hubbard. Now, with Hubbard aboard, the group had decided to meet every Tuesday for lunch in O'Neill's small conference room.

It was clear that Hubbard, a respected conservative economist from Columbia University, would round out a trio: it would now be O'Neill, Lindsey, and Hubbard hashing out economic policy. O'Neill knew Hubbard slightly—he had interviewed, at the White House's behest, for the deputy Treasury secretary's job that went to

Ken Dam—and felt comfortable with the soft-spoken economist's deliberative, academic demeanor. Yes, he had been one of the advisers to candidate Bush—and had his beloved models, as did Lindsey and so many economists—but Hubbard seemed more data-driven, more reflective.

Discussion at lunch swirled around the tax cut, which was fast enveloping the town. Democrats and some Republicans originally had said it was too large; now it was Democrats who were offering a plan of cuts about half the size of Bush's proposal. "We are for a tax cut, but we're for a tax cut that's affordable," North Dakota's Kent Conrad, senior Democrat on the Senate Budget Committee, told FOX News, summing up the opposing view. The President, Lindsey, and O'Neill, meanwhile, had been busy in various speeches and testimony through February, positing ways to make the tax cut more stimulative by accelerating the rate cuts or altering tax-withholding tables retroactively to January 1 in 2001.

At this point, the administration's plan was deeply weighted to the out years and provided only $20 billion in stimulus for 2001—a pittance in a $10 trillion economy. While Lindsey was pushing to accelerate the marginal rate cuts, O'Neill was focused on the out years, when surpluses might have long disappeared and the rate cuts would be all but impossible, politically, to countermand. Daniels and others mentioned the thorny issues proffered by a growing coalition in the middle ground. Two moderate Republicans—Lincoln Chafee of Rhode Island and Arlen Specter of Pennsylvania—had joined moderate and conservative Democrats in early February demanding that any tax cut be contingent on the projected surpluses materializing on schedule. This so-called centrist coalition was quietly growing.

At lunch, Hubbard spoke in a firm, measured tone about the economic problems presented by conditionality. It was an area he and his academic colleagues had investigated extensively. Studies showed it took between three and five years for a tax reduction to alter most spending and investment habits. People were creatures of habit—whether at the kitchen table or in the corporate suite—and any excuse not to change behavioral patterns was excuse enough. Making the tax cuts conditional on something the consumer couldn't control—such as the ebb and flow of deficit or surplus—would blunt the stimulatory effectiveness of any reduction in marginal rates.

Partially blunt it, O'Neill responded. He was familiar with the academic literature on the subject. And if the tax cut was made more progressive, angled toward middle and lower strata of the income scale—where each new dollar is most likely to be spent on basic needs rather than pushed into investment—the drag from conditionality would be further lessened. Yes, responded Hubbard, but a dollar invested is multiplied by its return on investment, bringing more stimulus, on balance, than a dollar consumed. . . .

And around they went. O'Neill realized that Hubbard was convincing and not easily swayed and that he was attentive to the data in ways Larry was often not. He backed up his arguments. Throughout the discussion, O'Neill never mentioned his support of triggers, his conversations with Greenspan, or his fears about the profligacy being justified by what he felt were "perceived" surpluses. Instead, he rounded out the lunch by mentioning Greenspan's testimony of a few days before in front of the House Budget Committee, where the Fed chairman had warned that the surplus was not money in the bank. However you put it, O'Neill said, spending more money than we've got is irresponsible—and we need to figure out a way to stop that from happening. Everyone nodded, and O'Neill wondered how much access Hubbard would have to the President.

• • •

WHEN HE RETURNED to his desk that day, Whitman's memo to the
President arrived. O'Neill read it carefully. It was straight talk of a
sort he was sure Bush rarely received.

> I would strongly recommend that you continue to rec-
> ognize that global warming is a real and serious issue.
>
> While not specifically endorsing the targets called for in
> Kyoto, you could indicate that you are exploring how to re-
> duce U.S. greenhouse gas emissions internally and will
> continue no matter what else transpires.
>
> Mr. President, this [global warming] is a credibility issue
> for the U.S. in the international community. It is also an
> issue that is resonating here, at home. We need to appear
> engaged and shift the discussion from the focus on the "K"
> word to action, but we have to build some bonafides first.
>
> We did win some issues at this meeting, i.e. recognizing
> cost, promoting children's health, and fending off some last
> minute end runs by the Germans and the Japanese.
>
> I'm available to discuss this further if you want.

O'Neill was surprised at the memo's frankness. Whitman was
laying down the gauntlet. Hers were fighting words, but certainly
true. As Whitman noted, Bush had "credibility" issues. O'Neill
thought about Gerald Ford. Was Ford smarter than Henry
Kissinger or James Schlesinger—or, for that matter, he and Greenspan? All four regularly struggled, openly and fiercely, on various
landscapes of public policy. And all could claim expertise that Ford
couldn't match. Yet everyone, eventually, had deferred to Ford's
judgment. Why? It wasn't just because he was the President, O'Neill
thought. If only it could be that easy. It was respect born from a
deeper constant. After Ford finally held forth, settling this issue or
that, each man had the same thought: *I like the way he thinks.*

O'Neill knew that Whitman had never heard the President analyze a complex issue, parse opposing positions, and settle on a judicious path. In fact, no one—inside or outside the government, here
or across the globe—had heard him do that to any significant degree.
And that, O'Neill decided, was what Whitman was getting at with
the word "credibility." It was not just the President's credibility
around the world. It was credibility with his most senior officials.

. . .

THE NEXT DAY, March 7, O'Neill walked over to the White House
for lunch with Bush and South Korean president Kim Dae Jung.

Lunch was preceded by a short press conference in the Oval Office. Bush officially snubbed Kim, saying that he wouldn't continue
the Clinton administration's policy of using carrot-stick negotiations
to stop North Korean dictator Kim Jong Il from building nuclear
weapons. Kim Dae Jung, a former political prisoner, had a "sun-
shine" policy of opening to the North, including economic trade,
and had managed a historic meeting with Kim Jong Il the previous
June. In large measure, those policies—upon which he'd staked his
legacy—were predicated on U.S. support for the idea of engaging
the dictator.

"I made it clear to the president we look forward to working toward peace on the peninsula, that we'll consult closely, that we'll stay
in touch, that I do have some skepticism about the leader of North
Korea, but that's not going to preclude us from trying to achieve the
common objective," President Bush said as Kim looked on grimly.

O'Neill had watched the give-and-take on Korea unfold during
the past month in what was becoming a familiar pattern. As with his
recommendation for "smart" sanctions against Iraq, Powell was,
again, on the side of hard-nosed internationalism, saying as recently
as the day before, March 6, that the Bush White House intended "to

pick up where President Clinton and his administration left off" in negotiations with North Korea to curb its production and sale of ballistic missiles. Rumsfeld, Wolfowitz, and the Vice President were quietly pressing the idea that we'd been appeasing a tyrant in North Korea's Kim Jong Il, that we were enabling him by supporting his teetering economy.

In his statements before lunch, the President noted of North Korea that "we're not certain as to whether or not they're keeping all terms of all agreements." It was widely known that there was only one agreement with North Korea—the 1994 accord that froze its plutonium processing—and almost immediately the White House was offering explanations of how the President understood that but inadvertently employed the plural.

O'Neill, meanwhile, sensed the consequences of haste—activity forced by South Korean president Kim's imminent arrival, in which the President had to digest unfamiliar facts, balance complex competing claims with little context, and make a snap decision. At lunch in the White House, O'Neill—who had been involved with South Korea during his years at both International Paper and Alcoa—engaged the dispirited Kim. He mentioned to Bush as lunch was served that "South Korea has among the highest literacy rates in the world, which demonstrates that all our children, here in the U.S., can succeed as well." Bush registered surprise. O'Neill, meanwhile, was thinking about the process of decision making in the White House. Ten years of delicately stitched U.S. policy toward North Korea—a sick man of Asia's economy (especially if its woes were to overwhelm South Korea) and, possibly, a rogue nuclear power in the making—had been torn up in what might have been less than a day. How, otherwise, could Powell have been out of the loop as recently as the day before? The prescription was clear: O'Neill couldn't end up out of the loop on the key, outstanding issues on the economic front. He needed to do more than edify Bush on the choices and consequences of various domestic policies—he needed to make his case for a prudent fiscal policy.

Once they bade Kim farewell, O'Neill and the President were due to walk over to Treasury and meet for an hour in the Treasury Secretary's office. This is something presidents sometimes do at the start of their term—visit the offices of cabinet officers, show the flag, and excite the troops.

It was also something that O'Neill thought was exemplary boss protocol. Visit the top lieutenants and the infantry, too. O'Neill regularly had gone on unescorted, and often unannounced, strolls through Alcoa factories. He did the same at Treasury. Once a week or so, he'd vanish from his suite and wander the building. People in cubicles would do a double take. He'd ask how they liked their job. What were things they might like to change? Did they feel they were doing meaningful work? He liked the way workers, at various levels, identified problems and posited solutions.

"Hey, let's take the tunnel to Treasury," Bush said, smiling. O'Neill laughed. He'd done this back in 1976 when they were conducting preparedness drills for those designated to keep the government running in case of calamity. Before he could respond, the President was on the phone to alert the Secret Service, and then the two men, accompanied by a few agents, were slipping out a side door of the Oval Office.

There was a winding stairwell into the subbasement and a labyrinth of lead doors and airtight rooms. They moved one way, backtracked, went down another hall, and then did it again. They were lost. Eventually, they found a hallway that stretched northwest, in the general direction of Treasury. "That must be it," Bush said, motioning to the agents. "Let's do it, team." And they walked the narrow tunnel, 150 yards at least through walls lined with dropdown canvas cots. They emerged into the basement of Treasury, where a maintenance worker, moving boxes, looked at them as though he'd seen a ghost. Bush laughed—"We made it"—and suddenly gave the startled worker a hug.

From there, they climbed a few stairwells into sunlight, causing turned heads and surprised looks. Bush engaged with the secretaries and clerks—joking and pointing, favorably noting men's ties and women's hairdos, and remembering the name of O'Neill's secretary, whom Paul had brought to his swearing-in the month before—the first time any of the four Treasury secretaries Annabella had worked for had honored her with a visit to the Oval Office. O'Neill recalled the way Bush had snapped at Andy Card during their cheeseburger lunch. Now, with folks a thousand notches below Andy on the pyramid of power and status, he couldn't be more magnanimous.

They entered O'Neill's office. The President made a joke about the furniture. They sat down. O'Neill thought the time was right after their walkthrough.

O'Neill made his case for triggers. He assumed that Lindsey or Hubbard already might have spoken to Bush. He explained the case for, and against, the conditionality of caps or triggers or sunset provisions. "It may blunt some of the tax cut's stimulus," O'Neill said, but the President would be eventually rewarded by the capital markets—both in lowered long-term bond rates and rising equities prices—"for continuing and advancing the virtues of fiscal prudence."

The conviviality had burned off. Bush looked at him with the flat, inexpressive stare to which O'Neill had become accustomed.

"I won't negotiate with myself," Bush finally said. "It's that simple. If someone comes to me with a plan for this, and they have a significant amount of political backing, I'll sit down with them—talk it out. But until then, it's a closed issue."

O'Neill's mind raced. He wanted to run through what was knowable about the illusory nature of any ten-year surplus estimate: how the $1.6 trillion number grew from a 1999 campaign proposal and no longer fit current economic reality; why, at this very moment, budgetary probity was being undermined—as it had been during recent years in so many corporations—by the *expectation of future revenue* . . . in this case, tax revenue. "I wanted to say to the President that all sound analysis is about negotiating with yourself," O'Neill recalled. "That Alan and I agree on all this, and we've been at it for forty years."

But he just nodded. The President made it clear that this was not about analysis. It was about tactics.

. . .

THE NEXT MORNING, at 8 a.m., Christie Whitman arrived at O'Neill's small conference room for breakfast. She brought some sobering news.

A letter had been sent to the President from a quartet of Republican senators—Chuck Hagel; Larry Craig of Idaho; Jesse Helms; and Pat Roberts of Kansas—who were at the vanguard of opposition to Kyoto and the regulating of carbon dioxide, along with many of the ideas that underpin regulation of industries in America.

O'Neill nodded. He had got around to reading the letter early this morning, though his copy had been faxed from Hagel's office two days before—on the afternoon of March 6—the same afternoon Christie faxed over her memo to the President.

The senators' letter, seeking a "clarification of your administration's policy on climate change," noted that they were aware that "your administration has recently begun a formal interagency review of climate change policies. Yet, on Tuesday, February 27, Environmental Protection Agency Administrator Christine Todd Whitman testified on this subject" before Congress. The body of the letter displayed several of Whitman's statements before, during, and after her testimony, including those she uttered during her CNN appearance with Novak, and reiterated exactly what the President had said during the campaign. It concluded:

> We look forward to working with you and your administration on the development of a comprehensive national energy strategy that is environmentally and economically sound, and a common sense, scientifically sound climate change policy. However, we need to have a clear understanding of your Administration's position on climate change, in particular the Kyoto Protocol, and the regulation of carbon dioxide under the Clean Air Act.

A frontal assault, Christie said. They'd wedged themselves between the President's sparse campaign pronouncements and her rounded, adjective-laden expansions.

O'Neill stiffened. This was not the soft turf of economic prognostication—where hundreds of billions are allocated based on speculative ten-year estimates. There were facts here. Tangible, measurable facts.

"We were of a like mind on the issue," O'Neill recalled. "Christie and I felt this was an issue we should own. Because it is one of the few issues of current policy that is subject to rational thought. One can collect facts. One can know in what areas there are not facts and put a process in place to collect them if they're necessary to figure out what to do. It's an area where you can fund research and demonstration work and get people together to listen to their ideas and hear what they know. Here, with so much at stake, you really can have a rationally based policy that represents what's good for the people.

"That was my notion, and I think Christie is that kind of a policy person, too," O'Neill said.

At breakfast, they talked about the report EPA had prepared for the President, which was similar to Treasury's report but more comprehensive, setting forth the mountain of evidence already assembled, along with proposals for action both outside Kyoto and, if necessary, within the framework of the international protocol.

And then they returned to tactics. The Hagel letter looked suspicious to both of them. The timing, the tone, the emphasis on the senators' desire to work with the administration on a "comprehensive national energy strategy," with all environmental issues as a subordinate clause beneath the dictates of energy and economics. That was right out of Dick Cheney's mouth.

"You know what?" O'Neill said. "I bet they didn't dream up the idea of writing this letter on their own. Looking at it here, with the cold hard facts, this is the kind of thing where somebody on the White House staff would have maybe called up Hagel and said, 'Chuck, why don't you ask us for a letter of clarification.'"

"No, I wouldn't be surprised if you found out that the White House requested this letter of clarification and that the Vice President was preparing the response."

O'Neill, like others who served with Cheney under different presidents, was almost always in the dark about his actual beliefs. But they'd sometimes pick up his method: quietly select an issue, counsel various participants, manufacture the exchange of seemingly impromptu letters or reports—the bureaucratic version of a media event—and then guide unfolding events toward the intended outcome. This was the puppeteer's craft, all done with strings and suggestions.

In the end, there are no fingerprints. No accountability.

• • •

WHITMAN RETURNED to her office and urgently called Andy Card. She wanted a meeting with the President as soon as possible.

It was becoming clear to her. The circle around the President was extremely tight: Rove, Hughes, Cheney, Andy Card, and, maybe,

Rice. She told Andy she needed an audience. It was already mid-March, she said—she'd been traveling the world representing U.S. policy, but she had yet to be told, by the President, what he thought about a central issue of national importance.

Whitman liked Card and trusted him. He didn't have the power of a Rove or a Hughes but he was frank and reliable. He said he'd see what he could do. Soon he called back. A meeting was set for March 13 at 10 a.m. Whitman assumed the President had read EPA's report and the one sent by Treasury. Over the next few days, she merged both reports—and her credibility memo—into talking points: a presentation of a plan of action for her most significant area of engagement.

This, she felt, entering the Oval Office on that Tuesday morning in mid-March, was what she had come to Washington for.

The President settled into the wing chair near the fireplace, Whitman on the edge of the mustard couch. She smiled and started right in, talking about the importance of promoting international cooperation, the areas of scientific evidence that were indisputable, the issue of U.S. credibility.

Bush cut her off. "Christie, I've already made my decision." He had a letter all ready to send back to Hagel, Helms, and the others. He read portions of it to her.

He would oppose Kyoto because it exempted 80 percent of the world, including China and India, and it was an "unfair and ineffective means of addressing global climate change concerns."

As for the campaign promise of regulating carbon dioxide in the United States, he'd changed his mind. The letter's few paragraphs on that subject mostly highlighted the primacy of energy policy.

The President said his letter mentioned a new Department of Energy report that showed how caps on carbon dioxide emissions would lead to an even more dramatic shift from coal to natural gas for electric power generation and significantly higher electricity prices. With the California energy shortage and other western states worried about prices and availability this summer, we just can't harm consumers, he said. It only took a moment for Bush to recount the high points of what he'd be telling Hagel, Helms, and the rest of the world.

Whitman just sat. It was a clean kill. She was running around the world, using her own hard-won, bipartisan credibility to add color and depth to *his* campaign pronouncements, and now she ended up looking like the fool.

With nothing more to say, Bush rose and thanked her for coming by.

She drifted, empty-handed, into the small atrium outside the Oval Office where several secretaries sit. One of them was speaking but not to her. "Mr. Vice President, here's the letter for Senator Hagel."

Dick Cheney suddenly appeared, pulling on his suit jacket. He plucked the letter from the secretary's desk and strode by Whitman on his way to Capitol Hill.

CHAPTER 4

BASE ELEMENTS

A FEW HOURS after her meeting with Bush, the EPA administrator was on the cell phone, livid. "He went further in this letter than anyone could have expected, even Hagel!" she said, incredulous. Kyoto was dead. Plans to regulate carbon dioxide emissions from power plants were abandoned. The United States was no longer engaged on any of these issues—it was back to let's study "this possible problem," she fumed. "Energy production is all that matters. He couldn't have been clearer."

"It just doesn't make any sense," O'Neill agreed. A decade of dialogue about the evidence of climate change and a responsible international response was shattered, along with the hard work to find a middle ground between economic progress and environmental good sense—a conversation that had been progressing with sound results since Nixon created EPA. "We just gave away the environment," O'Neill told Whitman. "For no good reason."

But there is always a "good reason," good enough for intent to flow to action. And as O'Neill and Whitman regained their composure, they began to review events, sifting for motives. What was clear was that the two of them, moderates on this issue, and the wider, in-

creasingly diverse environmental community had been outmaneu-
vered . . . and now bloodied. That last part was what left them slack-
jawed. What was the point of that?

"When Christie told me that afternoon, I was flabbergasted,"
O'Neill recounted. "But then we started to think through what
process was at work. . . . For whoever it was who called the shot on
this whole mix of issues, the real question is whether they had looked
at the facts and made an informed decision that all this stuff about
global warming was a bunch of crap and that we didn't need to think
about it. Or was it more narrowly based on simply 'The base likes
this and who the hell knows anyway.' "

The base likes this and who the hell knows anyway. . . . The sentence
was a direct assault on the worldview shared by Whitman and
Greenspan and a wide community of policy pragmatists who began
each morning with hard-boiled questions and fresh cups of analysis,
sure that discernibly correct answers would be found up ahead . . .
and that, in the end, *being right mattered.*

O'Neill felt like a man discovering that he has just bought
swampland in Florida. First move, reexamine the deed. "If, say,
somebody thinks that they've done all the hard work and looked at
all the facts—that their view of it is clear and it's a nonsense issue—
and it's not motivated by appealing to the base but, instead, doing
what you think is right . . . well, that's different."

It was different from what both of them knew had just occurred.
Whitman's recounting of the Hagel letter made it clear that there
was not a balancing of competing issues and interests: energy concerns and the thinly supported jeremiad by industry lobbyists that
the United States was in the early stages of an energy crisis had
eclipsed considerations about action on global warming. Period.

Still, there was the question of *who had called the shot.* Whitman
and O'Neill swiftly arrived at the same place: Dick Cheney. The
letter's brusque language, needlessly offending environmentalists,

sounded like the Vice President. The pertinent conclusions—that energy production was a first priority; that coal, the underappreciated national workhorse that produced half of the country's power, needed protection; that lifting the burden of regulation was holy writ, and any carbon dioxide emission caps were a constraint on free, unfettered, essential American commerce—were the precepts Dick had encouraged in early meetings of the energy task force. *His* energy task force.

As for the execution, O'Neill said, it was "the Cheney M.O., start to finish." Could it be, O'Neill wondered for the first time, that he had signed on to be the contrary voice, and odd-man-out, inside a team of ideologues? It seemed, suddenly, that there were no let's-look-at-the-facts brokers in any of the key White House positions.

A strict code of personal fealty to Bush—animated by the embrace of a few unquestioned ideologues—seemed to be in collision with a faith in the broader ideals of honest inquiry. He could barely keep that thorny assessment and his old friend Cheney in the same thought.

For a wide community of intellectual pragmatists, who had served Gerald Ford and George H. W. Bush, and who formed the core of old-line, traditional Republicanism, a query now took hold: Who is Dick, really?

O'Neill eventually posed the question to Roger Porter, whom he talked with a few times during late winter and early spring. Porter, the domestic policy chief for the first President Bush and professor of Harvard's popular course on the American presidency, started to get calls about this time from moderates in the Republican establishment. His office at Harvard became a sort of confessional booth. The question was often the same.

"At the start, there was a sense that Dick would be the pragmatic voice," O'Neill said, "handling a great deal, of course, and providing a wide avenue for clear thinking and discussion—that he would be the guardian for sensible policy and reasoned analysis. He had often filled that role for other presidents. He was never one to take a position and dig in, to be strident. Or so we all thought. We thought that we knew Dick. But did we? About this time people first started to ask—has Dick changed? Or did we just not know him before? Or, maybe, he can't do necessarily what *he wants*, because, after all, there is a President who is above him, and we've overstated his power? In any event, Dick seemed to become ideological—and not as attentive to deliberation and evidence—and people started to wonder what happened."

O'Neill started to wonder about the President.

He found himself flipping through a favorite book, *Beyond Human Scale*, co-authored by Eli Ginzberg, an expert, over the past fifty years, in organizational theory and utilization of human resources, and an adviser to nine presidents, and by George Votja. Near the start of this short book—which looks at how huge organizations, such as the U.S. government, major corporations, or the Vatican, often fail to provide leaders with the honest brokers and sober analysis that they need to make sound decisions—is an anecdote about John F. Kennedy's first days in office. After the new President reviewed a position paper on a particular issue, he said to some advisers that he found it persuasive but added that "he didn't know whether the government of the United States was in agreement with it."

The problem, O'Neill felt, was that this President's lack of inquisitiveness or pertinent experience—Jack Kennedy, at least, had spent a decade in Congress—meant he didn't know or really care about the position of the U.S. government. It wasn't just a matter of doing the opposite of whatever Clinton had done, which was a prevalent theme throughout the administration. This President was starting from scratch on most issues and relying on ideologues like Larry Lindsey, Karl Rove, and, he now feared, his old friend Dick. Not an honest broker in sight.

"Administrations are defined by their President," O'Neill said.

And, while it was already apparent to many inside the administration that this President ceded significant authority to others, he was "clearly signing on to strong ideological positions that had not been fully thought through. But, of course, that's the nature of ideology. Thinking it through is the last thing an ideologue wants to do."

. . .

THE NEXT MORNING, O'Neill pored over stories in the national newspapers with gritted teeth. *The New York Times* front page, under the headline BUSH, IN REVERSAL, WON'T SEEK CUT IN EMISSIONS OF CARBON DIOXIDE, reported that the President retreated on his pledge under "strong pressure from conservative Republicans and industry groups." The decision, the *Times* added, "left environmental groups and some Congressional Democrats angered at what they called a major betrayal. But the White House said a cabinet-level review had concluded that Mr. Bush's original promise had been a mistake inconsistent with the broader goal of increasing domestic energy production."

Cabinet-level review?

O'Neill fumed. Certainly it was one from which the Secretary of the Treasury and the administrator of the EPA had been excluded.

After all the secret twists inside the White House, everything was now in the open. The text of the letter to Hagel, with its pointed language about the scientific uncertainties of global warming and the untenable costs of any response, was liberally ladled into stories run by all the major papers. Cheney and Spencer Abraham were cited as the winners, alongside ebullient quotes from industry lobbyists. "Mandatory controls [on carbon dioxide emissions] would drive a stake through the heart of a balanced energy program," John Grasser, of the National Mining Association, told *The Washington Post*.

California Democratic representative Henry Waxman, mean-

while, told the *Post* that it was "an embarrassment" to blame this retreat on energy prices. "If the administration fails to act, it won't be
because of energy prices," he said. "It will be because special interests are dictating the president's environmental policies."

Whitman's epitaph was visible to all. "As recently as 10 days ago,"
wrote the *Times*, "Christie Whitman, the new administrator of the
Environmental Protection Agency, had described Mr. Bush's campaign promise as if it were already policy. Administration officials
would not say directly today whether Ms. Whitman had supported
the change in position but suggested that she had not." Tina
Kreisher, Whitman's spokesperson, said the EPA chief would "follow the president's lead."

Several papers went on to mention O'Neill as an administration
supporter of action on global warming who had also lost out.

No doubt, O'Neill reflected. But how do you follow the lead of a
President if you're sure he's on the wrong path and there's no process
to hash out differences? Why would you follow?

. . .

ANY STUDENT of the presidency knows it is extremely rare for a
campaign pledge to be broken in the first one hundred days, the time
when a newly elected leader carries, most forcefully, the banner of
vox populi, ready to do "what I was elected to do." The clarity of that
mandate usually results in a flurry of activity and a predictable arc of
policy. Beyond those three months, there are examples of presidents
who have veered from cherished principles or what they've publicly
promised to do, but that is almost always driven by a historic, unexpected change of circumstances—such as a war or a depression or
a scandal.

At this point in mid-March 2001, a very different model was
becoming apparent. It caused confusion for senior officials like

O'Neill, Powell, and Whitman, none of whom was part of Bush's small coterie of advisers from the campaign or his days in Texas. From November until March, there had been no significant shifts except, possibly, in regard to the economy. Here, where Bush was holding tight to his central campaign pledge despite advice from Senate Republican moderates, O'Neill and others believed that, in fact, a historic economic shift could well be under way, and current conditions bore no relation to the economic landscape in 1999, when the proposal for a major tax cut was fashioned.

As for global affairs, the end of 2000 and the start of 2001 had not been a time of dramatic shifts in world events. Yet Bush's campaign positions, that the United States would be noninterventionist—that we would hesitate to become embroiled in disputes as we had in Bosnia and Somalia; that we would be "humble abroad" and not "engage in nation-building"—were the very opposite of the policy that O'Neill, Powell, and the other NSC principals saw unfolding. Actual plans, to O'Neill's astonishment, were already being discussed to take over Iraq and occupy it—complete with disposition of oil fields, peacekeeping forces, and war crimes tribunals—carrying forward an unspoken doctrine of preemptive war. Was it, O'Neill wondered, a matter of Bush—"who had spent virtually zero time outside of the country"—speaking during the campaign without any personal experience in foreign affairs and then learning everything he'd felt was necessary to know during the short transition? Didn't seem plausible.

In the same fashion, the global warming debate had been all but inert since the summer of 2000, as the world community had waited for its leading player to change administrations and start again to become engaged on the issue.

O'Neill and Whitman knew precisely what information the President had received. "An intensive evidentiary hearing was well under way," O'Neill said, and policies, driven by Bush's campaign pledges, were being executed. It wasn't as though the President had been pre-

sented with new, credible evidence to dispute assertions that global
climate change was real; nor would the California electricity crisis,
which was fast easing and already being attributed to poor distribution of available power rather than short supplies, merit a policy
shift. Seeing so much of the policy analysis that was being conducted—in so many realms—left O'Neill befuddled about the real
intentions that underlay action.

Was it possible, O'Neill wondered, that the country thought
it had elected a centrist when in fact it had empowered an ideologue?

The incident with Whitman was the start of what O'Neill later
called "a rolling revelation of the way this administration was operating."

"What became clear to me at that point," he said in an interview
with me in his house in Pittsburgh, not long after he left office, "is
that the presence of me and Colin and Christie helped convince people that this would, actually, be an administration that would look
hard for best solutions, without regard for which party had claimed
an idea first or some passing political calculation. That's what the
three of us were kind of known for, for being non-ideological, for
walking across political borders and looking for common ground.
Thinking back about how all of us started to be banged up so early
on, from the inside, it now seems like we inadvertently may have
been there, in large part, as cover."

· · ·

LATER THAT AFTERNOON—still smarting from the defeat on
global warming—O'Neill dove into materials prepared for his meeting that same day on Capitol Hill with the Senate's "centrist coalition."

The tax battle was rapidly settling into a conflict of two teams. Liberals, moderates, and some conservative Democrats, like Conrad of North Dakota, were gathering around a proposed tax cut of $800 billion over ten years, with a more progressive blend of rate reductions to advantage the middle class. They were also looking to pay down a larger share of federal debt and to do it more swiftly. Their patron saint, Bob Rubin, and former Fed chairman Paul Volcker both came out against the President's tax plan, noting in a joint press conference on March 12 that the tax was "fiscally unsound."

Senate and House Republicans were angling for deeper tax cuts. House Majority Leader Dick Armey and Senate Majority Leader Trent Lott were pushing to add capital gains tax cuts to the President's proposal. Just this morning, Majority Whip Tom DeLay had said that the President's proposal was "a floor, not a ceiling."

One thing spurring that enthusiasm was the posture of the White House. Mitch Daniels, in an internal memo he sent to O'Neill and others in mid-February, had written that "there are very large opportunities and contingencies that could *expand* the surpluses over ten years," above the current projection of $5.6 trillion. This assessment, which O'Neill argued in various internal meetings was analytically specious, was leaked to senators and strengthened talk of deeper cuts and various additions, from child credits to marriage credits to the repeal of the estate tax.

With the two parties settling into camps and the Senate divided 50–50—Vice President Cheney holding the tie-breaking vote—the chamber's centrists felt like crouching tigers, their position increasing in value with each passing day.

And they'd embraced triggers. The seed planted by O'Neill and Greenspan had grown steadily with this group through February, even if it faced increasingly strong winds from both sides of the aisle.

Triggers are widely known as an imperfect device, a last resort, like an intervention with an alcoholic, for politicians who are proving to be fiscal libertines.

"It's bad economics, especially if you're trying to influence economic growth," said Dick Armey on February 18 to *The Boston Globe*, making the case that growth rests on certainty and predictability, not on conditions.

Robert Reischauer, former director of the Congressional Budget Office when it was under Democratic control, offered a more esoteric criticism in the *San Francisco Chronicle* two days later: "Putting a trigger into the tax bill is worse than no trigger at all, because it provides a false sense of security to those who worry about the possibility that the tax cut might prove to be too large."

A week later, on NBC's news program *Meet the Press*, White House chief of staff Andrew Card said, "There's no need for a trigger if you have responsible budgeting, and this tax relief plan is responsible in a responsible budget. You know, there's $5.6 trillion of surplus, and that's a very conservative estimate."

A week after that, on March 4, Leon Panetta, former House Budget Committee chairman and later budget director and White House chief of staff under President Clinton, explained in the *Los Angeles Times* that "when you establish triggers, what you're doing is saying you have to establish an automatic procedure because there isn't any political will. But any time you do that, politics ultimately prevails."

Fine, replied the centrists. At least with this mechanism, Congress would be forced to abide by it or disarm it, an act of political exposure that would publicly call the question of fiscal prudence.

In other words: not perfect, but better than nothing. On March 7, Maine's Republican senator Olympia Snowe and Indiana's Democratic senator Evan Bayh introduced a bipartisan resolution in support of a trigger mechanism that "will enable Congress to provide broad-based tax relief that is fiscally responsible and avoids a return to annual deficits." The resolution was structured to allow the first phase of the President's proposed tax cut to proceed unconditionally, while certain elements of the phased-in relief would be implemented as long as specified debt reduction targets were met. Joining Snowe and Bayh as co-sponsors were Senators Tom Carper (D–Del.), Lincoln Chafee (R–R.I.), Susan Collins (R–Maine), Dianne Feinstein (D–Calif.), Jim Jeffords (R–Vt.), Mary Landrieu (D–La.), Arlen Specter (R–Pa.), Debbie Stabenow (D–Mich.), and Robert Torricelli (D–N.J.).

That morning, when Olympia Snowe breakfasted with O'Neill, he was uncharacteristically circumspect on the issue, not letting on that he agreed with her stance and, in fact, had been behind the initiative from the start.

Yet, this afternoon in the lion's den, it would be more difficult to conceal his beliefs. The centrists would assume that he and Greenspan were of one mind, and they'd do their best to get O'Neill to admit it. A nod from him on triggers would be all they'd need to claim convincingly the President's support and officially post triggers as the compromise position. Insofar as he had already talked to the President about it the week before—and Bush's disfavor had convinced O'Neill that he'd never sign triggers into law—for O'Neill to show his support of the idea would amount to insubordination.

O'Neill held all calls and opened a folder of reports that the Treasury staff had prepared for today's meeting. On top was the summary:

> As you know, Congressional Centrists account for the critical swing vote in consideration of the President's budget and tax plan. Rather than reiterate the administration's position on the tax plan and fiscal policy, you should demonstrate to them that the lines of communication are open between Capitol Hill and the Treasury, and listen to their ideas. However, it is not a time to negotiate.

That, clearly, was the White House's position. Stay the course. Dig in. We won't second-guess ourselves. If Congress wants to accelerate the tax cuts as a way to speed stimulus to the economy, that will be fine. There was nothing to stop Congress from giving Bush more than what he'd asked for: the $1.6 trillion tax cut would simply happen more quickly. This had been discussed at countless meetings, many of them with the President in attendance. Any analysis of the economy's lethargic condition and what medicine it might actually need was a secondary issue. The staff memo reflected that. Consensus: *Don't negotiate.*

. . .

AT 4:15 P.M., O'Neill and his delegation—including Mark Weinberger, his tax specialist; Michele Davis, his communications director; and John M. Duncan, his legislative chief—entered Room 11 in the Dirksen Senate Office Building.

The room was jammed. Each senator had brought at least one senior staffer, along with aides from the staffs of Finance and Banking. Ten or so senators settled around the conference table, with O'Neill at the head. Staffers crowded along the walls. The principals quickly engaged. Apart from perfunctory nods, there were no cordialities. Olympia Snowe, among the Senate's early advocates of conditionality, led with comments about the propriety of triggers. Their proposal was to link tax cuts to the reduction in debt, currently at $3.2 trillion when Social Security was excluded. While always keeping the budget in balance, they wanted to use more of the surplus for debt reduction. Senator Joe Lieberman of Connecticut mentioned the President's misleading total of $1.2 trillion in unreduceable debt; most of the senators, including the Republicans, felt the number was closer to Gary Gensler's $500 billion. O'Neill demurred that "honest people can disagree on that total"—a dodge he had used in the past two weeks in various public pronouncements. He hated to do it, he recalled, "but I decided that contradicting the President on this one was a battle I couldn't afford to fight."

As the talk of triggers swirled, with senators citing Greenspan's recommendation for triggers in his January 25 testimony, and again in testimony before the House Budget Committee on March 2, O'Neill was opaque. Be like Cheney, he thought: Nod earnestly, show them nothing, don't speak. For O'Neill, this was something like "Don't breathe."

Lieberman, whom O'Neill liked and respected, tried to draw him out. "Are you saying you disagree with Chairman Greenspan on this?"

"I try to *never* disagree with the chairman," O'Neill said, drawing a welcome laugh, "unless absolutely necessary."

He had to move carefully. Under any imaginable scenario, these centrists would be crucial to the passage of a tax bill, a finished "product," as the legislative staff liked to say. The White House strategy was to let the centrists think that O'Neill—and, by association, the President—was open to suggestion on the triggers, though this wasn't true. But that would keep the centrists in the game until the end, all the way until the House and Senate, with separate resolutions, went into conference. Only then would it be appropriate for the President to roll up his sleeves, sit down, and maybe horse-trade. Until then, Bush wasn't budging, even if his tax package seemed, with each passing day, designed for an economy that had all but vanished.

O'Neill hated the idea of willfully misleading the centrists as "a kind of strategy that eventually catches up with you." In fact, he hoped they'd make it all the way to a House/Senate conference with their triggers held high and that the President, to get a bill through, would be forced to keep the conditional mechanism. It was what he and Alan had hoped for from the start.

But the longer the meeting went, the more he sensed that prospect fading. John Breaux of Louisiana, the Senate's master of shotgun marriages across party lines, said he had doubts about the triggers, but they needed to be "prudent in managing the federal budget, today and tomorrow." Snowe talked about Greenspan's position that the surplus wasn't money in the bank and that soon we'd see more clearly how much money there was to work with. Max Baucus from Montana, a conservative Democrat trying to hold on to his seat in a Republican state, was sober and deliberate: "We just need to look at the hard budgetary facts, and the trigger, at least, encourages us to embrace real numbers—not fictional ones."

Yes, everyone was posturing a bit, O'Neill felt, but mostly it was straight talk from pragmatists—senators, from both parties, seeking the most responsible path based on the known facts, just as he and Whitman and others had done on global warming, just as Powell was attempting his pragmatic internationalism in foreign policy. This faith in open, reality-based deliberation would, O'Neill was realizing, soon make them vulnerable to the cynical counteridea: *The base likes this, and who the hell knows anyway.* It would be a rout.

"That meeting was the start of a turning point for me," O'Neill remembers. "I knew I'd have to be guided by the principles of sensible policy, not what was expected of me."

He cut off the discussion on triggers. "I think we understand where people stand on the issue of conditionality," he said. "Let's talk about how to create economic stimulus."

It was a discussion that he had started in his confirmation testimony—his first break with the President, who was at that point advertising his package as providing economic stimulus. O'Neill had said otherwise, much to the White House's dismay.

Now, for the senators, he elaborated. If the tax package was passed today, he said, even with an accelerated schedule of rate cuts, it wouldn't provide meaningful stimulus any time before late 2002.

"But whether stimulus is needed, well, that's a different question. I think we do need stimulus." They launched into a discussion of the latest economic numbers. They ran through inventory figures for automobiles, the highest credit-to-income ratio on record, and latest indicators of how job losses were continuing. Clearly, the terrain was soft. A stimulus was needed. Today. In six months, we might be desperate for one. That was reality.

"Well, I have about $125 billion of surplus in Treasury's checking account. Why don't you just use that for an immediate tax rebate?" O'Neill asked.

The room was quiet. No one said anything for a minute, not wanting to jinx it. Everyone could do the math: the last thing the President would want was a separate bill, a onetime rebate to target current economic conditions, possibly at the expense of his package of long-term reductions in marginal rates. But an immediate, substantial rebate was indeed what was needed. They could have a proposal together in a week, maybe sooner. And the President would now have to defend his $1.6 trillion plan to reduce marginal rates on its merits, instead of pretending that it would stimulate a wavering economy.

At that moment, Paul O'Neill wrestled economic policy from whoever was calling the shots inside the White House.

"I guess I kind of said, 'Screw it,' " he recalls. "And it turned out to be one of the best things I ever did."

. . .

THE NEXT MORNING, Greenspan was waiting in his conference room, eating his oatmeal with raisins, when O'Neill arrived.

"I'm one up on you today," he said. O'Neill smiled. In the past month of their breakfasts at the Fed, the pair had been joined by Ken Dam, the deputy Treasury secretary, whom Greenspan had known almost as long as he'd known O'Neill. Dam was also in the Nixon White House and had served like Greenspan on the Alcoa board.

The door was shut and O'Neill settled in, feeling, as always, that he was in a protected place, a safe haven for clear thinking. As Dam sat by, taking a few notes, Greenspan and O'Neill offered their "What do we have to roll around in this morning?" and off they riffed.

Today's news, they agreed, might as well be served on ice, like a dead fish. Every major paper led with the declining stock market. The Dow had dropped for three of the last four trading days, and yesterday had closed below 10,000 for the first time in a year. The *Washington Post* headline pointed to GLOBAL SLOWDOWN. The *Los Angeles Times* blamed JAPAN'S WOES. *USA Today*, which O'Neill had added to his morning habit, went in a different direction. Its front-page story emphasized how the market's collapse was hitting the U.S. Treasury. The paper cited several respected private forecasters whose analyses suggested that, owing to the resultant loss in corporate, capital gains, and other tax revenues, a fifth to a half of the projected ten-year, $5.6 trillion surplus could be wiped out.

They talked about how the next round of budget projections, due out in mid-July, would show the surplus reduced but agreed that the tax bill debate should be well over by then.

"I hear you were making some trouble on the Hill yesterday," Greenspan said.

O'Neill smiled. "I'm not sure if the triggers will survive, but I suppose I created some bargaining position for the center."

Greenspan thought about the arc of their conversations since December. "I'm not sure that a tax cut of that size and long schedule is appropriate without some mechanism of conditionality," he said. "These surpluses, or the perception of surpluses, is proving to be surprisingly corrosive to the maintenance of spending discipline."

O'Neill nodded. "Corrosive to the very standard of fiscal responsibility." He talked about how a tax rebate of $125 billion could be a crucial, near-term boost to the economy—"it's front-loading our efforts to where they are needed"—and could result "in a reduction in the size of the President's long-term tax package or an urge to make it conditional on surpluses."

Both men took this in and sat quietly for a moment. Dam listened. "White House can't be too happy about all this," Greenspan said finally, and looked with concern at his friend.

"What are the real choices, here?" O'Neill asked. "If we don't exert some discipline on spending and taxes, we may find ourselves at day's end without the one trillion we need for Social Security."

The $1 trillion figure had evolved over the past year into a central feature of the President's plan to move Social Security from its safe, sleepy, government-run home to higher-yielding private accounts that individuals could help direct. In May 2000, candidate Bush had championed the idea of private accounts and embraced a proposal to create a bipartisan commission that had been advanced by Senators Daniel Patrick Moynihan, a Democrat from New York, Bob Kerrey, a Democrat from Nebraska, and Republican John McCain of Arizona. Under their plan, the commission would propose a solution for reforming Social Security within a tight timetable, and Congress would then take an up-or-down vote on the proposal.

For a period of time, Bush's bridge proposal would mean funding two retirement systems at once. During heated give-and-take in the fall, Bush had suggested that workers under about age fifty could set up new accounts—where a portion of their payroll taxes would go into a private investment account, while most would be paid into the traditional government coffer—but the benefits promised to older workers and current retirees would be protected. Part of that calculus was a recognition that current benefits would have to be paid for at least twelve years before anyone in the new system had reached retirement age and was entitled to benefits that otherwise would be inadequately funded—a shortfall that the government would then have to make up.

The $1 trillion would cover costs of the parallel programs and the shortfall. Greenspan and O'Neill, though, saw the $1 trillion allocated differently. They did not think the new accounts should be a mix of private investments and safe, low-yielding government securities, a blended approach the President seemed to endorse. Once again, without the benefit of a few extensive discussions with the President about his thinking on this issue, his position was unclear. O'Neill and Greenspan, however, believed in a clean break. Those who remained in the old Social Security system would see no change; those in the new plan would be *fully invested* in large, indexed private equity or bond funds. Only thus could the latter group fully benefit from what Warren Buffett calls the "miracle of compounding returns" on their portfolios.

The two men talked through all this over second cups of coffee.

"So, what did you get for our number?" Greenspan asked expectantly.

O'Neill had come ready. At their breakfast the week before, they wondered about what $1 trillion would buy. More specifically, what a bridge fund of that amount would permit in terms of how many Americans could be brought into a new, private investment plan. They agreed there should be a clean break—everyone above a certain age would be fully funded under the old system. Everyone below would be part of a new plan "of wealth accumulation rather than generational transfer," as O'Neill often preached.

"I got a cutoff age of thirty-seven," O'Neill said.

Greenspan laughed. "Me too."

They threw a few math queries across the table—Did you consider this? Did you factor that?—then jotted a few double-checks on the backs of envelopes. Ken Dam looked on and wondered if he should run across the hall for a calculator. No, they'd be fine. It all figured. With a bridge fund of $1 trillion, they could now have everyone thirty-seven or younger move to the new plan.

"Okay," Greenspan quipped, "all you have to do now is take $1 trillion and lock it in a safe."

. . .

FOUR DAYS LATER—Monday, March 19—was Social Security day in the Capitol. O'Neill, as Treasury Secretary, was chairing a meeting of the Social Security and Medicare board of trustees. Statute dictated that the Treasury Secretary be the chairman and that the Secretaries of Labor and Health and Human Services act as trustees. The agenda was rigid, always the same, and year by year it had revolved around an ever tightening bind: the system was in trouble. Now, it was threatened by a declining economy. It was a mighty tree, rotting from within.

After a morning of brain-bending give-and-take on such consequential calculations, O'Neill emerged for a midday press conference in Treasury's Diplomatic Reception Room, across the hall and down the steps from his office. The news that was released from today's Social Security trustees' meeting was in the form of a document: the *Annual Report on Social Security and Medicare.* The key conclusions: that the Medicare Trust Fund will run out in 2029. The Social Security Trust Fund will run out in 2038.

Reporters grabbed copies of the report. These days, they were always sure to turn up for an O'Neill press conference. The freewheeling, and sometimes disastrously frank, statements of January and February made O'Neill an act not to be missed, especially in an administration that, reporters were fast discovering, controlled candor the way the EPA handled toxic waste.

O'Neill stepped to the podium.

REPORTER ONE: Mr. Secretary, when does the administration anticipate sending its Social Security reform proposals to Congress?

O'NEILL: Well, we'll see. The president is going to announce his commission in the near term, and I expect we will see something, hopefully, in the early fall. And then there will be preparation time.

And so I can't answer your question specifically. But we're working apace on it, and, hopefully, we're going to be able to get tax reform done in the next couple of weeks, and then we can work specifically and almost exclusively on Social Security.

REPORTER TWO: Given the decline in the market of late and the nervousness with which even blue-collar workers are looking at their 401(k) funds in shock and disbelief, how could you convince the American public that a program that has been the source of ultimate security should now be turned over to a more risky private investment formula?

O'NEILL: Well, first of all, we're not here today to design a new Social Security program. And I have to accept your premise of a particular form and composition in order to even be tempted to answer your question, which I am a little bit.

O'Neill paused and took a sip of water. He was trying to be more circumspect in his public comments, and his hesitations often created Greenspan-like gusts of constructive—or, in this case, unconstructive—ambiguities. He made a mental note to send Alan a transcript of that last response; he thought he'd get a chuckle out of it. He cleared his throat and picked up the question.

> O'NEILL: Let me do a short answer, but not to deal with specifics of how one might design a program. If you look at the recorded history of economic activity in Western society—I guess I need to define it that carefully, let's say over the last 100 years, what you would find over—I think it's fair to say over any 40-year period you could imagine—that is to say, I leave the composition of the 40 years to you, that real returns to private investment have been higher than the zero-risk government investment alternative. That may be more complicated than you want.

> REPORTER TWO: Yes, sir.

. . .

LATER THAT AFTERNOON, March 19, O'Neill and members of the Vice President's National Energy Policy Development Group filed into the cabinet room to present their findings to the President about the state of energy production and consumption in the United States.

This presentation marked the completion of the first of two phases (the second would be creating policy recommendations) that had been decided on in late January, when the President officially empowered Dick Cheney to handle energy.

The Vice President, upon receiving his charge, had vowed it wouldn't be the way it was before. In this case, *before* meant the energy task force that the first President Bush called to action in 1989 to assess what powered America and how to wean the country from dependence on foreign oil.

Back then, Energy Secretary James D. Watkins was in charge. There were eighteen public hearings. Four hundred ninety-nine individuals from forty-three states participated in the forums. The dialogue, the General Accounting Office found, "represented an unprecedented effort by DOE to solicit the nation's views on energy policy." In fact, the response was so overwhelming that the Department of Energy missed its deadline for compiling draft recommendations. The report, submitted to President Bush in December 1990, listing options—such as deregulation of gas pipelines or a 50-cent-a-gallon tax on gasoline—was called the most ambitious energy study ever conducted by the government. Nearly a year later, a bill drawn from the report, carrying the bipartisan stamp of the President and leading Democrats, failed in the Senate on a procedural vote, mostly due to a provision to open the Arctic National Wildlife Refuge (ANWR) to oil drilling—an evergreen issue, so to speak, for the oil lobby, which had been pushing for opening ANWR since the late 1970s. Some senators said there were other places to find oil at far less risk to the environment. "Furthermore, the provision symbolized the bill's mindless bias toward energy production as opposed to conservation," *The New York Times* maintained in an editorial after the bill's defeat in November 1991. "Still, the Senate's failure has produced useful lessons to guide the next attempt at a national energy strategy. Keep it simple. And make it balanced."

In this Bush administration, Dick Cheney looked to keep it simple. Also quiet and efficient. He had been in both the Nixon and Ford administrations in periods of energy crises. He had witnessed sound and fury on energy policy during Bush I that in the end amounted to nothing. He'd run an energy company, Halliburton, for five years in the 1990s, and—all things considered—viewed himself an expert. That meant that no public hearings or debate from opposing factions were required. Cheney was sure he knew all he needed to know.

The National Energy Policy Development, or NEPD, was structured *not* to entertain public discourse or contrary positions. At the first working meeting at 10 a.m. on February 9, Cheney and his staff, eight cabinet officials and their staffs, sat at a long mahogany table in the Vice President's meeting room, a dark, high-ceilinged chamber in the Old Executive Office Building.

There was much discussion of the California energy crisis. Internal documents between Treasury and the White House show that in the preceding week the U.S. government was considering a Chrysler-like bailout of the California utilities. After heated deliberations, the administration had decided that a Clinton administration order forcing energy suppliers to sell their excess power to California utilities would be extended for two weeks, giving the state more time to deal with the crisis. The move provoked a barrage of letters to Treasury and the White House from outraged suppliers, claiming that those orders forced them to sell without any prospect of getting paid by the insolvent utilities. California used the two-week reprieve to pass a $10 billion bond issue to prop up the companies. The orders expired two days before the first NEPD meeing; within days, those outraged utilities were at the table with state utilities negotiating long-term contracts. But at that point, even with the $10 billion, the state was cornered. It was a forced market, and utilities had to sign, and quickly, at almost any price.*

O'Neill thought Cheney's task force was oddly constructed: made up solely of government officials. Most task forces go in the other direction: their strength is in creating a structure for government officials to mix with leading experts, former top public officials, or respected businessmen. Such entities are covered under the Fed-

---

* Two years later, the Federal Energy Regulatory Commission (FERC) charged that the energy providers engaged in illegal market manipulation in the period preceding and following the signing of the long-term agreements. Whether this was the result of encouragement from federal authorities, or of a sense that energy producers and brokers viewed their relationships with senior administration officials as protective, is a question that various lawsuits are now examining.

eral Advisory Committee Act, or FACA, which mandates that the activities of groups that combine governmental and nongovernmental officials be fully disclosed to the public; lists of members, advisers, agendas, and minutes of meetings must be made available.

Because this was a task force with only government employees, there were no reporting requirements. O'Neill knew Cheney liked it that way—he had often groused about prying questions and transparency and how information released under the claim of right-to-know became ammunition for a host of political enemies. This task force, Cheney's, would operate in utmost privacy.

Not that other voices didn't join in the conversation. Industry representatives—in bureaucratic language, the "nonfederal stakeholders"—were just outside the door. Before and after the formal task force meetings, principals and staff, often moving in small, interdepartmental groups, would meet with lobbyists from all the major energy concerns. For the most part, environmentalists were nowhere to be seen.

According to documents in O'Neill's files, along with those obtained in various disclosure actions filed against the Cheney task force, Secretary of Energy Spencer Abraham met with corporations and trade groups, including Chevron, the National Mining Association, and the National Petrochemical and Refiners Association, each of which delivered policy recommendations in detailed reports. On the meeting roster for Secretary of the Interior Gale Norton were Rocky Mountain–based petroleum companies looking to lease federal land and an Indian tribe from Nevada interested in building a power plant. Cheney met with Enron chairman Kenneth Lay and received detailed policy recommendations from one industry group whose central concern was not allowing carbon dioxide to be regulated as a pollutant, as well as from another—called the Coal-Based Generation Stakeholders—whose central position was lifting pollution controls on coal-fueled electric generators.

Even Whitman sat down with a few industry representatives, including executives from the Alliance of Automobile Manufacturers and Edison Electric Institute, which represents investor-owned utilities.

O'Neill, for his part, received three short phone calls that late winter and early spring from Enron's Ken Lay. In one, Lay advocated federal support of a derivatives trading market for fuels. In another, he voiced support for global warming initiatives because they would favor natural gas, a big part of Enron's trading business. O'Neill also received a strongly worded letter of protest from Goldman Sachs's CEO, Hank Paulson, about how the federal price controls in California were injuring the investment firm's subsidiary J. Aron & Company, an energy supplier to California utilities. J. Aron pulled out of the California market and was not among the companies later to be charged by the Federal Energy Regulatory Commission with price manipulation.

If process drives outcomes—an axiom O'Neill and his fellow pragmatists live by—this combination of confidentiality and influence by powerful interested parties would define the task force's analysis of energy issues.

"It meant," O'Neill says, "that environmental concerns went virtually unrepresented."

So, on March 19, at an hour-long meeting in the cabinet room, the President was hearing dark predictions about the economic effects of a looming energy crisis.

Everybody played their parts: literally. For this President, cabinet meetings and the many midsize to large meetings he attended were carefully scripted. Before most meetings, a cabinet secretary's chief of staff would receive a note from someone on the senior staff in the White House. The note instructed the cabinet secretary when he was supposed to speak, about what, and how long. When O'Neill had received his first such note, he was amazed. The idea of a cabinet meeting or any significant meeting between the President and his

seniormost officials being scripted seemed to kill off the whole purpose of bringing people together. He had been in many White
Houses. He had never heard of such a thing.

But by now he didn't question it. At least, he figured, he had his
regular one-on-ones with the President. Virtually no one else in the
cabinet had that sort of inside track, except for Rumsfeld.

For today's meeting, the stage direction had come from the Vice
President's office and, as expected, Dick went first, sitting in the
chair directly across from the President. He talked about the task
force's structure, its methodology, and the sources it had relied upon.
He said that the goal of phase one had been to "assess more clearly
what the energy needs are of a growing country and how to meet
them."

O'Neill then talked, as scripted, about the way rising energy costs
would cripple the economy and how the California crisis could
spread to other regions, driving up energy costs for the coming
summer.

Spencer Abraham addressed the beleaguered coal industry, which
still produces half of the nation's energy, and how rising gas prices
could be caused by "unfolding supply constraints" in the United
States.

Secretary of Agriculture Ann Veneman offered a short rendition
of how rising fuel prices would affect agriculture. Larry Lindsey described how energy costs washed through many parts of the U.S.
economy and hit certain areas of manufacturing particularly hard.
And around the table they went. Whitman was not asked to speak.

O'Neill was watching Bush closely. He threw out a few general
phrases, a few nods, but there was virtually no engagement. These
cabinet secretaries had worked for over a month on detailed reports.
O'Neill had been made to understand by various colleagues in the
White House that the President should not be expected to read re-

The PRICE of LOYALTY • *149*

ports. In his personal experience, the President didn't even appear to have read the short memos he sent over.

That made it especially troubling that Bush did not ask any questions. There are so many worth asking about each of these areas, O'Neill thought as he sat quietly, dozens of queries running through his head.

"This meeting was like many of the meetings I would go to over the course of two years," he recalled. "The only way I can describe it is that, well, the President is like a blind man in a roomful of deaf people. There is no discernible connection."

· · ·

OVER THE NEXT DAYS, on the tax cut initiative, the White House worked to distance itself from the arguments about triggers and the rebate compromise that O'Neill was working out with congressional centrists. But it was getting more difficult by the hour. The rebate proposal was gaining strength. On March 22, Republican moderates in the Senate agreed to an immediate $60 billion tax rebate to stimulate the economy. The sense in Congress was that the size of the rebate would grow.

During an appearance in Portland, Maine, on March 23, Bush was asked about the trigger proposal, which was also gaining strength. "There's a lot of ideas now being floated out in the Congress, and I'm open-minded to any good idea," he said. "Any suggestion that people give, I'm willing to listen to."

In comments later that day, Senator Snowe could barely contain her optimism. "I think, ultimately, he'll accept this trigger. He didn't say so, but I sense that."

Meanwhile, more senators were signing on to the rebate.

It needed to be addressed. On March 27, the President gave a speech in Kalamazoo, Michigan, where he warned against passing the $60 billion rebate plan as a substitute for an overall tax plan. "Our economy needs more than a pick-me-up, more than a one-time boost," he said.

Late that day, O'Neill received a memo from Michele Davis about the press conference the next morning that was to unveil the President's budget.

Davis, who gathered each morning with other communications directors, was taking heat from the White House—as was O'Neill's chief of staff, Tim Adams. Rove and Card were still smarting from O'Neill's unilateral maneuver with the centrists. The message: Control your man.

Davis's memo was terse.

> You and Mitch Daniels are scheduled to unveil the President's budget at a press conference in the Old Executive Office Building at 10:15 tomorrow morning. *This event, more than anything you've participated in to date, requires that you be monotonously on-message.* . . . Your role is to 1) repeat the message that we will pay off all the debt available to pay off and 2) state clearly that we must cut taxes because we take more from people than we need to fund these new priorities, and if we don't give it back to the people who paid it, we'll end up wasting it in Washington.

O'Neill read the memo. This was the sort of advice he did not take well, especially the suggestion to be monotonous. Yes, he could say that last thing about waste—in his own words, of course—not the rest. But maybe, he thought, he'd also find a way to mention the threat of deficits.

. . .

"HEY THERE, Pablo, how ya makin' out?"

"Just fine, Mr. President. And yourself?"

"Never better."

It was 3 p.m. on March 28, the afternoon after the press conference—a meeting scheduled for forty-five minutes. O'Neill's weekly
standing meeting with POTUS had, for the most part, been kept up.
On balance, with travel and intervening events, they were averaging
about once every eleven days. While the meetings sometimes left
O'Neill troubled about how disengaged the President seemed, he
was grateful, nonetheless, to have a regular spot on the schedule.

Last week, O'Neill had brought his tax specialist, Mark
Weinberger, to give the President a tutorial on the intricacies of tax
policy, so this was the first time in several weeks the two were to be
alone.

O'Neill assumed his regular spot on the mustard couch, the President on the wing chair near the fireplace. O'Neill thought today
would be a good day to talk about Social Security. Two weeks before,
he had chaired the trustees' meeting, and in a month or so, the President was expected to announce the formation of his Social Security
Commission, co-chaired by Daniel Patrick Moynihan and AOL
Time Warner executive Richard Parsons, a close friend of O'Neill's
from the Ford administration.

"Fixing Social Security is the issue that could create the historic
part of your presidency."

Bush nodded.

"We need to make that happen, no matter what else we do,"
O'Neill said emphatically.

O'Neill was ready to continue his monologue—he'd come to
expect that the President would say little, or nothing, in these encounters.

"Fact is, the dramatic stance I made on Social Security, pushing for these private accounts, is what got me elected. It was the key thing. People saw me as dealing with one of the real big problems—figuring it out," Bush said.

In case the President had any further thoughts, O'Neill let a bit of silence hang between them.

"Okay now, Mr. President, it's time for follow-through."

O'Neill laid out the various options on how private accounts might be structured and how the "blended" approach was a compromise "that gets you the pain of having to sell people on change, but no gain."

He said that he and Greenspan had come up with a cutoff age: thirty-seven. For $1 trillion, everyone below that age could be fully vested in the new private accounts, which would mix widely indexed equity and bond funds, so that their growth would all but correspond to the country's economic growth. "And I think that cutoff age, thirty-seven, corresponds pretty well with a cleavage age line that exists right now in the population, between those who don't want anything to change and those who believe they won't get anything *unless* things change."

Bush seemed to shrug it off. "I didn't go with that approach in the campaign."

O'Neill tamped down his frustration. This wasn't just any issue. It was the most important contract between the government and its citizens, a program angling toward crisis at a moment when a unique surplus—driven mostly by tax receipts from people cashing out their once-in-a-lifetime stock market winnings—had fallen into their laps. A surplus that was evaporating by the hour.

He decided to explain to the President the calculations he and Greenspan had done. They were complex, multiplying a typical American's annual payroll tax payments by the average indexed investment returns of the past forty years.

"Mr. President, here's an example. A person vested in a true, private accounts plan at eighteen would have, at sixty-five, one million dollars in assets."

O'Neill paused, to let it sink in.

"Imagine how that would change what's possible in the lives of people in this country—to arrive at sixty-five with assets of one million."

Bush showed no response. He had checked out, and time was up.

"I just thought we needed to have a real discussion," O'Neill recalled. "We needed to do some actual questioning and thinking. I'm the Treasury Secretary and I happen to have spent forty years studying Social Security. The Fed chairman and I are in agreement. I've even had real discussions with other presidents about the choices and consequences on this issue. . . . But he just sat back in his chair. His attitude was, 'I said this during the campaign, and whatever I said in the campaign must be right.' "

O'Neill, who had come to Washington dreaming of reforming Social Security, left feeling confused and deflated.

· · ·

THE VICE PRESIDENT'S energy task force was well into the second, or recommendation, phase by its April 11 meeting.

The gatherings—which included the Vice President; eight cabinet members representing Treasury, Commerce, Interior, Health and Human Services, Energy, Agriculture, EPA, and Transportation; Larry Lindsey; and, frequently, White House staffers including Karl Rove—had taken on an edge in phase two. The recommendations of energy lobbyists were now routinely embraced by the task force. And the group would soon make its recommendations to President Bush.

In many areas, Whitman and O'Neill were articulating the environmental and conservationist views—the basic idea that thirty years of regulations to protect land, water, and air were of value.

"This is a slaughter," Whitman said to O'Neill after one meeting. "It's ten on two, not counting White House people and all the advisers to the group from the various industries."

Some proposals on the table, which would be in the final report, included opening ANWR to drilling and a host of rule changes and tax credits for the coal, natural gas, and nuclear industries.

One topic of discussion on April 11 was an EPA proposal to simplify the process of obtaining permits for new power plant construction. The President would direct federal agencies to coordinate with local and state officials to streamline the licensing system. In order to speed construction, the government would also "identify in advance the types of pollution controls that would facilitate fast-track approval of air permits," according to memos from the meeting.

Whitman had pulled together the EPA's proposal in response to the group's criticism of the present uncertainty that complicated the process. O'Neill had noted in a memorandum from Treasury for that day's meeting that "regulatory uncertainty adds needless cost and delay to the development of new generating capacity. Much of this uncertainty derives from the current piecemeal approach to environmental regulation, in which each regulatory proposal is developed independently. Agencies, and even offices within agencies, generally do not coordinate the mandates they impose." EPA's proposal would remove this uncertainty by forcing regulatory agencies to enforce the uniform regulations.

For Whitman, this was an answer to a modest problem—but it was a fix that could ignite a dangerous overhaul of the regulatory structure. After six meetings of the task force, in which EPA was blamed for virtually every problem facing America on the energy front, she presented it with a kind of resolve—"Yes, we recognize our problems and are attacking them." Much of the rest of the group—and especially Abraham, Cheney, and Lindsey, the most strident of the anti-regulatory contingent—was ecstatic. Every energy producer was pushing for this: with the proper application of pressure from industry and the White House, it could mean the rewriting of vast swaths of regulation—across many departments—in the name of coordination and simplification.

Lindsey, who had been attacking Whitman, the EPA, and the very idea of environmental regulation with ideological zeal from the start, leapt in with enthusiasm.

"This could be the start of real change," he said. "There have been thousands of power plants, literally, that have not been constructed because of these jumbled regulations, and immeasurable amounts of energy that the country has been denied because of it, energy we've needed."

Whitman could take it no more.

"With all due respect, Larry, do you have any facts to back up these assertions of yours? I'm driven by facts, and I'd like to see any facts that show that *any power plants* were not built because of these regulations."

Lindsey rolled his eyes and whispered something to the task force members on either side of him. They all snickered, along with some aides around them.

Whitman blew. "If you have something to say to me, Larry, say it to my face!"

The Vice President intervened and moved the discussion along. There was a long agenda to complete.

In the end, almost none of Treasury's recommendations made it into the final report. But over the next few weeks, O'Neill and Mark Weinberger worked to cut out nearly a dozen major tax credits to the energy industry in the final draft of the recommendations.

"We killed off our share," O'Neill said. "We viewed almost all of them as just a waste of money. Companies that are already doing something don't generally do more of it if they get a tax credit. And the ones that aren't doing the thing you want will probably just take your money and then drag their feet or figure out a way not to do it."

He felt there were some good ideas aired in the meetings—including a national energy grid, so utilities could operate across state lines without facing a jumble of state regulations; and the passage of mandatory safety and reliability standards for pipelines and electricity infrastructures, both of which made the final report.

Yet on balance, he viewed the Vice President's task force as an example of what happens when "good process" is not embraced. "When you have people with a strong ideological position, and you only hear from one side, you can pretty much predict the outcome.

"Let's just say the recommendations generally did not meet the high standard of 'in the broad public interest.' "

. . .

ON MAY 2, the President announced the formation of the Social Security Commission. All of the members of the commission had been preapproved by Larry Lindsey or Karl Rove as supporters of private accounts.

O'Neill, who was a vigorous supporter of private accounts, objected strenuously to their screening. "It meant we gave away our most valuable asset, credibility. If you're certain you're right—and I think we are [right] on the private accounts—you shouldn't be afraid to include the opposing voices at your table. If you can't convince them, there may be more facts you have to gather, or something you're not thinking clearly about. In this case, we should have been confident enough to engage the other side."

The commission, which would conduct studies over the next six months, was immediately attacked by Senate Minority Leader Tom Daschle as "a stacked, completely orchestrated effort to come to a desired result, and I'm very disappointed that that is the decision they've made."

On May 16, O'Neill entered the Cabinet Room at 2:30, a few minutes early for a meeting with NSC principals on the Mideast. Powell and Rumsfeld were already there. The President was uncharacteristically late, so the three men sat around the table and chatted like old buddies—which in Rumsfeld's and O'Neill's cases was true. They and their wives had socialized since the early seventies. But Powell was also in familiar company. In the early seventies, he'd worked for O'Neill as a White House fellow—a plum assignment for an officer on the rise—and they had many mutual friends.

Now they were all rich, older men, powerful and prickly, who'd accomplished much before arriving at their elevated stations and, lately, had endured a requisite dose of scrutiny. When one is selected for a high post, humility is demanded, especially in disclosure of one's personal business. All of them had been through the process— having their income, assets, and partnerships revealed during confirmation—but O'Neill's passage had been troubled. His situation was, indeed, a bit more complicated. He made $25 million in his last year as chairman of Alcoa and left the company with 2.37 million shares worth $80 million and options for another 4 million shares. He could sell the stock, but his initial assumption was that he would have to give up his stock options. He estimated the options to be worth $250 million, basing that on a particularly optimistic view of Alcoa's fortunes after his departure. However, well-established pricing models valued these options at less than half that amount.

In any event, Treasury lawyers told O'Neill in January 2001 that he could keep his stock and options if he exempted himself from decisions that might affect Alcoa, which is what he had decided to do. He had been such a white hat at Alcoa, spending the 1990s putting an end to expense accounts and embracing transparency, that he couldn't imagine anyone accusing him of ethical confusion. The appearance of impropriety, moreover, strikes O'Neill as a foolish standard. Either you act improperly or you don't—appearances, in the O'Neillian worldview, don't *really* matter. But of course they do. Since February, when the stock issue surfaced, he'd endured a thousand small cuts on the matter—including a graphic on the Democratic National Committee web site with his image surrounded by money bags. "I realized I should have walked away from all of it and not listened to the lawyers," he eventually told *The New York Times*, and on March 25, he said on ABC's *This Week* that he'd sell the stock.

But, again, the matter became more complicated. O'Neill, as a huge shareholder of Alcoa, felt he could significantly alter the company's stock price if he dumped all his shares at once. Maybe, but if so, only modestly. In any case, he left the transaction to investment managers, who finally began to sell his Alcoa stake piecemeal starting on April 28, at $37.20 a share. In February, when most administration officials had divested, Alcoa stock was in the mid-30s. The day before the meeting, May 15, it closed at $42.09. Now, the price was rising precipitously into the mid-40s and looked as if it would close near $45.

For a holder of more than two million shares, this distinction amounted to tens of millions of dollars. O'Neill, who checked the stock often, felt that his options would have been worth much more than a sale—even if the price was rising nicely—and, again, he looked past appearances. He was certain that some journalist would note this incidental windfall. He expected to face questions on the transaction prices, and God knows there was plenty of interest. But he made no move to just dump the stock rather than have managers work over months to get the best prices—or to engage in any preemptive, public relations damage control. Was he itching for a fight? Not exactly. It was more a kind of cognitive dissonance, an almost truculent impulse to not give in to what he considered the "tyranny of perceptions"—an itch to incite battles on this broad philosophical terrain of appearance versus reality. Losing battles, mostly. It didn't have anything to do with me, O'Neill groused; it was about giving away my kids' legacy.

But this matter ate at him like few others. If he had been more attuned to how things looked—as Powell certainly was—he would have dumped the stock in February and been done with it. This was one incident when he should have played the game like everyone else. He'd messed up.

Now it made him uncomfortable—as the three men chatted around the cabinet table about the niggling indignities of public life—that they all knew he was in a bind on his Alcoa stock, and it was something even these old friends would talk *around* rather than talk *about*.

As they sat, he thought back to a similar conversation the three had had at a mid-February NSC principals meeting in the Situation Room. They had all come early to that one—just to make sure they were there before the usually punctual President—and the talk was jocular and easy. The Internal Revenue Service had just finished auditing O'Neill's tax returns, a process they had started during confirmation when it became clear that O'Neill had failed to declare as part of due compensation Christmas presents he and Nancy had given to their housekeeper. Results of the expensive, three-year audit were in, he told both Powell and Rumsfeld that day. "And, guess what? I now have to pay a grand total of twenty-eight dollars to the IRS!" This drew hearty laughs—a topper.

"And think of it," Powell had joshed, "the guy who handled that audit, he works for you now."

"Not anymore!" Rummy had chortled. "Not anymore!"

Yes, it was sort of funny, even farcical. Sometimes in Washington you have to just play the game, O'Neill thought now, and not be focused in every case on who's right—he or the IRS, he or the lawyers, he or the people who said back in February that he should just dump his damn stock because that's the way most people around town did it, *whether or not it was the right thing to do in a perfect world.*

The President entered the cabinet room and looked over. Rumsfeld was talking at this point about how much he liked the Teddy Roosevelt portrait on the wall—Rumsfeld sees man-of-action virtues in TR that he admires—and Bush moved toward the trio. He moves toward conviviality like a heat-seeking missile. But the moment passed. These men knew each other, after all, since the President was barely out of college—an intimacy he could never match. And, in any event, they worked for him.

So now it was all business, and a stiff formality quickly took hold. Bush's cabinet members addressed each other as Secretary Rumsfeld or Secretary O'Neill in his presence. The President might zing them with a Pablo or a Balloonfoot, Powell's nickname, in greeting. But then an arm's-length conversation prevailed, a stand-and-deliver mode.

This was the tone as the President went around the table this afternoon and asked key principals their views on the best course in Iraq. The State Department had, by now, produced dozens of reports about the situation in Iraq. Defense had done the same, examining military options and how to secure the country after a coup or an invasion. Treasury was attempting to seal off the borders to transactions—all but impossible—by pressuring banks in Jordan and Syria to avoid doing business with Saddam. Each cabinet member spoke in an order and on a subject that had been designated in advance. At one point, Bush asked Rumsfeld to comment on something Powell had just said, but that was the extent of the interaction. When George Tenet gave his report on intelligence—it was still only speculation, he told Bush, whether Hussein had weapons of mass destruction or was starting any weapons-building programs—Rumsfeld, looking at the many aides lining the walls, interjected, "I'm not sure everyone here has clearance to hear this."

The President nodded. "Okay, let's get into it at another time."

But despite the concern about clearance, there was little to tell or to hear. O'Neill had reviewed a pile of CIA intelligence dossiers prior to this meeting. "Everything Tenet sent up to Bush and Cheney about Iraq was very judicious and precisely qualified. The President was clearly very interested in weapons or weapons programs—and frustrated about our weak intelligence capability—but Tenet was clearly being careful to say here's the little that we know and the great deal that we don't. That wouldn't change," O'Neill recalled, *"and I read those CIA reports for two years."*

. . .

THE LAUNCH of the administration's high-powered, carefully vetted Social Security Commission received little attention. O'Neill blamed the scripted nature of the enterprise that tapped only supporters of private accounts. "Imagine if you had both those for and against," he said to Michele Davis, who hoped that the rollout of an initiative to change Social Security would generate more heat. "Imagine if it were people who believed in the pure wealth generation of private accounts and others who thought we should just hold tight to the old system. That would have drawn real attention, because it would have been a commission that reflected the reality of where people stand on the issue."

The problem was also timing, and that, O'Neill was certain, revealed much about the White House's priorities. Social Security was for later. Now was the time for a historic tax cut. Congress, at this point in mid-May, was deep into negotiations on the tax bill. The final figures started to harden. As O'Neill had predicted to Greenspan, the overall tax proposal was shaved down and the rebate held. The final mix: a $1.35 trillion, ten-year tax cut and an $85 billion immediate, across-the-board rebate.

On May 18, Senators Olympia Snowe and Evan Bayh offered an amendment to this tax package that would "trigger a delay in the scheduled cuts and new spending programs if targets for reducing the nation's $3 trillion in public debt are not met." Three days later, the amendment lost in a 50-to-49 vote. It was a last major hurdle.

Throughout the rest of May, the White House's lobbying of senators was fiercer and angrier than many members of Congress had ever experienced. Vermont senator Jim Jeffords, murmuring he'd been "battered and disrespected" by White House officials, defected from the Republican Party—handing the majority in the Senate back to the Democrats.

The morning of May 22, after the Snowe and Bayh triggers were defeated, Greenspan arrived at the Treasury for breakfast with O'Neill. Their secret trigger pact had come up one vote short.

In both foreign and domestic policy, O'Neill was looking each day at policies and legislation that emerged from one-sided "dialogues" inside the White House—from what his military friends often called "incestuous amplification."

"We did what we could on conditionality," O'Neill said with momentary resignation, then mentioned to Greenspan that the Social Security Commission was starting its slow deliberations and that the President's schedule would lighten for the summer. "The first big battle is over, really. I think we fought well, we made our points vigorously."

Greenspan said that that wasn't enough. "Without the triggers, that tax cut is irresponsible fiscal policy," he said in his deepest funereal tone. "Eventually, I think that will be the consensus view."

On June 7, the bill, at $1.35 trillion and $85 billion, was signed into law by the President. Cheney said it "was close to what the President wanted."

CHAPTER 5

THE SCALE OF TRAGEDY

NOW IT WAS TIME for everything else, once the main campaign proposal, a massive tax cut, was signed into law. That is, once the logistics were handled. O'Neill had always been good at that—implementation and execution, moving men and machines. This was tangible: the task of printing checks and mailing them out by the truckload. There could be performance markers and a way to measure outcomes. So, with some enthusiasm, he and Mark Weinberger sat in the Oval Office talking about the *hows.*

"So, how long do you think it will take for the checks to go out?" Bush asked a few days after the tax cut was passed. The summer stretched before them. A time to spend on disposable items and vacations and easy living. "It seems like the economy might need that boost more than ever."

O'Neill merely nodded. The retroactive rebate of $100 billion—officially measured at $85 billion because $15 billion was in a retroactive refundable child credit that was booked as an expense—had been launched, after all, by O'Neill's insurrection with the centrists. This was something Bush certainly knew. It had been noted in the papers. At this point, he didn't think the President actually read the papers, but someone—Card or Rove or Hughes—must have been keeping him informed. In any event, the President's good cheer on the subject seemed to indicate that that was all in the past.

"Yes indeed, Mr. President," O'Neill said, ticking off some fresh economic figures showing that the economy had slowed steadily since early March. "I think our timing is particularly good."

"So, what will that timing be, exactly?" Bush asked.

Weinberger, who was a prominent tax lobbyist and had run Ernst & Young's tax division beore joining the administration, noted that, using the full force of the U.S. government to push funds into the right accounts—handling the printing and then the mailing of 91.6 million checks—it would take three months to get them into the mailboxes.

Bush frowned. "That's taking us into fall."

"We can do it in three weeks, Mr. President," O'Neill said. The Texan let out a little hoot.

"There's the CEO talking," Bush said as Weinberger looked on in disbelief. "You bet. A *can-do* attitude. I love that."

O'Neill immediately dove in, worked the mechanics himself, slicing off edges, cutting out steps of "the way things had always been done" with relentless, razor-edged questions.

On July 23, seven weeks after Bush signed the tax bill in early June, the checks went out.

This was process, too. A rethink of a basic act of government—the mailing of checks—that meant bringing all the key players into a room, locking the door, and having everyone start firing the most pointed questions imaginable at one another. Only the secure survive in this pressure chamber. But, in the end, everyone will have something to show for the pain. After one of these sessions, a battered participant returned to O'Neill's office with a gift, a small steel plaque that read: WHAT WOULD YOU ATTEMPT TO DO IF YOU KNEW YOU COULD NOT FAIL? O'Neill stuck it on his desk, front and center.

. . .

GOD KNOWS the administration would need some rigorous analysis, O'Neill alerted his senior staff—now that the hard work of domestic policy was about to begin. In some ways, the tax cut was about execution: the administration had managed to kill off the *whys* at every turn. *Why* do it? Because the American people elected me to do it, Bush had said in countless utterances in the first six months.

It would be hard to have that precision with education reform or health care policy. It wasn't clear what the public expected or what, exactly, had been promised by candidate Bush. The mandate to justify each policy on its merits would be unavoidable.

O'Neill was still bruised over how that process had been hijacked on global warming. Was it, he wondered, a pattern: either no process, or a truncated one, where efforts to collect evidence and construct smart policy are, with little warning, co-opted by the White House political team, or the Vice President, or whoever *got to the President* and said something, true or not, though in any case effective, that no one else was privy to? The value of open deliberation *inside* the White House—public discourse is another matter—is that everyone, in the end, can do the math and point to the good reasons that carried the day. At lower levels, where assistants or undersecretaries hashed things out, there often was real debate. The problem came when matters reached the highest level, where the decisions were made. At that level, the President, really, has to lead.

When a president doesn't offer explanation, even to his most senior aides, the problems are many. Bush often ascribed action to a general "I went on instinct" rationale, leaving O'Neill and others in the cabinet or White House staff to ponder the intangibles that create "gut"—from some sweeping, unspoken notion of how the world works, to a one-size-fits-all principle, such as "I won't negotiate with myself," to a squabble with a family member over breakfast.

Senior officials, guiding large ships in the fleet, were starting to feel they might *never* get to understand the way the President thought. After all his one-on-one meetings with Bush, and scores of group encounters, six months into the administration O'Neill realized that he didn't know the man's mind—something he could usually pick up in a good, long interview with a prospective hire.

For presidential scholars, there is a long-standing chestnut: Does a president need to be smarter than his advisers? The key is how to define "smart." A president can hardly be more *expert* than, in sum, a collection of advisers, who have deep specialties in domestic or foreign affairs. Yet during a president's engagements as synthesizer, provocateur, direction-setter, clarifier, and, in the end, decider, he displays telling qualities of character and intellect. While the public persona of a president is evermore the product of stagecraft— scripted to the word and gesture and camera angle—the way the President *thinks* is usually discernible to his senior advisers.

The process, in the formulation of O'Neill and countless others who've spent time at the top of administrations, goes both ways: the staff presents an array of thoroughly constructed choices and consequences to the leader, and the President lets his senior staff see what he's thinking and why or, at very least, *how he thinks* about large or complex issues.

Previous presidents, O'Neill had sensed, held up their end of this exchange. Sitting in his office in mid-July, he sketched some notes for a meeting he wanted to have with Cheney, another serious talk about effective process—a way to handle decision making so that policy didn't get served half-baked and larded with political calculations. Both he and Cheney had been advisers to Richard Nixon and

Gerald Ford, and there were lessons to be drawn from those days. Nixon, for one, presided over the creation of the modern OMB, a burgeoning government's answer to the goal of sound process. OMB, which went from 30 professional managers when Nixon created the office in 1970 to nearly 130 by the time he left, gave the President control over the administration without having to, himself, work the levers of power. What Nixon had quickly realized was that an enlarged, powerful OMB wasn't so much an extension of his own brain as a companion brain—inhaling data from every department, distilling it, and making assessments as to effectiveness of policies. Once OMB presented in writing its often voluminous rendition of choices and consequences, Nixon tried to absorb them.

But even Nixon, a lifelong student of Washington policy and politics, found that, in the end, he was himself favoring whoever could best manage a rather difficult trick: making a good oral presentation in the rarefied atmosphere of the Oval Office. "He didn't consider that skill a material issue," O'Neill recalled. "He was afraid of oral presentation, because he knew he could be swayed by it, that a strong presentation on only one side of an issue by an expert could cause otherwise sensible people to make bad decisions."

So Nixon called OMB and other major departments to give him "Brandeis briefs" on all pertinent issues. Supreme Court Justice Louis Brandeis is often cited as the most thorough and balanced among justices in the writing of briefs, works of analytical craft and clear thinking.

And, soon, the President was sitting with bound leather folders. "Our briefs weren't one-pagers—they were fully realized analyses of ten or so pages, and pray God you didn't leave out some important point or counterpoint; Nixon would call you on the carpet. He forced us to not only collect the data, and be completely thorough about where all sides stood, but to really think deeply about the ideal of good government and how to get there," O'Neill said. "After he'd read them, Nixon could hold the center in any room on any issue, no matter how fractious the debate, and the combatants would usually walk out the door with conclusions, with a clear direction. Nixon, for all his faults, had an incredible analytical mind and a grasp of the central issues of his times. We could add depth and rigor to those natural talents."

O'Neill wanted to talk to Cheney about the Brandeis briefs—and about Nixon's take on the type of analytical support he most needed. It was one way to get to a discussion of what this President needed.

Ford, he judged, also relied on the Brandeis briefs but was certainly more like Bush in that he preferred oral presentations. But Ford never had much trouble holding the center, even with strong personalities like Kissinger and Schlesinger battling around him. After twenty years in Congress, he had a mastery of issues in domestic affairs and many areas of foreign policy. O'Neill remembered that when the proposed federal budget for 1976 was released, Ford presided over an hour-long press conference with his senior officials lined up behind him. He turned, at one point, to O'Neill to answer a question on housing policy. It was a memory O'Neill had long cherished.

Now, as O'Neill jotted notes about to add fiber to the policy process in this White House, and about how to persuade Cheney to take the lead, he reflected on how different the tentative, quip-ready Bush was from the secure, magnanimous Ford. "I realized, thinking back, that Ford didn't need me to answer that question—it was just a way to get me noticed and say something nice about me to the press. Hell, he knew the ins and outs of the damn budget better than any of us.

"I realized it would be hard to find things we did with Nixon or Ford that would be applicable for this President," O'Neill added. He thought of Bush's unresponsiveness in large and small meetings. "This President was so utterly different from those men."

He stopped by Cheney's office. The fears he had harbored during the transition—about "kids rolling around on the lawn"—had been confirmed.

"There is more that we have to do to bring analytical rigor, sound information-gathering techniques, and real, cost-benefit analysis to bear on what government does—or what it ought to think about doing—otherwise we're just flying blind. You can't just move on instinct. You end up making too many mistakes," O'Neill told the Vice President. "We also need to be better about keeping politics out of the policy process. We need firewalls. The political people are there for presentation and execution, not for creation."

As before, Dick nodded earnestly. He thanked Paul, as always, "for his sharp insights."

When he left the office, O'Neill remembered one area from their shared experience that he had failed to mention: the last days of Nixon.

In that tumultuous last year, Nixon closed ranks. He no longer wanted to innovate on policy. OMB and other departments kept producing the Brandeis briefs. As John Herbers pointed out in a lengthy 1974 story in *The New York Times*, Roy Ash, head of OMB, along with the senior team of O'Neill, Fred Malek, deputy director of OMB, and Frank Zarb, OMB's associate director, were running the government by default.

And who, O'Neill wondered, was really in charge now? The current incarnation of OMB was more narrowly engaged with managing the huge, unwieldy federal budget—and Mitch Daniels, despite his quick-study capacities, had a background that was mostly in politics, which spoke volumes. In some ways, O'Neill recognized, there was a small group—Cheney, Rove, Hughes, and, increasingly, Rice—who seemed to be in charge, again by default.

"The biggest difference between then and now is that our group was mostly about evidence and analysis, and Karl, Dick, Karen, and the gang seemed to be mostly about politics. It's a huge distinction."

. . .

As O'NEILL WAS MEETING with Cheney, a senior administration official who had similar concerns about process was preparing to act on his frustrations. John J. DiIulio, Jr., the University of Pennsylvania professor who ran Bush's Faith-based Initiative, a project to support the faith-based institutions that have so long provided a bulwark against chaos in underserved areas of the country, announced in August—a few days after O'Neill and Cheney talked—that he was leaving the administration, the first senior official to depart.

Though DiIulio and O'Neill knew each other only from a distance, there were similarities visible to even the casual observer: both were outspoken, cerebral, referred to as mavericks, and, after a fashion, process men. DiIulio, much like O'Neill, became celebrated by embracing a fierce, regenerative standard of inquiry. And a faith in the data, wherever it may lead, even if it meant discarding a publicly held view.

After eight months in the White House, DiIulio felt his initiative had been revised from Bush's campaign rhetoric about "compassionate conservatism"—a way to support those in need—into a political and financial prop for those evangelicals who were in "the base." O'Neill thought it was another hijacking of a promised policy.

The concerns DiIulio voiced to a few close friends in the administration went well beyond matters of the faith-based program: "There is no precedent in any modern White House for what is going on in this one: a complete lack of a policy apparatus. What you've got is everything—and I mean everything—being run by the political arm. It's the reign of the Mayberry Machiavellis." DiIulio made this statement nearly a year after he left the White House and enlarged on it in a letter to *Esquire* magazine for its January 2003 issue. His points matched almost exactly what had so deeply concerned O'Neill. "I heard many, many staff discussions but not three meaningful, substantive policy discussions," DiIulio wrote.

> There were no actual policy white papers on domestic issues. There were, truth be told, only a couple of people in the West Wing who worried at all about policy substance and analysis, and they were even more overworked than the stereotypical nonstop, twenty-hour-a-day White House staff. Every modern presidency moves on the fly, but on so- cial policy and related issues, the lack of even basic policy knowledge, and the only casual interest in knowing more, was somewhat breathtaking: discussions by fairly senior people who meant Medicaid but were talking Medicare; near-instant shifts from discussing any actual policy pros and cons to discussing political communications, media strategy, et cetera. Even quite junior staff would sometimes hear quite senior staff pooh-pooh any need to dig deeper for pertinent information on a given issue.

. . .

As the summer progressed, O'Neill pressed everywhere he could for what he called an "authentic discussion." One problem was that he didn't have a chair at the White House senior staff meeting, where the top two dozen or so officials in the West Wing met each morning at 7:30.

Robert Rubin, when he was Treasury Secretary, had considered attendance at this meeting—in which cabinet secretaries were rarely permitted to bigfoot—among his most important victories. It placed Rubin's finger on the White House's pulse each morning—and gave him a glimpse of where the political machinery was headed on any given day. Six months before Lawrence Summers succeeded him in the Secretary's job, Rubin started bringing him to the morning meeting, just to be certain his chair was grandfathered to his successor.

O'Neill wasn't going to ask, himself; he had his chief of staff, Tim Adams, inquire several times whether the Secretary could attend. "There was foot-dragging and then no response—the way most things get killed in a White House," he said.

While no one would head-on confront an official as powerful as the Secretary of the Treasury, overseer of a vast swath of the U.S. government, it was clear that O'Neill was viewed as armed and dangerous by the White House's political staff. His "unmanaged" comments during the first winter and spring's tax battle—even if they did result, at day's end, in sound policy—had placed him on the wrong side of Karl Rove and Karen Hughes.

"By summer, certainly, you could feel the chill from both of them. I wasn't going to be controlled by the political crowd, or say things that were half true to fulfill some strategic mandate or simply to please the base," O'Neill said. "And, by then, they knew all that."

Several memos from O'Neill to the President had leaked in the preceding few months, including his global warming memo, which resulted in a blistering screed from Paul Gigot in *The Wall Street Journal*.

Under the head, O'NEILL MAKES A NOT-SO-HOT IMPRESSION, Gigot ran through a litany of "off-message" public statements and chastised him for suggesting Michael Oppenheimer as someone who should advise Bush on climate change. "This," wrote Gigot, "is like asking James Carville to design the Bush tax cut."

The article was a signal to the far right that O'Neill was fair game.

So O'Neill offered them more ammunition. The financial crisis in Argentina was erupting. After a burst of prosperity in the mid-1990s, a slow and agonizing economic depression had devastated the country's economy. By midsummer, millions lost their jobs, Argentina's standard of living went into free fall, and the country was on the brink of insolvency.

For the Bush international economic team, Argentina emerged as its first major test—and another chance to distinguish this administration from its predecessor. Rubin and Summers had pursued an interventionist foreign economic policy, pushing the International Monetary Fund (IMF) to lend money to prop up the economies of Mexico, Russia, and the nations of Asia. The U.S. Treasury and IMF had lent billions of dollars. A country like Argentina, a loyal ally and an important emerging democracy, could have expected favorable terms from the Clinton team.

This President had come to the White House promising to scale back the U.S. role in financial crisis management. Many conservative economists, including Larry Lindsey, felt the international lending of the Clinton era had placed too much of taypayers' money at risk and done more harm than good. Providing money allowed recipient countries to put off tough economic reforms, the reasoning went, which only prolonged their problems and made it more likely they would seek more loans in the future. It had also ended up bailing out banks and investment houses that offered loans that might not be sound. The Rubin and Summers gravy train, they felt, created a "moral hazard" problem, a situation in which developing countries were encouraged to make bad decisions because they knew the IMF would bail them out.

This line of thinking masked significant splits within the Bush administration. O'Neill generally opposed bailouts, but he wasn't dogmatic. He could be swayed by facts. He could be flexible. In his confirmation hearings in January, O'Neill had praised Clinton's Mexico bailout of 1995, a policy that many GOP conservatives, including Lindsey, held in contempt. To O'Neill, decisions that affected the livelihoods of millions in the developing world deserved a case-by-case approach rather than rigid prescriptions.

Argentina's specific request the summer of 2001 was relatively
technical. The country's president and finance minister wanted to
delay repayment of $9 billion of its IMF debt in a deal that required
Washington's approval. Despite Argentina's political importance to
the United States, on this occasion O'Neill joined fiscal conservatives in opposing the deal. But then he wanted to explain the reasons,
the rationale underpinning his decision. A few weeks before the Ar-
gentinian delegation was due to arrive in Washington, O'Neill was
quoted in *The Economist* saying, essentially, that the country's economic problems were, in large part, of its own making. "They've
been off and on in trouble for 70 years or more," he said. "They don't
have an export industry to speak of. And they like it that way."
O'Neill's point, as the rest of the interview attests, was that Argentina had choices. It could engage more forcefully in international
trade. It could stop supporting national monopolies and open its
markets. It could exhibit the discipline that other countries had successfully embraced.

Immediately, the White House's attack machine went to work—
against O'Neill. Officially, the administration said little. Unoffi-
cially, Larry Lindsey's office went into overdrive.

"Up to this point, they'd been attacking O'Neill regularly with
off-the-record stuff and 'senior official' comments," recalls one of
O'Neill's top aides. "Now, it went to almost a daily footing. I mean, it
was amazing before. But then it got crazy. We would get calls every
couple of days, all of them pretty much the same: a reporter would
call with some out-of-context thing Paul had said at the weekly economics lunch or some meeting with Larry. It wasn't even subtle.
From the first month of the administration, every reporter in town
knew they could get some inside punch at O'Neill just by calling
Lindsey's office."

Senior officials of the administration responded anonymously to
the *Economist* quote, affirming that, this time, O'Neill had gone too

far. President Bush placed a phone call to placate Argentine president Fernando de la Rua.

In a meeting with O'Neill, Bush said that he understood what his
Treasury Secretary was saying to the Argentinians, even if it was a little sharp-edged. He was going to grant the IMF package in any event,
a decision O'Neill felt was sound. Putting aside his past criticisms of
the Clinton record, Bush gave his blessing to new IMF aid for Argentina on August 22, 2001. This decision established what would be
a pattern on international finance: talking tougher than in the past
and delivering an ultimatum that a last chance had arrived, but quietly keeping a teetering country from a full collapse. Bush knew that
O'Neill didn't want Argentina to implode, and neither did Condi
Rice or Colin Powell. In pushing through the IMF loans, he sided
with that trio and overruled Lindsey and Hubbard, who felt that if a
country got itself into trouble, it should figure a way to get out of it.

In the confusion of rhetoric and action, Lindsey saw Bush's move
as a reversal and blamed it on O'Neill—and on the pressure his comments had brought on the administration.

The view, from Gigot to Lindsey, was that O'Neill was dangerous
because his positions were nonideological and he had a tin ear for
politics. He was unaware of the repercussions of his public acts.

Those closest to O'Neill at the Treasury Department, some of
them seasoned Washington mandarins, dispute this. What was unfolding, they say, was a sweeping philosophical battle, in placing a venerable—and, for the most part, successful—idea of pragmatic governance
against a counterclaim of ideology and political mobilization.

"Paul doesn't come at questions of policy with a political design.
The White House *defines* questions of policy by political design," said
David Aufhauser, general counsel of the Treasury Department and a
longtime Washington hand. "That's the tension. That's not simply a
statement about the Bush administration—it's a statement about
Washington. What makes Paul unique is that he addresses policy by

assessing the real consequences of an action, not political design. He would get accused, wrongly actually, of being politically tone-deaf. He was well aware of political consequences. But his conclusion was that the force of a good idea could trump any imagined adverse political consequences. And that kind of position of governing takes courage that you've got the answer right. I'm not talking about moral courage. I'm talking about that you actually are good at your job, that it's genuine talent that you've brought to the table. No one would ever say anything to the contrary—no one. O'Neill is one of the most talented men any of us has ever met. That's why . . . there was so much cognitive dissonance."

Aufhauser is a soft-spoken man who gets paid for his words and chooses them with great care.

"People think he was politically tone-deaf. He wasn't!" he all but yells. "He knew full well the political consequences. But he would say, This idea will prevail because it has been developed on fact—and to do good.

"That's why O'Neill stirs such strong passions in this town. It's not just about him. He's utterly fearless in representing an idea of how we should be. And how we could be, still."

. . .

THE IMPERIAL HOTEL in Tokyo, one of the world's great hotels, offered an oasis of luxury and comfort for the U.S. delegation after an exhausting week of meetings in Beijing with Chinese leaders in early September.

O'Neill slumped into his suite at 10:00 p.m. and got ready to call Nancy. Tokyo time is eleven hours ahead of New York, so he thought he'd check in as she started her day. After preparing for the uplink, he flipped on the television to CNN.

And sat on the edge of the bed.

He stared at the flaming building, and his mind reeled backward to 1945, when he was a kid in Missouri and saw a newsreel at the movie theater of a plane hitting the Empire State Building. The plane looked so small, like a penknife stuck in a sequoia.

Good God, O'Neill thought, this must be the worst FAA mistake in history—some air traffic controller guided a plane into the Twin Towers.

But how could a pilot let himself steer into a building on a clear, sunny day? Maybe it was a mechanical issue out of La Guardia. On the television, eyewitnesses swore it was an internal explosion. Then they said it was a rocket.

Tim Adams knocked on the door. "Yes, I'm watching it," O'Neill said. Adams and the rest of the entourage were monitoring the situation. "I'll just stay here," O'Neill said. Then, as he watched smoke billow into the Manhattan sky, the second plane hit. Time became compressed.

He just sat, halfway around the world, feeling disembodied—as if watching his own life through Saran Wrap. He'd been to the World Trade Center more times than he could count, and the visits started to flood forth from memory—hazy, passing glimpses of the near and distant past. That meeting on 102 last year; a lunch he and Nancy had in the eighties, racing through the cathedral foyers toward the elevator banks, filled now with soot and ash.

On the television a couple jumped holding hands. God.

A knock on the door. Tim Adams again.

"Mr. Secretary, I guess you've seen now . . . the Secret Service is talking to the intelligence folks. We've set up a staff room where everyone is operating, down the hall."

"Tim, we need to go home."

Adams left to find a flight.

O'Neill called home in Pittsburgh.

"It's just the worst ever," Nancy said. "I'm so glad you're not in the country. It's crazy here."

And then Paul wished her well and asked that she make the day as good as it could be. September 11 is his wife's birthday.

Adams was back. There were no commercial flights available back to the States, many airports were closed. "How do we get our hands on a military plane?" O'Neill asked him.

. . .

THE TREASURY DEPARTMENT'S chief counsel, David Aufhauser, was under a tent on a golden afternoon in England. It was the annual meeting of the International Symposium on Economic Crimes, held on the empyrean grounds of Cambridge University. Chief justices and attorneys general and regulatory chiefs from around the globe had gathered for sober discussions about flows of illegal capital and global enforcement initiatives.

Speeches were made by the chief of Interpol, by the head of the German version of the FBI, and then by Aufhauser. Strides had been made in international cooperation. The tracking of laundered money represented one of the few areas where tangible global action had occurred in the past two decades. Drug dealers and criminals of many flavors were on alert, having to innovate constantly to stay ahead of regulators—and that's where the bad guys make mistakes. Not that all that many are caught, because they *do* innovate.

Nevertheless, the atmosphere was self-congratulatory. Ensconced in the ancient temples of the old university—an immovable philosopher's stone of the civilized world—this peerage of the most senior members of the international financial system felt safe, and correct, and relevant. Later, cocktails would be served.

Then a murmur went through the crowd of nearly three hundred. In a moment, a thirty-foot screen—which seconds before had carried bullet points of victories—filled with images of the trade towers burning.

An awful and appalling silence descended. The scene, freshly taped from a television, had no audio. Everyone watched the towers disintegrate into fire and dust, as the birds chirped.

"You intuitively knew what everyone was thinking: that we had been looking at the world through the wrong end of the telescope," Aufhauser recalled. "That the chief enemy of peace was not criminal proceeds seeking a way to launder in a place of hiding. But, actually, what you might otherwise describe as clean money—actually money given to charities—which had been spirited around the globe to kill people."

· · ·

MILITARY CARS ARRIVED at midmorning the next day to pick up the O'Neill delegation. As the entourage emerged from the main entrance, they saw hundreds of Imperial Hotel employees—bellmen, desk clerks, cooks—lined up to the waiting vehicles, applauding loudly along the way. An hour later, the Secretary led his entourage of about two dozen onto an Air Force C-17 transport. Everyone was issued a smallish wool blanket, earplugs, and a box lunch as they stepped into the flying cavern—like an airborne collegiate field house—and settled into the canvas jump seats lining the walls. O'Neill was offered a seat in the cockpit. "No," he said. "I'd rather sit with the troops."

Once they were airborne, O'Neill dug through his briefcase for some folded sheets from the trip to China. He ran through a daunting schedule of business conferences and trips to schools, with Jiang Zemin in the Great Hall of the People; with the finance minister, who said that the Chinese currency would be allowed to float, a bit, but not too much. It was still a command economy, after all. To unleash the forces of market capitalism would tear China apart. He and Jiang both said, Let's be patient, and let's work together. O'Neill was happy to affirm that cooperative spirit. It had been a tough year in Sino-American relations, starting when the Bush administration deemed China no longer a "strategic partner" but a "strategic competitor." The neocons in the White House and Pentagon were, from the first, listing China as a country with weapons of mass destruction that was poised to challenge U.S. interests. Then, in April, a U.S. spy plane was downed over China. Now, it was time to make up. . . .

But all that was past, as was the agenda of Japanese-American meetings that had been slated for today. He folded the sheets over and began to write on the clean back.

> *Memorial—rebuilding*
> *Confidence measures for the market*
>
> *Lessons learned from these events*
> *Greenspan/O'Neill joint news conference*
> *Meeting with P. TV visuals.*
> *Honest Assessment of the import*
> *of the people/capability lost in lower Manhattan.*

Already, he was thinking of how tempting this would be to spin, to euphemize—for the White House to give in to temptation, as O'Neill had often seen it do, to tell the public a politic half-truth rather than the hard verities that needed telling. Never has it been more important to be brutally and exhaustively candid, he thought. The stakes are too high for any other course. He drew a box around the words "Honest Assessment."

He knew immediately that a key for Treasury would be tracking the financial web behind the terrorists who wreaked this destruction.

Throughout the summer, there had been disputes on how the United States tried to stymie money laundering and other financial crimes. O'Neill found, digging through budgets, that the United States spends $1.1 billion a year to fight global money laundering and illegal offshore bank transactions and to freeze the accounts of felonious individuals. Most of the funds go to the collection and management of oceans of data from financial institutions around the globe and to the screening of that data for irregular activities. In congressional testimony during the summer, O'Neill had fenced with Senator Carl Levin, a Michigan Democrat, who headed the Senate Subcommittee on Investigations, about whether that money produced any reasonable return. In fact, the sum spent, O'Neill discovered, was closer to $700 million—a rounding error of nearly half a billion—and the results were modest. O'Neill said he'd like to get agreements with countries that have offshore banks or loosely regulated banks to be more transparent about their transactions and help fight fraud. Levin said it was all but impossible, they'd been trying for years.

"You looked at bank data and you saw countless transactions at $9,999. Of course, the amount to trigger some regulatory notice is $10,000. It's no surprise that the crooks and launders know these thresholds better than we do," O'Neill said. "These huge data grabs take time and enormous resources and yield very little. We've invested a lot in this technique, but it doesn't mean it works. I knew that 9/11 would change that—that we were going to have to rethink the way we did things."

Then he thought of the couple he had watched jump, holding hands, and began, again, to write.

> Scale of this tragedy (compared to Hiroshima and Nagasaki) inflicted by so few on so many.
> Economic matters are important, but they must take their rightful place in our thoughts at a time such as this and clearly they are not foremost now.

Striking at a symbol of our market system is a pathetic
act of an evil mind that fails to understand that the genius
of our system is in the hearts and minds of the people—not
in the buildings we work in.

O'Neill slid off the slim canvas seat onto the aluminum floor, a
high-grade, special alloy, he couldn't help but notice. He'd slept only
an hour the night before, and it was catching up with him. It was
thirty degrees below zero outside, at thirty-five thousand feet, and he
could see his breath. The cargo hold was getting colder by the hour;
had to be below fifty. When O'Neill was a kid, his father, an army
sergeant and attendant in a veterans hospital, often moved to find
work, and the family—two parents, four kids—lived one frigid winter in a single room, a summer kitchen, with a hard floor and no heat
or plumbing. After that, they moved to a barracks in Hawaii that
once was a Japanese detention camp. It was a point of pride that he'd
not been raised in comfort, that he was one of those rare instances—
ever more infrequent, the data showed—where someone from the
bottom made it all the way to the top.

The floor of the plane was grooved and porous—to lock in equipment for transport—and icy cold. Not a problem. He'd slept on
worse. So the leading domestic official of the U.S. government
pulled the blanket around his shoulders and—in his blue suit, red
tie, and wingtips—shivered off to sleep as the C-17 raced toward
America.

. . .

SIXTEEN HOURS LATER, the plane flew over D.C. O'Neill looked
out the porthole window at Reagan National Airport and then the
burnt wall of the Pentagon. The C-17 was conspicuous, sharing the
sky only with fighter jets.

At the same time, Aufhauser and Greenspan stood shoulder to shoulder as their plane banked wide around New York City. Along with an assortment of generals and officials of the U.S. government, they had caught an air force cargo going west. It stopped at bases in Europe like a city bus at rush hour. Greenspan had been in a conference in Switzerland. Aufhauser had rushed over from Cambridge. And now, after ten hours with box lunches and earplugs, their plane arced over Manhattan. Below, the rubble of the towers smoldered, sending smoke into their fuselage and an electrical fire stench into the cargo bay.

"We all felt a great sense of resolve," Aufhauser recalled. "Resolve to do something about this."

An hour later, at Andrews Air Force Base, Aufhauser disembarked and saw a familiar motorcade pulling away. It was O'Neill's. He gave chase, calling out to the Treasury Department sedans. A few minutes later, barely catching his breath, he looked desperately for a cab.

. . .

"THE PRESIDENT WANTS to open the New York Stock Exchange tomorrow—that's the word I'm getting," said Peter Fisher, undersecretary for domestic finance. "I think he made his wishes known to several people on the senior staff."

O'Neill listened patiently, his mind racing. He had been taken to a secure phone at the Hotel Washington, where he was still staying. It was Wednesday night, September 12, and he didn't get off the phone. Greenspan and Josh Bolten, deputy chief of staff. Frank Zarb of the NASDAQ. Now, Fisher.

"We only get one chance at this, Peter. I understand that the computers up there are under thirty feet of water. The phone and electrical systems are compromised. We'll only get one chance to re-open the market, and it has to work. If it falters, or goes down again, the terrorists will have won. When it opens, it has to be clear that it's not closing again."

O'Neill and his deputies made some calls to electrical engineers, systems analysts, and tech support teams "to get a real estimate on how long it would take to do the job right."

The next morning, September 13, at 9:45 a.m., the NSC met with Bush in the situation room. The president had made four public statements—two during the day on September 11, telling the country that the government was fully engaged in discovering what occurred and prosecuting whoever was behind it; and another, that night, from the Oval Office. He spoke again from the cabinet room on the morning of the 12th, describing the attacks as "an act of war . . . in a monumental struggle between good and evil." Neither address was particularly reassuring: Bush stumbled on a few words; he looked tired and tentative.

O'Neill had received a short briefing before the meeting. What was guiding the discussion thus far was whether this was a war against al-Qaeda and its host, Afghanistan's Taliban regime, or the first step in a broader struggle against worldwide terrorism and the numerous states that support terror. At an NSC meeting the day before, just as O'Neill's C-17 was landing at Andrews Air Force Base, Rumsfeld had raised the question of Iraq. The Pentagon had been working for months on a military plan for the overthrow of Saddam Hussein. Any initiative against worldwide terrorism would surely, at some point, Rumsfeld had argued, take the United States to Baghdad. Powell, for his part, opposed striking Iraq at this point, pointing out that the American people were focused on al-Qaeda, which had, after all, attacked the United States, and that public support was a prerequisite for any war. The President, having pressed his administration from the start to focus on Saddam—with little, at this point, to show—was against a strike on Iraq.

At the NSC meeting that morning—the 13th—Bush was looking for more reliable, thorough information about options. George Tenet began the meeting by describing how to fund and strengthen Afghanistan's Northern Alliance, with its twenty thousand or so fighters, to oust the Taliban and ferret out al-Qaeda. That alliance was deeply factionalized, especially after the assassination on September 9 of its charismatic leader, Ahmed Shah Massoud. But with an infusion of arms and CIA paramilitary units, it could become a cohesive unit that could be augmented by the U.S. military and special forces.

Tenet then introduced his "closer"—the dynamic, swaggering Cofer Black, a lifelong CIA operative who ran the agency's Counter-Terrorism Center, who proceeded with a half-hour show of how Tenet's plan would catch and kill the terrorists—who have a no-surrender policy—in the mountains and caves where they'd hidden. "When we're through with them," he told Bush, "they will have flies walking across their eyeballs." But, he cautioned the President, there will be U.S. casualties, and "it could be a lot."

Bush said he understood—that "this is war," that "we're here to win"—and asked Black how long it would take to achieve victory. Black said it could be weeks.

O'Neill and others at the table responded with arched brows but saw that Black had revved up the President.

"Mr. President, the fastest we can get stock markets open is Monday morning," O'Neill said. "We only get one chance at this. It has to be done right—and then we won't have to do it again. To have the markets open, and then have to stop trading for fixes, would be disastrous."

With the memory of O'Neill's performance on the rebate checks still fresh, Bush nodded. "Okay, if you say so. Monday, then."

• • •

THAT WEEKEND, O'Neill and his wife arrived at Camp David. Bush had created a war cabinet, a subset of his senior officials, to carry forward the war against al-Qaeda. He included Cheney, Rumsfeld, Rice, Powell, Tenet, Joint Chiefs Chairman Hugh Shelton, Attorney General John Ashcroft, and O'Neill—and invited them, with their spouses, to the presidential retreat in the Maryland mountains.

Everyone had checked in by Saturday morning, Paul and Nancy in one of the older cabins. Meetings started at 9:30 a.m., and the war cabinet was joined by members of the White House staff, including Karen Hughes and Ari Fleischer.

In one long day of meetings, they'd figure out what to do—that was the plan—but first the President said he would listen to all competing positions.

They began, as the President now opened all meetings, with a prayer. This had put off many cabinet secretaries when Bush started the practice in the first days of the administration. Today it seemed, for the first time, almost a necessity.

Powell started in with the status of various conversations with the Pakistanis and then the status of coalition building.

Then O'Neill spoke about the opening of the markets on Monday and progress in tracing the path of the hijackers. Investigators were now convinced that fifteen of the nineteen men were Saudi nationals, and they had left a trail of transactions in the United States that Treasury investigators and other departments were gathering and analyzing. "It could yield an awful lot about who they were dealing with—when and where. The money trail doesn't lie. These are real facts."

Tenet passed out a thick packet with intelligence documents on worldwide terrorism and the CIA's plan for a covert war against terrorists, in Afghanistan and elsewhere. The plan focused on expanded powers for the agency and a kind of global charge—under which the agency could attack every aspect of terrorist networks using any means necessary without specific, case-by-case clearance from the President or other senior administration officials. This included an assault on the financial infrastructure of the terrorists.

After a lengthy explanation of the CIA's plan to energize Afghanistan's Northern Alliance, Tenet ran through specific plans, some of them already under way, for attacking terrorists in dozens of countries. The President, O'Neill recalled "seemed very engaged by George and his plan."

The morning proceeded with more presentations, from Attorney General John Ashcroft, about expanding law enforcement powers to fight terrorism, and Robert Mueller, the FBI chief, before General Hugh Shelton took the group into military plans he'd drawn up for Afghanistan, including a comprehensive operation employing bombers, cruise missiles, and significant U.S. ground forces.

Bush said that running terrorists out of Afghanistan would "persuade other countries to change what they've been doing" by harboring or supporting terrorists. He gave Iran as an example.

The widely accepted idea was that Afghanistan could act as a "demonstration model" of what other countries that were considering actions hostile to the United States might face. This gave Condi Rice an opportunity to discuss threats beyond Afghanistan and how they might be met.

At the ready was Deputy Defense Secretary Paul Wolfowitz, who turned the focus to Iraq. Afghanistan could develop into a mess, with U.S. troops mired in the country's remote mountains, seeking elusive al-Qaeda cells. Iraq, on the other hand, was a corrupt, anti-American regime waiting to be toppled. Though intelligence coming from inside Iraq continued to be thin, the Defense and State Departments, responding to the President's intense interest in Saddam Hussein, had produced dozens of reports since January on what might be done to oust Saddam and the Baathist regime. Wolfowitz seemed to dance across that pile of speculative analysis, touching the high points. The thrust: If you want to do something, Mr. President, Iraq is doable.

O'Neill thought of Rumsfeld's January memo, which had listed Iran, Iraq, North Korea, China, Russia, and others as trying to exploit lapses in U.S. capabilities—and then, in its conclusion, cited the need for some action to *dissuade* nations from challenging American interests.

"I thought what Wolfowitz was asserting about Iraq was a reach, and I think others in the room did, too. It was like changing the subject—Iraq is not where bin Laden is and not where there's trouble," O'Neill said. "I was mystified. It's like a bookbinder accidentally dropping a chapter from one book into the middle of another one. The chapter is coherent, in its way, but it doesn't seem to fit in this book."

Andy Card finally headed Wolfowitz off, saying that there didn't seem much new in these arguments. They broke for lunch.

O'Neill returned to his cabin. Nancy watched her husband carefully, protectively, at moments like this. She knew his enthusiasm for this President was muted. She'd seen him with other presidents—or other people whose intellect he deeply respected—and knew how his voice changed when he talked about them. She remembered his going on and on about how bright Nixon was, how skillful Ford was at distilling competing positions, how open-minded and judicious the first President Bush was. This was different. "Paul just seemed to leave meetings with the President and shake his head," Nancy said. "It was like, 'I'm not sure if this guy's got what it takes to pull this off.' "

Nancy had met the President only briefly, during the inauguration; now, at lunch at Camp David, he made her the object of his attentions.

"You're sitting with me," he told her, kissing her on the cheek as she entered the Laurel Lodge dining hall. He looked much better in casual clothes—in this case, jeans and a sweater—than in a suit, she thought. He had an unlit cigar in his hand.

And, soon, she was sitting next to Bush at a long, chattering table—more than a dozen people—as they ate homemade chicken noodle soup and sandwiches on freshly baked bread.

"I just love the food here," Bush said. "It's real comfort food. A good thing to be eating right now."

She asked what kind of comfort food he'd grown up on, what was the favorite thing he'd ask his mother to make on a special occasion.

Bush shook his head. "You got to be kiddin'. My mother never cooked. The woman had frostbite on her fingers. Everything right out of the freezer."

The President paused. "We're having more comfort food tonight. I can't wait."

. . .

AT 3:30 p.m., everyone returned to the lodge's meeting room for summations. Bush said he'd listen to everybody and then, in the next day or two, he'd make his decision. He went in a circle, asking the principals what they thought the United States should do. Most replied that we should opt for the covert/overt military operation sketched out by Tenet and dislodge the terrorists from their Afghan haven, killing as many as possible. There was talk about the broader war on terror and some sense that Iraq would be next, but no one was willing to commit, at this point, to an Iraq invasion. The President listened and nodded, his expression flat—placing all energy, it would seem, toward grasping the complexities at hand.

When his turn came around, O'Neill spoke for a moment about tracking terrorists' financial assets and choking off their sources of funds, and then he looked intently at the President. "I told you where we are or where we ought to soon be about the things I know

about," he said. "I don't have enough information to have a thoughtful position on what we should do militarily."

The meeting broke up as evening descended. It had been a long
day of intense give-and-take. That night it was fried chicken, corn-
bread, mashed potatoes and gravy—heavy, country food and a time,
afterward, for everyone to relax.

Nancy's friend Joyce Rumsfeld, and her husband, Don, left early;
another friend, Alma Powell, hadn't come. So Nancy worked with
Laura Bush and Janet Ashcroft on a wooden cutout puzzle of the
White House and the First Family that an artist had made for them.

After a while, Laura said she was turning in. Condi wondered
aloud whether anyone wanted to bowl.

"I'm not bowling tonight, no way," Bush called back in a jocular
tone, and followed Laura to Aspen, the presidential lodge.

Across the room, Ashcroft started playing the piano. Rice wandered over.

"Do you know any hymns?"

"Do *I know* any hymns," Ashcroft said in stagy surprise. And
started pounding out "Amazing Grace."

Rice sang—she has a lovely voice. For the next hour they both
sang as Ashcroft played.

In the corner, O'Neill sat in a wide leather chair, devouring the
pile of documents that George Tenet had passed out in the meeting.
It laid out a span of covert activity around the globe, including plots
and assassinations—a plan to neutralize people disposed against the
U.S. government by any means necessary. At its core was the enabling provision that there be virtually no civilian oversight. The
concept: Tell us how you want to look, Mr. President, and we'll handle the rest.

"What I was thinking is, 'I hope the President really reads
this carefully,' " O'Neill recalled. "It's kind of his job. You can't

forfeit this much responsibility to unelected individuals. But I knew he wouldn't."

. . .

ON MONDAY, September 17, the markets opened successfully. A fireman, a few cops, and an EMT rang the bell to open the New York Stock Exchange. It opened and stayed open. The Treasury Secretary and other dignitaries worked the room.

Business as usual suddenly felt like a call to arms.

While he was on Wall Street, O'Neill toured the rubble. Up on the sixth floor of a building that housed the American Stock Exchange, he and a delegation walked through a sprawling financial office that had been abandoned in a panic. Papers covered the floor, wires and light fixtures and assorted accoutrements drooped from walls and ceiling. Workmen, walking alongside the group, pulled plywood sheets off the tall windows. The sun shone through the awning of dust. He looked down at the carnage that had once been the financial district and saw along the high ledge an accumulation of fine powder, like snow after a storm. O'Neill grabbed a handful and let it sift through his hands.

"It was heart-stopping. The towers, the people in them, they were in that dust."

The President held an NSC meeting that morning, Monday, to give everyone assignments to prepare for the invasion of Afghanistan and the war on terror. He wanted the military's tripartite—bombing, cruise missiles, "boots on the ground"—plan; he wanted Tenet to move forward, under new, broadened authority, with covert operations in Afghanistan, first, and across the globe. O'Neill, meanwhile, would head up the first active assault: the financial war.

But how? Over the next few days, O'Neill met with David

Aufhauser, who, he decided, should act as an honest broker, overseeing the "financial war" activities of the FBI, CIA, and Treasury.

It was Aufhauser's first stint on a government paycheck. But as a senior partner at the Washington-based law firm of choice, Williams & Connolly, he'd spent decades advising administrations. His initial entrée to the Bush team had come during the campaign, when he was hired to handle a long-forgotten kerfuffle: that Dick Cheney and George Bush both had residency in Texas, and the Constitution doesn't allow both a president and a vice president to come from the same state. Aufhauser managed to finesse a Wyoming residency for Cheney, even though he hadn't lived in his home state for years. When the administration started, Cheney referred Aufhauser to O'Neill.

Now, Aufhauser would have to prove his worth, organizing a fractious interagency group to track terror assets, under a weight of high expectations that had few precedents. "Everyone wanted results, two days ago," O'Neill told him. "Tell me what you need, I'll make sure you have it. And keep me engaged."

Quickly, the group, which did not yet have a name, moved on two tiers: setting up a new legal structure to freeze assets on the basis of evidence that might not stand up in court; and raising the "standard of care" that was expected of individuals, businesses, and fiduciary agents around the world. That means the funds of anyone associated with a person or entity linked to terrorism could be frozen.

That meant a strict liability standard for directors, managers, or officers of a company and significant shareholders. Because the funds would be frozen, not seized, the threshold of evidence could be lower and the net wider. Yet "freeze" is something of a legal misnomer—funds of Communist Cuba have been frozen in various U.S. banks for forty years.

In any event, the call to action at this moment—a week after the attack—meant that conventional barriers vanished. An executive order was quickly signed, attaching the lowered legal standard to a broadened mandate, and then a parallel UN resolution gave it force worldwide.

Now all there was to do was seize some assets, and quickly. The President was to announce the new executive order on September 24, launching the war on terrorism. He needed some assets to point to.

"It was almost comical," Aufhauser said. "We just listed out as many of the usual suspects as we could and said, Let's go freeze some of their assets."

. . .

O'NEILL HAD ALWAYS been a fast walker—but he was walking so fast these days that aides started to complain. He was only sleeping a few hours a night at this point, his last few days at the Hotel Washington—renovations on the Watergate apartment were almost completed.

And he was talking almost nonstop on CNBC, FOX, NBC's *Today* show, the ABC Evening News, and any outlet with a signal. The idea was to say things—anything—that would instill confidence. He told FOX viewers that it was their patriotic duty to buy stocks. On CNBC, he was asked about the stock market: the Dow Jones Industrial Average had dropped 500 points since 9/11. Could it go up? "Yes, the market could reach a new high in twelve to eighteen months." Financial commentators hooted. Lindsey and his people were on the phone lines, priming reporters: There he goes again. And O'Neill was accused of inappropriate cheerleading.

He had little time even to read what they were saying. Michele Davis read the barbs to him and, again, said he had to be more careful. "Michele, if you look at the data points," O'Neill said, racing between interviews in New York on September 17, "over the past forty years when the market has fallen sharply, it has risen within a year and a half."

Michele was dumbstruck. "You actually got that from a factual analysis? Why didn't you say that?"

O'Neill shrugged. "No one asked."

. . .

AT 9:05 on the morning of September 19, Greenspan was on the phone.

"So, what did you think of [Glenn] Hubbard's column [in *The Wall Street Journal*, September 17, 2001]?" Greenspan asked. "He sounded as though he wasn't expecting significant effects" from 9/11.

"I think there's some cheerleading in there, Alan. On the inside, he's much more pessimistic. And you can figure what Larry is saying."

The two men talked about another conflict, fast unfolding, where they'd have to once again join forces.

"I hate to say this, but Larry and the ideologues, and even Glenn, may be seeing in this terrible mess what they've been looking for—a new rationale for enormous additional tax cuts," O'Neill said. He mentioned that Lindsey was already throwing around numbers—north of $100 billion—for an immediate stimulus plan. "I think we may have to bring them back to earth."

"We need to wait to see what the facts tell us about how the economy is responding," Greenspan said emphatically. "It's the responsible course.

"To push for deep tax cuts, now," O'Neill said, "would look politically opportunistic, because it *would* be politically opportunistic. Maybe, working together, we can get them to listen to reason."

Their counterpoint was presented the next day in front of the Senate Banking Committee.

"We cannot tell at this stage which is a physical problem which will be reversed in a manner similar to a hurricane or a flood and which is a more deep-seated, underlying problem," Greenspan intoned, noting that O'Neill, sitting to his right, said it would be about ten days before the economic effects became clear. "While there is an obvious, strongly desired sense to move rapidly, it's far more important to be right than quick."

O'Neill, meanwhile, urged a delay while the Bush administration looked at stimulus proposals. "We are looking at every instrument that's ever been used and some that haven't been . . . some that are suggested are of dubious value," O'Neill said. Among the options on the list, he said, are increases in the minimum wage, a "supplement" for people who pay no income taxes, and a reduction in the capital gains tax. "We are not excluding anything," he said. Possibly the most useful thing the government could do would be to lower corporate taxes, O'Neill added. That could encourage investors to raise their estimates of companies' after-tax income, and the subsequent increase in earnings estimates would have the effect of boosting stock prices.

Echoing the idea of caution—that we need to let the data speak before we jump to a remedy—O'Neill took a veiled shot at Lindsey and company. "We need to proceed in good faith without a predilection toward 'We already have this tool and we already know the answer and now is an opportunity when we can go ahead and put it in place' without careful consideration of what are the consequences and does it have lasting value to the economy?"

Then, as Greenspan looked on, O'Neill offered some freshly dug data, just the kind he and Alan might serve for one of their breakfasts.

"Yesterday I talked to one of the major credit card companies, and they told me that on a year-to-year basis their credit card activity was off 20 percent in the period since a week ago, Tuesday," he told the senators. But, when you think about it, "that's clearly to be expected, because people stayed home and looked at their television; they were heartbroken." Everyone, from their own experience, knew that now, starting the second week after 9/11, people were pulling away from their televisions and starting to get on with their lives.

There was a pause. "We will recover," O'Neill said.

. . .

ON SEPTEMBER 24, Bush strolled into the Rose Garden for a press conference: "This morning, a major thrust of our war on terrorism began with a stroke of a pen. Today, we have launched a strike on the financial foundation of the global terror network." Then the President unveiled a list of twenty-seven entities—thirteen terrorist groups, eleven individuals, and three charities—whose assets the United States would work to freeze at home and abroad. Some of the organizations were linked to Osama bin Laden, but others were said to be independent of him and active in the Philippines, Kashmir, and elsewhere.

O'Neill followed Bush to the microphone. His two-minute statement ended with a promise: "We will succeed in starving the terrorists of funding and shutting down the institutions that support or facilitate terrorism."

He stepped down from the podium. Now, he thought, all we have to do is figure where the hell to even start.

The interagency task force on terror financing was stymied. The activities of the nineteen terrorists from 9/11 could be tracked in the United States, but then the trail vanished into a mist of the Arab world with its loosely regulated financial institutions. Banks and financial firms in nondemocratic Arab states often are the personal province of ruling families. The interwoven elite of sheikhs, oil barons, and assorted royalty—and their network of friends—is the community from which characters as disparate as Osama bin Laden and Saudi Arabia's erudite, savvy Prince Bandar both emerge. At the center of it all, of course, is the kingdom: a country with the world's largest oil reserves, named for its founding family, the Sauds. It also has a deeply rooted Islamic fundamentalist movement that is fiercely anti-American and anti-Israel and that is funded—in a sort of extortive symbiosis—by the Saudi royal family. After 9/11, the clarion call to hunt terrorists and their money—with Bush's neat division of "with us or against us"—immediately ran into the complexities of *"our"* extortive symbiosis with the Saudi rulers.

O'Neill, who had to report regularly about the "financial war" at meetings of the war cabinet, oversaw the situation intently. Ken Dam, who was a deputy secretary of state under Ronald Reagan, was directed to start calling senior Arab officials. He called the Saudi vice minister of finance on September 28—four days after the press conference with Bush and O'Neill—to gauge Saudi Arabia's cooperation. The vice minister, according to internal Treasury documents, told Dam that "he did not think that they had any accounts that might help terrorism."

Dam was flummoxed. He reported to O'Neill, and a few weeks later, an interagency meeting among Treasury, State, and the NSC spent much of a day hashing over the so-called Saudi problem. Despite the urgent public purpose, the group agreed—in a note sent to O'Neill—that "due to domestic Saudi political sensitivities, a more private and consultative approach was needed on achieving specific action." Translation: The Saudis feared the blossoming dissent from Islamic fundamentalists that accused the vast royal family of being addled with materialist excess and Western entanglements. The "private and consultative approach"? The Saudis could offer no publicly detectable assistance.

. . .

ON OCTOBER 7, 2001, the United States began the war in Afghanistan with an air assault combined with covert operations on the ground. During the next month, with the focus on the military campaign, the Treasury terror-financing task force developed operations in countries other than Saudi Arabia.

The progress was often slow, the signing of treaties of cooperation with 130 countries, including the Kingdom of Saudi Arabia, and there was not much to show for the displays of documents and goodwill.

A break occurred in late October, however, and the President, O'Neill, Powell, and Ashcroft gathered for a press conference at FinCen, the center for the financial war on terror in Vienna, Virginia, on November 7. The quartet announced that Treasury had blocked the U.S. assets of sixty-two individuals and organizations connected with two terrorist-supporting financial networks—Al Taqwa and Al Barakaat. Al Taqwa was an association of offshore banks and financial management firms that had helped al-Qaeda shift money around the world. It was based in the Bahamas, and virtually all the known money of al-Qaeda at that point—$20 million— was housed there. It was identified thanks to a break that was anything but exotic: a Bahamian banking official simply blew the whistle on the group. Internal Treasury documents estimated that another $80 to $100 million of al-Qaeda funds was tucked into other, undetected accounts around the globe.

Al Barakaat, on the other hand, was a group of financial and communications companies owned by a friend and supporter of Osama bin Laden. It was based in both Mogadishu and Dubai. Al Barakaat managed, invested, and distributed funds, and provided terrorist supporters with Internet service, secure telephone communications, and other ways of sending messages and sharing information. The group even arranged for the shipment of weapons. Shutting it down meant that assets were frozen from Minneapolis to Switzerland, where an Al Barakaat director lived.

The President lavishly praised O'Neill at the press conference in northern Virginia and said that "by shutting these networks down, we disrupt the murderers' work."

Then the four men toured the northern Virginia facility, where several hundred agents were working on tracking and freezing assets.

"You've done a great job, Paul," Bush said as they walked among the honeycombed desks, lit screens, and ardent workers. "I really feel progress here. At least, I think it's the start of real progress."

"Yes, it's a start," O'Neill said, "but we know there's a lot more money out there that we just can't seem to get to. It's clean money, in charities, and we don't know where it is until long after it has been allocated and spent. By then, it's too late."

He was speaking of the money coming from—and moving through—Saudi Arabia. Without active investigations inside the kingdom, without the full cooperation of the Saudis as true co-investigators, much of what remained was just sniffing the transactional trail of the dead 9/11 hijackers, a trail that was going cold.

• • •

A WEEK AFTER the FinCen press conference, Paul and Nancy were in their just finished apartment at the Watergate, preparing for a gala evening. Tonight, two months after jetliners hijacked by mostly Saudis had wreaked havoc without precedent on the U.S. mainland, the Saudi ambassador Prince Bandar was giving a party at his northern Virginia compound.

Officially, the fête was hosted by Laura Bush, along with the Mosaic Foundation—an organization comprising the wives of Arab ambassadors to the United States—and the United Nations Foundation, to raise money for AIDS in Africa. The guest of honor was Nelson Mandela.

But the celebration was as much in the cause of the Saudis, at a moment when they desperately needed to remind Washington's ruling elite of the abiding nature of their friendship.

Virtually the entire American power structure was represented. The underwriter for the evening was ExxonMobil. Benefactors included ChevronTexaco and the Ford Motor Company. Patrons or sponsors included General Dynamics and General Electric, Kuwait Investment Partners, Raytheon, Saudi Aramco, Citigroup, Marriott, Black Entertainment Television, Merrill Lynch, and Pfizer. On one of the undercards—the Mandela Challenge Grant Sponsors—were the names Paul Newman, Joanne Woodward, and David Rockefeller.

The O'Neills sat at the head table, with Mandela and his new wife, and Ted Turner and the thirtyish brunette he was dating after his breakup with Jane Fonda. As three hundred or so guests dined on noisettes of lamb with lavender and oregano on a bed of leeks, and basmati rice with pine nuts and almonds, Miriam Makeba, the legendary South African singer and anti-apartheid activist, sang. At one point, Mandela rose and danced, a native South African step, as the crowd swooned.

Mandela's ties to the Kingdom of Saudi Arabia have prompted some controversy. He has been quoted as saying that the kingdom is, in many ways, a more honorable and exemplary society than the United States. It is, in fact, a relationship of traditional construct, familiar to many in that room and around Washington. In the late-1990s, King Fahd gave the African National Congress one of its largest gifts ever: $50 million. So, forever, they are friends. In fact, whether a high-ranking official in the State or Defense Department, or a senior aide in the Senate or House, or a congressman who just lost a tough race, or a former President who has signed on with the Carlyle Group, everyone in the know in Washington is aware that Saudi munificence is vast. A job is always waiting.

For O'Neill, who had only visited Washington in the past twenty-five or so years, the clarity of the dilemma, the Saudi dilemma, was stark. He was seeing it clearly for the first time as the chocolate orange-blossom marquise and mint tea were served.

Prince Bandar stood and the room hushed. He spoke of how the friendship between the United States and Saudi Arabia will "last for all time." He said his country is "doing everything possible to help America in these trying times."

As O'Neill sat in this warm wash of goodwill, he thought about the town's soft, enveloping clasp of influence.

"The Saudis, well, they're like the AARP—they both represent an interest and they don't see it as an issue of Democrats or Republicans. They see it as how can we get more for us, for our interests. So the AARP can get more money for its people and call it Medicare reform, and the Saudis can get what they want from us—they want our bases, a source of protection, they want security and for us to not put our nose into their business. . . . It's all the same crap. They want to rip off the general population of the United States. They want to get something that they shouldn't fairly get."

Bandar sat down to applause and on cue, a distinguished guest rose and smiled at the Prince. He nodded.

It was Roberta Flack. Still elegant in her sixties, she crossed the room, sat at a grand piano near the picture window, and, tapping the keys expertly, sang a haunting rendition of "Killing Me Softly."

CHAPTER 6

THE RIGHT THING

A CROWD BUSTLED into the Oval Office at 9:10 a.m. on January 10 and looked for seats. O'Neill, as the senior official, sat on the chair in the room's centerpiece ensemble of furniture, and others hustled in a game of musical chairs. Secretaries Donald Evans from Commerce and Elaine Chao from Labor were there, along with Hubbard and Lindsey, Andy Card, his deputy Josh Bolten, and the political team of Rove, Hughes, and deputy communications director Dan Bartlett.

Today's agenda was "Corporate Governance and Pension Protection," and the reason was that Enron had exploded and the debris was everywhere. The company had started its public stumble back in mid-October 2001—a few weeks after chairman Ken Lay told employees that the company's stock was "an incredible bargain" and the "third quarter is looking great." Enron had then reported a third-quarter loss of $618 million, started looking for a suitor, and received notice of a Securities and Exchange Commission (SEC) investigation. By late November, the SEC probe had expanded to include Enron's outside accounting firm, Arthur Andersen. On December 2, the energy trading company had filed for bankruptcy.

If it was going to happen, it couldn't have occurred at a more politically fortuitous time. President Bush was riding a wave of popularity that made even natural enemies wonder where they could pick up some Levi's and a pair of boots. The Afghanistan campaign had started with bombing and incursions by Special Forces on October 7. By mid-November, the Taliban had fallen and flags were being waved in the Afghan capital, some of them the Stars and Stripes. U.S. casualties were modest. Though Osama bin Laden had not been caught or killed, there was a general sense that this swift war had been handily won and it was now just a matter of consolidating victory.

O'Neill had been busy with meetings of the war cabinet and the NSC—sometimes sending his deputy, Ken Dam—while focusing his energies on the financial war on terror. Some headway had been made, even without significant help from the Saudis. By January 2002, according to an internal Treasury memorandum, $104 million in suspected terrorist assets had been frozen. Now, with victory in Afghanistan, the administration focus was returning to Iraq—with Rumsfeld and Wolfowitz pointing to the ease with which the Taliban had fallen as evidence of how doable Iraq would be.

It was almost a comfort, this morning, to return to domestic business. It felt like housecleaning—manageable issues that responded to good, honest effort. Bush seemed particularly relaxed.

"What are we going to do about this pension problem?" he asked the group, with purposeful good cheer. Enron shareholders were crowding the airwaves, discussing their ruined lot. Thousands of employees had lost their life savings and much of their retirement accounts when the stock became worthless in November.

Tentative plans had already been hatched, memos exchanged. The President would call for the formation of two groups, both headed by O'Neill. One, in which he would be joined by Evans and Chao, would analyze the pension system and the rules and regula-

tions that governed it and would propose reforms to protect em-
ployee pensions from bankruptcy. In the other, O'Neill would be
joined by Harvey Pitt, chairman of the Securities and Exchange
Commission, and Alan Greenspan. They would look at the broader
issues of corporate governance and disclosure.

Bush was to announce all this in twenty minutes, when reporters
would be invited into the Oval Office—a moment of perspicacious
confidence during which the President would be available to them in
an unmanaged way, with his key advisers clustered around him.

Talk in the meeting ranged from some ideas for pension reform
to a rehash of the Enron mess. There was a sense of incredulity. The
administration was every bit as surprised by Enron's collapse and
exposed wrongdoing as Wall Street brokers and the beleaguered
Enron pensioners. Bush, Card, Hughes, and others suggested that it
was too bad that no one in the administration had talked with Enron.
There might have been a better way to manage the fallout. The conversation crested forward from there about the subject of advance
planning and crisis control.

"Wait a minute, Mr. President," O'Neill said, breaking in. "I *did*
talk to Ken Lay not long before Enron filed for bankruptcy and I
know Don did, too. Because Don called me to talk to me about what,
if anything, he ought to do for Ken Lay."

Lindsey and the political staff looked at O'Neill with disbelief.
Was O'Neill self-immolating?

The President raised his hand. "Tell me all about it."

O'Neill laid it out. In late October, Enron—already conspicu-
ously troubled—was looking to be bought by Dynegy, a competitor
energy firm. Moody's was examining Enron's books, and Lay feared
the bond-rating agency would downgrade Enron's debt, scuttling
the deal.

Lay had called O'Neill on the last Friday in October. He had described Enron's financial problems and asserted that because it was

the country's seventh largest company in market capitalization and a market maker in the trading of nearly a thousand commodities, its bankruptcy could cause widespread economic repercussions. While he made no request, Lay was laying out a case for a federal bailout.

O'Neill recalled telling Lay that although he'd look into the matter, he didn't think an Enron failure would have broad effects on the U.S. economy. That next Monday, Don Evans received a similar call. This time Lay was more direct, asking Evans if he could help out by intervening with Moody's and convincing them not to downgrade Enron.

Evans had called O'Neill. "Secretary Evans, clearly, can speak for himself," O'Neill went on, "but Don called me to find out what I thought. I told him, 'Absolutely, under no circumstances, call up a rating agency. Absolutely not.' And I think that was the end of it."

As O'Neill described this chain of events for the President, the others sat mute. He added that undersecretary Peter Fisher—who'd handled the Long Term Capital Management collapse during the Clinton administration—did make a round of calls to Wall Street and various companies and determined there would be no significant economic effects from an Enron bankruptcy.

Evans affirmed O'Neill's account.

Bush paused. "We should tell the media that this happened, immediately . . . get it on the record."

O'Neill almost laughed out loud. "I couldn't agree more, Mr. President. Truth is best—always best. The principle is transparency."

A moment later, with the reporters, Bush spoke about the general issues of pension protection and corporate responsibility, the formation of the two committees to be chaired by O'Neill. He mentioned Enron and said that Lay and he had had only one recent encounter and had not discussed the trading company. There was no mention of Lay's calls to O'Neill and Evans. He then answered a question about Afghanistan. It was left to Ari Fleischer, at a midday press conference, to mention the phone calls to a half-empty briefing room as an afterthought. The reporters snapped to attention.

Afterward, Fleischer huddled with O'Neill. The press secretary was anxious that a damaging scandal was unfolding. "We really need you in front of the cameras," he told the Treasury Secretary. Not to worry, O'Neill said. "We didn't do anything wrong by receiving the call and saying, 'Sorry, Ken, get lost.'" O'Neill spent part of the evening at the podium in the White House Briefing Room, doing interviews with CNN and CNBC. Early the next morning, he taped for ABC's *Good Morning America*.

And then it was done. For the most part, the story—a complex but discernible tale—lasted only one news cycle. What's more, O'Neill felt it showed the worth of transparency, of straight talk. Had the calls been covered up, or relegated to the shadows and then revealed, it would have raised a cloud of suspicion not easily dissipated. Instead, the incident showed merely that a major contributor and friend of the administration had asked for help and hadn't gotten it.

O'Neill left ABC's Washington bureau satisfied that things were starting to work out . . . not in spite of his often bracing candor, but because of it.

O'Neill, who was still regarded, for the most part, as unmanageable, believed that the public wanted truth and transparency and determined to do his best to give it to them. The miracle, in the mind of many of the Capital's observers, was that he'd survived this long. Something here didn't add up—according to the conventional understanding of how Washington works. That meant it was time for a reappraisal.

The first note had been struck back on October 7 by Glenn Kessler, *The Washington Post*'s longtime White House reporter. In a front-page story headlined FIRST IMPRESSIONS, LASTING INFLUENCE; O'NEILL HAS MORE PULL THAN MEETS THE EYE, Kessler wrote:

The conventional wisdom in Washington is that O'Neill is some sort of supernova, a spectacular, doomed explosion. The truth is more fascinating and complex—and also revealing about the Bush White House.

Within the Bush administration, O'Neill appears to have not only survived, but thrived. His zest for combative language and his zeal for new ideas has made him a favorite of President Bush, though his style has rankled some officials. The president meets with him privately for a half-hour about once a week, a privilege that President Bill Clinton did not grant his Treasury secretaries for fear it would give them an unfair advantage in interagency discussions. O'Neill is also a key member of the president's war cabinet.

"The president likes his big thinking, even when it's way out of his realm of responsibility," said a senior White House official directly involved in policymaking. "The chemistry between him and the president is very good."

The truth, O'Neill had mused when he read Kessler's story, was more complicated. There really wasn't much chemistry. But this last incident—straight talk about the Ken Lay phone calls—lifted his spirits. Presidents, like it or not, need candor, even if it threatens the best-laid plans of their protective counselors.

And now the President seemed to be bending, if only slightly, in the Treasury Secretary's direction. O'Neill detected a change in the past few meetings they'd had together. With approval ratings at close to 90 percent and his gaze still cast abroad, Bush had slipped into a kind of repose on the domestic front. The big issues were elsewhere—war and peace, a titanic struggle of good and evil. So, for the host of largely tabled issues such as corporate responsibility, pension reform, steel tariffs, O'Neill later said, "the President seemed to be saying, Let the evidence speak—then we'll decide what to do."

Or, on a few of these issues, let O'Neill—sitting atop two heavy-weight committees—figure it out.

Two days after he finished telling of Ken Lay's calls on television, the fullest profile of O'Neill to date hit the public doorstep: an eight-thousand-word cover story in *The New York Times Magazine* by Michael Lewis. O'Neill read the story on Sunday, January 13. Lewis had been working on it since the previous summer. The account was anything but a puff piece—it described most of O'Neill's now famous verbal explosions and conjectured that he might have been fired by the time readers saw the article; it also noted how the Treasury Secretary "violates the central tenet of Washington financial life: never use the English language to convey meaning." This, of course, was a game Greenspan had played artfully for years, generating a mystique with his dense ambiguities—a suggestion of brilliance and inside knowl-edge—that allows financial markets to indulge the fantasy that some-one, somewhere, knows more than they do and can fix things in a jam.

For better or worse, O'Neill—both at Alcoa and now at Treasury—"instinctively takes the opposite view," Lewis wrote, "that people are more likely to prosper if you develop positive opin-ions on subjects and tell them what you think in plain English." Most of the so-called gaffes, the author noted, fell into that category.

O'Neill read the story with his morning coffee, in the predawn, at his house in Pittsburgh. Then he woke up his wife. "I think someone finally got it," he told Nancy, still half-asleep. "That I'm conducting an experiment in trusting the American people with the truth. And I'm the guinea pig."

• • •

PAUL O'NEILL HEADED INTO THE NEXT WEEK—the start of year two of the Bush presidency—in full sprint.

Opportunity now beckoned: one thing he knew was corporate America. After the astonishing collapse of the nineties stock market, the reversal of the dot-com and telecommunications booms—the neat, decade-aligned end of an era—followed by evidence of corporate perfidy on a vast scale, O'Neill was now duly empowered to innovate, to redraw the map. He had credibility to spare for this job. He'd lived in the executive suite for twenty years. Now, he'd have a chance to change it.

On January 17, Greenspan arrived at O'Neill's small conference room for breakfast. It was Greenspan's turn to venture into Treasury's turf—a fitting change of venue since O'Neill was afire with purpose about changing the way corporations did business.

The Fed chairman had strong feelings on the subject as well. He felt that stock analysis was often misleading, that accounting practice should be fundamentally redesigned, and that boards of directors needed to show proof of independence or face consequences.

O'Neill nodded along. He told Greenspan he'd been thinking about these issues for more than twenty years. He described an early and seminal experience. In 1981, when he was a senior vice president of International Paper, he served on the board of National Westminster Bank, a financial institution that operated primarily in the United States but was owned by a large British bank. Each month, the chairman would fly to the States for a long day of meetings with the bank's CEO. "And even there, Alan, the chairman, a smart, committed guy, had no real idea what was going on inside that bank."

Over twenty years—through various attempts to reform the governance of corporations and their directors—O'Neill kept getting nudged toward the same conclusion: It was all about the CEO. "The solution is to make the CEO responsible for the company he runs. Period," he said. "And I mean legally responsible. Everything else will flow from that. The accountants will either do their job or the

CEO will have to fire them—he can't take the risk. That goes for the senior executives, too. And for the board. Tie a high standard of accountability to the man in charge, and everyone will fall into line."

Greenspan sat for a moment, turning it around in his head. "You may be right," he said. "But I'm not sure if it's not a little more complex than that." He paused. "Then, again, it may be the thoughtful solution. Nothing else has worked."

And the more they talked, the more they agreed. O'Neill looked across at his friend.

"So, I guess we're a team again," O'Neill said. "Let's see how we do this time . . . or maybe intellectual pragmatists have no more place in Washington."

. . .

O'NEILL WAS SITTING at the table on February 7 before the Senate Budget Committee, but it might as well have been the Rules Committee because the discussion that transpired was about the rules that govern Washington. O'Neill, as much of the town had learned, was a rules-hater. Every rule he encountered prompted a *why* and a corollary *why not*? The habit of asking questions had guided him to success in life, including a personal fortune. But *why* questions are exhausting—they necessitate the reexamination of what has, for better or for worse, been accepted, and they're disruptive, and they often start fights.

Staring down at him was the Senate's thorny parliamentarian—the town's king of rules—Senator Robert C. Byrd, Democrat of West Virginia. Byrd has written, over his fifty years in Congress, more rules to guide the conduct of men and women—in the legislative chamber and beyond it—than a biblical scribe. He was the protector of an ancient order.

On this morning in Washington, Byrd was holding up a copy of the proposed Federal Budget of the United States, a 1,030-page compendium of rules with dollar signs attached. O'Neill was there to present it to Congress. The dollar signs are, in a sense, value judgments by the administration of the worth of various rules that will govern environmental protection or Medicare payments or the manufacture of attack helicopters in the coming year. Congress's core power, in the founders' wisdom, is to control the dollar and crunch those value judgments, and a matching set that Congress provides, into transactions that will fund society's wishes.

What Byrd was pointing to, though, was not a dollar sign—it was a cartoon. O'Neill thought that this cartoon of Gulliver being tied down by an army of Lilliputians was funny, so he had approved its inclusion. It was an allusion to a controversial comment he'd made the previous year to the National Association of Business Economists that Congressional rules—including the Byrd Rule, which generally requires sixty votes on key elements of tax bills—are "created by just ordinary people" and are "like the Lilliputians tying us to the ground." Of course, Byrd saw the cartoon as a value judgment, which it was, about everything he stood for, about the worth of rules and of senators. They were the foolish, nearsighted Lilliputians.

O'Neill's comment had been gnawing at Byrd for nearly a year. Holding up the cartoon, he said, "I'll not dwell upon this longer, except to say we're senators, and you've been in this town one year. I've been in this town fifty years. I've seen many secretaries of the Treasury. And I just want to tell you we senators are here to look after the interest of the people of our states."

He, paused, looking hard at O'Neill in his tailored suit, and a capsule bio, with Alcoa at the top, seemed to flash into his head. "They're not well-to-do people, not all of them, in my state. They're not CEOs of multibillion-dollar corporations. They can't just pick up a phone and call a cabinet secretary. In time of need, in drought, in floods, in famines, when a bridge is near collapse, when safe drinking water is not available, when health care services are endangered, they come to us. The people come to us. Yes, they're ordinary people. They're coal miners, they're farmers, they're schoolteachers, they're ministers, they're lawyers, they're bankers. But this cartoon on page fifty-one and comments throughout this budget suggest that this administration believes that so-called experts at bureaucratic agencies should determine the priorities of this nation, not the Congress, not the people they represent. That suggests that the problems of the people are too little to deserve the attention of the administration."

He turned the document around to read from the text.

"Here's what the paragraph says, by Dr. Gulliver: 'At a time of national emergency, it is critical that the government operate effectively and spend every taxpayer dollar wisely. Unfortunately, federal managers are greatly limited in how they can use financial, human, and other resources to manage programs. They'—meaning the federal managers—'lack much of the discretion given to their private sector counterparts to get the job done.' . . . Well, so you say federal managers are greatly limited in how they can use financial resources? That's a good thing. These people, so-called federal managers, are not elected by the people. We're talking about the taxpayers' dollars, the taxpayers' dollars. That's why there are rules. That's why we have rules!"

Then Byrd launched into a ringing endorsement of steel tariffs, an issue dear to West Virginia.

As O'Neill listened to the tirade, he clenched his jaw and stared directly at the owlish eighty-four-year-old, and at some point during the fifteen-minute monologue, he decided to break another Washington rule: *Don't get into it with Byrd.* Just let him go on for a while, then change the subject.

"Well, Senator, what I said to the National Association of Business Economists I stand by, because what I had in my mind and what

I deeply believe is this, that where we have rules made by men that restrict the realization of human potential, they should be changed."

Still smarting from Byrd's implication that he was a fat-cat, born-to-privilege CEO with no experience in Washington, O'Neill recalled that the senator, in his youth, had been a member of the Klu Klux Klan.

And, after all, this was about rules that constrain. "We had rules that said 'Colored don't enter here.' That was a man-made rule, and there are lots of those same kinds of rules that limit the realization of human potential. And I've dedicated my life to doing what I can to get rid of rules that so limit human potential, and I'm not going to stop!"

Then it got ugly.

BYRD: Mr. Secretary, I've been around a long time, and I try to live by the rules. You were specifically talking about the Byrd Rule.

O'NEILL: I was talking about all rules that limit human potential and the realization of human potential. And inferring something different is fine, if you wish to do so. But I'd also like to say—because there was an inference in your remarks that somehow I was born on home plate and thought I hit a home run—Senator, I started my life in a house without water or electricity. So I don't concede to you the high moral ground of not knowing what life is like in the ditch.

BYRD: Mr. Secretary, I lived in a house without electricity, too—no running water, no telephone, a little wooden out-house.

O'NEILL: I had the same.

> BYRD: I started out in life without any rungs on the bottom of the ladder.

Byrd withdrew from the clinch, wild-eyed and flushed. Who would have figured that this CEO grew up in a shack? He seemed to shake his head, trying to regain his bearings. How did this get started? Wasn't this about rules?

> BYRD: I'm talking not about putting any halter or brake on anybody's self-incentive, anybody's initiative. I've had that experience and I can stand toe to toe with you. I haven't walked in any corporate board rooms. I haven't had to turn millions of dollars into trust accounts. I wish I had those millions of dollars. I grew up in a coal miner's home. I married a coal miner's daughter. So I hope you don't want to start down this road, talking about our backgrounds and how far back we came from. I'm citing to you what you said in response to a question about the Byrd Rule.

And then he rambled toward closure, just to finish it.

> . . . the Byrd Rule has saved millions and millions and millions of dollars for this government, and we ought to live up to it. You perhaps ought to study the Byrd Rule a little bit, if you haven't, to the point that you can explain it. And just remember that when you are out talking about those ordinary people, you're talking about senators. They're ordinary people. And we're not going to let you get away with it. We're not going to let you get away with it.

When O'Neill had spoken about his modest upbringing, his voice quavered with rage, his eyes filled. In this exchange about the rules of the game in Washington, he had broken a few unwritten rules about mixing it up with Byrd and about the expected deportment of a man who signs the dollar bill, someone whom people—many of them wealthy, born to privilege, who run the American financial system—look to for comfort, as kindred. But he was never, really, one of them. As he left the hearing, a reporter asked if those were tears. "That was fire," he said.

Fire that in time would consume him.

• • •

ON SUNDAY, February 10, O'Neill and Greenspan went to the Vice President's house for lunch. They sat in elegant wicker chairs on the sun porch while Cheney talked to them about steel. As O'Neill warned the President in their very first meeting, steel had become a problem. Cheney, Rove, and Robert Zoellick, the U.S. Trade Representative, were now deeply involved. The issues were complex, and O'Neill's deep understanding of this industry had finally been tapped. There was dumping of steel onto the market by other countries, marked by so-called surges of lower-priced foreign steel.

There were ways, O'Neill said, to get major steel makers from the United States and overseas to the table to make trades. Over the past months he had joined Don Evans in meetings with U.S. steel executives. O'Neill knew many of the men in the room and spoke bluntly to them. He had commissioned independent research, and the conclusions were what everyone already knew: They needed to reduce production of steel that was overpriced or, in its manufacturing process, environmentally damaging. This would give the steel companies a way—an excuse, really—to do much needed retooling and would give the United States leverage to stop other countries from dumping. Prices would stabilize; overcapacity would shrink.

The executives replied with a legalistic brief showing that their products were cost-efficient and environmentally sound. O'Neill's response—"If you want to deal in this kind of bullshit, you can all go to hell"—left the CEOs stunned and ready to deal. They started to patch together a plan.

But another view was advancing—the view that steel was mostly about politics, not about economics or the principles of free trade. There were political debts to pay. During the campaign, Cheney had made a commitment of support to steelworkers in West Virginia, a state the ticket carried. Rove was looking at Pennsylvania and Michigan as crucial states in the upcoming midterm elections. The aim was not only to energize the base but, in discrete instances, where it was affordable, snatch portions of the opponent's territory. This was something Clinton did regularly as he cobbled together centrist coalitions on various issues. Now, it was Rove's turn to try.

What's more, the White House legislative staff was hoping that it could trade support for steel tariffs for a vote or two in the Senate approving Trade Promotion Authority for Bush. The Republican-controlled House had passed its trade promotion bill in December 2001, giving the president authority to reach trade agreements that are largely immune from congressional tinkering.

All this set the agenda for Sunday's lunch. Cheney told O'Neill and Greenspan that Bush and he were going to make a decision on the steel issue. But, clearly, Cheney didn't want to end up in open debate with O'Neill, whose stance on steel was well-informed, or with the unmanageable Greenspan.

So, he had granted them an audience. They could both make their case to him on the issue of steel tariffs. They were getting in early, he told them, before the battle started in earnest. Both men knew that the debate would be intensely political. Now was their chance, Cheney told them, to discuss their view of "the right thing to do." Their positions would be duly noted; there would be little more that they needed to say. Cheney said, "We'll make our decision and then, that'll be that."

O'Neill and Greenspan both made the case that the largely bipartisan consensus on free trade was one of the great victories of the last decade; that the President would confuse many constituencies by flouting that consensus. O'Neill explained that tariffs would do little to offer long-term support to the U.S. steel industry. Greenspan pointed out that tariffs might actually violate certain World Trade Organization agreements and would weaken our hand at the bargaining table at upcoming WTO negotiations.

• • •

AT 2 p.m. the next day, February 11, a small army entered the White House Situation Room for a showdown. It was officially an NSC meeting, but the chamber was crowded with people who didn't spend too much time at this long table—Elaine Chao from Labor, Don Evans, Mitch Daniels, U.S. Trade Representative Robert Zoellick, Lindsey, Hubbard, and then the regulars—Powell, Rice, O'Neill, Card, Ashcroft, and, lending weight to the proceedings, the Vice President.

Zoellick and Evans laid out the issues. The International Trade Commission, or ITC, had recommended a range of tariffs in response to the surge in steel imports that occurred in 1999 and 2000. A range of options was before them—with the prospect of trade wars and an undermining of one of the key principles of general consensus, free trade, hanging in the balance. These were the options: Either reject the ITC-recommended tariffs; or set tariffs triggered only by surges; or set a limited, rolling tariff schedule; or impose tariffs of 20 percent on certain products; or, finally, set tariffs of up to 40 percent on all products, which was what the steel companies and their various allies in electorally precious rust-belt states were pushing for.

Before getting into the main battle, a few of the players laid down markers for key constituencies. Rice emphasized the importance of exemptions for Canada and Mexico as our partners in the North American Free Trade Agreement, or NAFTA. Zoellick discussed the idea of a pilot program to assist with the health care and pension benefits of steelworkers who lost their jobs—something he could trade for votes for Trade Promotion Authority. Then the conversation widened to a generally agreed upon fact—namely, that protection of this industry hadn't, historically, helped firms. If they couldn't manage to compete globally—or if they couldn't be directed to be competitive—protection was just a Band-Aid on a deep wound. Zoellick made several oblique references to "political realities."

Cheney asked what is "the excess capacity in the U.S. compared with the OECD" (Organization for Economic Cooperation and Development, mainly European countries). He was looking for a bit of us-versus-them capital with the Europeans, some of whom were accused of dumping. In fact, almost three-fourths of the world's overcapacity was with the United States and Japan. It became clear, quickly, that the facts seemed to be going against Cheney.

Don Evans, who had been having regular tutorials with O'Neill, mentioned that "we actually have seen a 6 percent increase in price in the U.S.," a healthy increase and a fact that undercut claims by American steel producers that dumping was driving down prices. "Whatever we do," Evans added, striking a note for free trade, "we have to be true to our principles."

Mitch Daniels became agitated. He blurted out, "Well, yes, but if you can't do the right thing when you're at 85 percent approval, then when can you do the right thing? I think it's time to say no."

Everyone looked with surprise at Daniels—he has a way of expressing what others are thinking but won't say. Often, he'd find himself doubling back when he got an arched brow from Cheney or Rove, but once his opinion was out, it was out.

His comment seemed to tip the room. Is there any point, Daniels's outburst implied, where the political team says they have enough capital, enough advantage, that they are satisfied with their franchise and not constantly twisting the arm of policy? O'Neill wondered about this as he broke his agreed silence, which was so out of character it was drawing notice.

"Well," he said quietly, "certainly, there should be a high hurdle before we take this step" of imposing tariffs. Cheney looked at him impatiently.

But O'Neill's cue seemed to embolden Rice, and soon the meeting was a free-for-all. "I think we have a split here," she said. "Do we take this to the President?"

This was what Cheney had been hoping to avoid—a split. In fact, it was anything but a split. Nearly everyone seemed on one side; Cheney and Zoellick were on the other, trying to hold their position. A consensus on sound policy was colliding with a political favor.

Finally, it was Powell's turn. "Why are we thinking about doing this?" he asked in frustration. "I have heard good reasons today not to do it, but I haven't heard one good reason to move forward with tariffs. This will hurt downstream producers. We can't even say this will improve our steel industry."

With Mitch Daniels's comment still hanging above them all—if not now, then when?—Zoellick said halfheartedly, "We have to think about the Pension Benefit Guaranty Corporation." Zoellick's point was that the PBGC is underfunded, and it won't help if a lot of steel companies fail and their pension obligations come due; it would make the situation worse. O'Neill shook his head. That, he recalled, "had absolutely nothing do with the issue of whether tariffs should now be U.S. policy."

Finally, it came back to Cheney. He mumbled that "imports are, in fact, way down from the surge. . . . Our minimills are competitive," and, whatever we do, the tariff-empowering statute, called Section 201, says "we can review this in eighteen months."

In other words, if what we do now is go with tariffs, it will be political bait, and in eighteen months—after the midterm elections—we can effect the switch. Meeting over.

. . .

THE NEXT DAY IN HIS OFFICE, O'Neill pulled up a file he'd been sent on his computer and noticed it was rather long.

It was from Greenspan. In the cover note, Greenspan wrote: "I have gone further than originally intended, but I thought it might be useful nonetheless."

O'Neill opened the attached document.

Alan Greenspan
February 12, 2002

CORPORATE ACCOUNTING AND DISCLOSURE
A DIAGNOSIS OF THE PROBLEM

Corporate governance has evolved over the past century to more effectively promote the allocation of the nation's savings to its most productive uses. And, generally speaking, it has served us well. We could not have achieved our current level of national productivity if corporate governance was deeply flawed.

And yet, our most recent experiences with the bankruptcy of Enron and, preceding that, a number of lesser such incidents, suggest that the practice of corporate gov-

ernance has strayed from our perceptions of how it is supposed to work. By law, shareholders own our corporations
and direct the allocation of corporate resources in an en-
deavor to maximize the value of the firm. To the extent they
succeed, they foster the optimum allocation of capital in
our economy.

But as our economy has grown, and our corporations
have become even larger, de facto shareholder control has
diminished: ownership has dispersed, and few shareholders
have sufficient stakes to individually influence the choice of
boards of directors or chief executive officer. The vast majority of corporate share ownership is for investment, not
to achieve operating control of a company, notwithstanding relatively infrequent instances of "hostile" takeover attempts.

Thus, it has increasingly fallen to the CEO to guide the
corporation, hopefully in what he or she perceives to be the
best interests of shareholders. . . .

Over the next pages, Greenspan took O'Neill's concept and bol-
stered it with supporting analysis, noting that boards of directors are
mostly selected from slates provided by the CEO; that auditors
are selected by the CEO; and that the business strategy of a company, set by the CEO, "strongly influences the choice of accounting
practices that measure the ongoing degree of success or failure of
that strategy.

"Thus," he wrote, "the markets have no alternative but to depend
on the CEO to ensure an objective evaluation of the prospects of a
corporation."

Greenspan then ran through a litany of commissions and omis-
sions perpetrated of late, under the CEO-dominated model, by various parties from securities analysts (who, research shows, "have
been persistently overly optimistic") to CEOs (who, "under increasing pressure from the investment community to meet elevated ex-

pectations," have been "drawn to accounting devices whose sole purpose is to obscure potential adverse results").

With each passing page, Greenspan's despair at the current state of corporate America deepened, going further, even, than O'Neill's concerns.

"In this environment," Greenspan summed up, "a disturbing amount of corporate accounting has come to rest on little more than conforming to . . . GAAP [Generally Accepted Accounting Principles], without endeavoring to judge whether the companies' accounts in total do, in fact, represent a full and accurate portrayal of the current financial state of the corporation.

"So long as the corporate duty to disclose is viewed as limited to conforming to GAAP, disclosures will remain inadequate. . . ."

Well, O'Neill thought, Greenspan just flushed the entire system of Generally Accepted Accounting Principles—long a baseline of what corporations must consider in their operations and then disclose to the public. Those rules had been steadily bent out of shape.

This manifesto, O'Neill believed, represented a Greenspan only a privileged few had any direct experience with. It was logical, as clear as a sparkling lake, and without the layers of hints and suggestions that characterized his public utterances on the economy and interest rates. A pleasure. Too bad the public doesn't get a chance to meet *this* Greenspan, he thought.

He put the memo aside.

If the CEO was to represent an ideal of probity, and guide all those in a company's orbit to the highest standards of decency, transparency, and disclosure, he'd have to be motivated by fear—fear of the abyss. Contemplating Greenspan's sepulchral assessments affirmed for O'Neill that the standard to trigger litigation and censure should no longer be recklessness. That was too narrow, too rare—a standard that doubtless would apply to Ken Lay when he was CEO of Enron. But Lay was one in a thousand. No, the new standard should be negligence. If you do not present to investors an accurate picture of the company you run—an illustration that a "reasonable person," or in this case a "reasonable investor," can understand and, thus, know to be true—you are negligent.

A moment had arrived. Historic events had created a sudden, stark recognition of what had slowly and steadily been going awry in corporate America for twenty years. Pin a negligence standard to the CEO, who would be kept honest by the "reasonable investor," and the tide would turn. Profits for the boss and the shareholder would flow from a new standard, a kind of integrity competition— rather than what *my* company and *I* can get away with. As for the negligent CEO, O'Neill thought, settling into the role of scourge, *watch out!*

· · ·

REPORTS WERE FILED. Opinions offered. The staffs at the Fed, Treasury, NEC, and SEC had prepped their champions.

On February 22, at 1 p.m., a collection of the top financial officials in the United States met in the large conference room at Treasury: O'Neill; Greenspan; Harvey Pitt, the SEC chairman; Glenn Hubbard; Lawrence Lindsey; William McDonough, president of the Federal Reserve Bank of New York; and Ken Dam, David Aufhauser, and several assistant secretaries from Treasury.

Yes, it was a crisis. Three weeks before, Global Crossing—the large fiber-optic backbone provider—had declared bankruptcy. An SEC investigation swiftly commenced. Dennis Kozlowski's Tyco, Inc. was beginning to look shaky. Large fiber providers such as Qwest were in trouble. Each day, new revelations emerged about what AOL did or did not reveal to Time Warner prior to using its wildly inflated stock price to capture the media giant. It was all coming due, the thing known but long denied: that there had been an on-going shift, across nearly two decades, of what is acceptable conduct for corporations. The men in this room had agreed in previous meetings on that premise and on its consequence: that there were tens of thousands of companies in America—more than any agency could police—that were operating with virtually no proactive standard to compel probity.

Now, the question was what to recommend as remediation, as a new set of standards. O'Neill, as chairman, was due to make his presentation to the President in the next week or so. It was time for decisions. For the moment, he would sit back and let those assembled fight it out, weighing in only when he felt needed. When the group had settled around the baronial table, O'Neill nodded to Greenspan, who asked, "Where are we on agreements on principles?"

O'Neill, not wasting a moment, articulated his standard, which was to guide the discussion: "We have agreement to tighten the structure of responsibilities for the CEO."

Pitt, a bearded and sometimes volcanic former regulator and securities lawyer, sized up the two older men—O'Neill and Greenspan, who were so often in concert—and offered a counterweight. O'Neill had mentioned his proposed new standard—negligence—for regulatory, or legal, action in a previous meeting. "Shifting the standard to negligence is a huge problem," the SEC chairman said. "We just can't go there. There's no doubt that we have to prevent gaming of the system. But we need a high standard, otherwise we'll be overwhelmed with litigation."

Greenspan was cognizant of Harvey's problem. A negligence standard would ensnare more CEOs—at least initially, many more than the SEC staff could handle. There'd been talk of creating a new agency to deal with accounting and disclosure issues. Harvey was talking turf.

The Fed chairman wanted to take that concern off the table. "We are talking about ambitious changes," Greenspan said, "but we should put enforcement at the SEC and only the SEC."

The responsibility today is simply to meet the legal burden of proof, which is GAAP, the Generally Accepted Accounting Principles. This was not the best incentive. He had been persuaded in his conversations with Secretary O'Neill, Greenspan said, that they needed to shift the burden of proof to the CEO to inform the "reasonable person."

"Paul, what is the current standard for a CEO?" Glenn Hubbard asked.

"The standard is developing in case law, but some CEOs have gone out of bounds."

After some discourse about specific ways that CEOs were disregarding boundaries, Pitt said, "The CEO must say what he sees for his company, and this must match the disclosure."

Greenspan listened to the give-and-take with impatience. Yes, yes, we know all that. "I get back to corporate financial policy: dividends, stock options, incentives."

He wanted the causal logic he and O'Neill embraced to be so compelling it could not be denied. "Before 1980, share buybacks were discouraged," Greenspan said. "Returns were driven by dividends. Earnings are a very dubious measure . . ." And he began to pull apart the gold standard—earnings per share—that drove markets, expectations, hope, and fear. There are so many tools a CEO can use to "craft" an earnings statement, so many ways to mislead. "All asset values, after all, are just based on a forecast. . . ." The group was following his every word, but the chairman did not see in their gazes an outrage to match his own. He clapped his hand on the table and raised his voice. "There's been too much gaming of the system until it is broke. Capitalism is not working! There has been a corrupting of the system of capitalism."

The room was silent. Several of those present recall feeling a physical reaction—a chill in the spine—to the reasonable, oracular Greenspan, so measured and calm in every storm, lifting his voice like Lear, railing at heaven's vault.

O'Neill, too, was silent, respectful of a friend's indignation. His deputies moved to fill the awkward silence.

"I think we need to get back," said Aufhauser tentatively, "to what is the standard of care for a CEO that should, specifically, be required by SEC."

Peter Fisher, the undersecretary for domestic finance, said: "If a CEO knows a fact, and a reasonable investor would like to know it, that fact should be disclosed."

Pitt was ready again: "Let's discuss remedy—the power to remove a CEO, the power to bar him or her from future employment in a public company." He ran through methods of disgorgement—making an executive pay back ill-gotten proceeds. But talk about penalties was premature; the question of a standard of conduct had to come first. Pitt tried to parse it once more. "The CEO has an obligation to inform investors of material information that he knows that investors would like to know. There cannot be 'conscious avoidance.'"

O'Neill frowned. Conscious avoidance was just a hair's breadth from recklessness—you'd have to prove intent. At this very moment, top executives and directors at Enron were claiming they had been unaware of the financial woes that led to the bankruptcy. Under current standards, that claim largely protected them against penalties, since they were asserting they hadn't knowingly, recklessly, misled stockholders. Under a negligence standard, a judge or arbiter could determine that, whether or not executives knew about problems, they *should have known* about those problems and should have worked to fix them.

As Pitt spoke, O'Neill looked over at Greenspan, who he had

hoped would lead the charge today—an expectation already exceeded.

"If not the present system, then what?" Greenspan said. "There's a hole in the present system, that much is clear." But then the Fed chairman sidestepped into his pet concern—securities analysts, their persistent and remunerated optimism, and the idea of tracking and publishing the ex-post performance of analysts' recommendations (what they predicted versus what occurred) so that their credibility and that of their firms could be assessed. He was slipping into the thicket. "But everything we talk about will be in the world of 'second best,' " Greenspan added, referring to the General Theory of Second Best, which posits that focusing on one variable and changing it could cause unforeseen alterations of related variables.

Pitt seized the opening. "It's not the job of government to protect shareholders from the risk of bad management. We need to focus on the quality of disclosure, not the quality of judgment." Then he moved the discussion back to "conscious avoidance." Not that there wouldn't be some affirmative duties by executives and directors; such duties would pertain to reporting "unquestionably significant" information.

"Unquestionably significant"? These were lawyer terms, fuzzy, debatable words, and Greenspan reached again for the wider mandate.

"This is a moral and ethical issue. The President needs to speak to the nation about the moral issues—something he does so well. There needs to be a meeting between Secretary O'Neill and the President to discuss what our system of capitalism needs." And Greenspan started listing standards—transparency and auditor ethics and the disclosure of what officials knew and relied on in making their decisions.

Larry Lindsey, sitting quietly, self-protectively, in a meeting that was thoroughly in O'Neill's realm, responded to Greenspan's litany with the evergreen "We need to tighten standards, to really just enforce existing laws."

Greenspan shook his head. It wasn't about enforcement—it was about an affirmative duty to uphold a higher standard of integrity, he said. He returned to O'Neill's mantra, the only way, he realized, to keep this debate in focus. "If the CEO is lined up, the rest of the company will follow."

Glenn Hubbard tugged back.

"No, no, no. . . . We need to talk about institutional investors, auditors, and analysts," he said, and started running through the particular agendas of each group.

O'Neill had had enough.

"We need CEOs to certify financial statements, and that will create a system of internal controls," he said—an idea whose clarity, coming from the only one in the room who'd ever run a large company, cut off a host of escape routes. Then he went a step further. The key, as with so much else, was creating a process of constant improvement. You could do that only by setting a standard of "best practice" and then grading how close a firm got to the optimal. This must be added to the architecture of thresholds and sanctions—a path to self-improvement. "Every investor should know, is the company following best practice? Auditors must disclose to a company's audit committee if the company is following best practice, and the committee must certify and disclose if best practice is not being met—and, if not, why not. This gives a context to the standard of negligence, a set of parameters for that discussion. I am going to brief the President in preparation for a speech he's giving in a few weeks. These ideas will be at the centerpiece of that briefing."

O'Neill's tone had the beat of conclusion. It was his committee, after all, and he and Greenspan—who had done the most analysis—were clearly together. Everyone nodded. Everyone except Larry Lindsey.

"There's always the option of doing nothing," Lindsey said with the breezy free enterpriser's faith in the self-correcting powers of the markets. "Should we change incentives? Listen, the markets are moving ahead. They are already discounting the stocks of companies that show accounting irregularities." Others in the room were dumbstruck. It was as though Lindsey had been sitting in another room; as though he paid no mind to the course charted by O'Neill, or to Greenspan, who, after fifty years studying American business, had spoken with daunting fervor.

"We have to be concerned with the law of unintended consequences," Lindsey continued. "Better incentives for better behavior by CEOs can, I think, be achieved in the existing framework."

Midway through this monologue, O'Neill took out his pad and began to write. A moment later, he cut Lindsey off. "An outline for my brief to the President starts with this: 'The financial system depends on transparency and on investors having information they need to make informed decisions. What is needed is a new standard of disclosure, a higher standard to which a CEO must certify.' "

"It's important that we use the existing authority of the SEC," Pitt said—a last word on his key issue.

"This is an important opportunity to lock in these higher standards," O'Neill said firmly. "Maybe the only goddamn chance we'll ever get."

. . .

THREE DAYS LATER, a story ran in *The Wall Street Journal* about O'Neill's position on corporate governance and his desire to lift the standard from recklessness to simple negligence.

It mentioned that Pitt and Hubbard were against the new standard, "concerned that no matter how it was crafted it will lead to more lawsuits."

Mentioned as an internal voice for restraint was Larry Lindsey. "From a historical point of view, when one looks at these periods, there's always too little regulation on the way up, and there's always the temptation to do too much regulation on the way down," he had told the *Journal*. But [the story continued]

> . . . the iconoclastic Mr. O'Neill—a former Alcoa Inc. chairman who has long delighted in chiding fellow CEOs for failing to adhere to his high management standards— appears to revel in the role of corporate scold. He said that when he raises the notion of tougher governance standards with CEOs, "their eyes get real big, which is OK with me." If executives look at the White House reforms and "say, 'oh yeah, piece of cake,' then we probably haven't raised the bar high enough," O'Neill added.

• • •

EARLY THE NEXT MORNING, February 26, O'Neill sent his memo to the President, keeping it to three pages, designed for the President's study habits.

"The challenge," he wrote to Bush, "is to restore a value system of responsibility and accountability oriented toward sustained, long-term growth, not short-term market gain."

After describing what he called "required reforms"—such as realigning corporate disclosure practices with the long-term needs of investors; enforcing and expanding the duties of corporate leaders and auditors without inviting frivolous lawsuits; ensuring auditor independence and the creation of sensible accounting rules—he wrote that there was consensus in the working group that "companies must enable their investors to view the same picture management sees."

It was in the next category—"still open" issues—that he mentioned the change from recklessness to negligence. "Now," O'Neill implored the President, "may be a once-in-a-generation opportunity to lock in higher standards for corporate disclosure."

The memo, like others he had written, was, O'Neill thought, an honest broker memo. Especially in this case—as chairman of the working group—he wanted to show how an honest broker might operate. As he had written those even-handed paragraphs, he wondered if he should be more strident and polemical—do what Greenspan seemed to suggest: persuade the President with an airtight case.

Instead, O'Neill included a section about how a raised standard of care could invite frivolous litigation. The way to address that possibility, he added, was to limit enforcement of the negligence standard to the SEC and prohibit private actions arising from the new standard.

· · ·

A WARM ATLANTIC BREEZE blew through the open lobby windows of the Ritz-Carlton on Amelia Island, Florida—about thirty miles northeast of Jacksonville on the beach—as O'Neill and Michele Davis arrived at midday on February 26.

Now, the very day he had sent his memo to Bush, O'Neill would get a chance to road-test some of what he'd suggested to the President. The luncheon speech at the hotel was to the Financial Services Forum, a high-powered group of the heads of the country's twenty-one largest financial services companies.

Waiting for him in the Mayport Room was Phil Purcell, chairman and CEO of Morgan Stanley. "Thanks for coming all this way for lunch in the lion's den," Purcell quipped.

"I guess I'm the entrée," said O'Neill. "I think it's now or never on corporate governance, on raising the standard for the CEO."

Purcell, an avuncular Notre Dame grad who had run Dean

Witter Discover before moving to Morgan in 1997, leaned in sympathetically. "It just may be a tough sell with a lot of chiefs. They're already feeling pretty banged up by the economy. And I'm sure they'll be calling the White House."

A few minutes later, at an enormous round table of lunching financial executives, O'Neill ran through issues from 9/11 and the repair of Wall Street to the economy to foreign aid to, finally, corporate governance.

He laid out the case for high standards. "Simply knowing what's going on in your company—and being responsible for it—is a standard no one in this room would have any trouble meeting. It would not even be an issue for most CEOs."

The story in the previous day's *Wall Street Journal* had telegraphed the issue to everyone in this room of religious *Journal* readers. In this case, forewarned meant forearmed.

Comments were almost universally negative. Lindsey's point about the self-corrections already occurring in the market—the short-selling of stocks in companies that had had regulatory or accounting problems—was a favorite response.

"The discounting of those companies is an issue now, at a time of historic scandals, but it'll pass. It'll be business as usual before you know it," O'Neill said. "What we're looking for is a way to create lasting change." Many of the CEOs seemed to have consulted already with their chief counsels. The one thing they didn't want was even the slightest uptick in litigation.

The discussion roiled for half an hour, until a financial services CEO, sitting about six feet from O'Neill, said emphatically, "I would resign rather than be expected to know everything that's going on in my company. It's just not tenable. That's what I have a board for, that's what I have a chief financial officer for. I simply can't be held responsible for what all of those people do."

O'Neill said little in response. He thanked the executive for his opinion. In any event, it was time to head off for a town meeting with customs officials at the Naval Air Station in Jacksonville.

As he speed-walked through the lobby of the Ritz-Carlton, Michele Davis trotted up next to him.

"I can't believe that guy said that. That he'd rather resign than be held responsible for what's going on," she said.

"God knows," O'Neill said, "I wouldn't invest in that guy's company."

. . .

THE NEXT MORNING, as his plane approached Washington and angled toward Andrews Air Force Base, O'Neill thought about the negative reactions of the CEOs in Florida. He was sure executives from far and wide were calling the White House. It would take courage for the President to stand up to them. Many had been major fundraisers for the 2000 campaign. If they had their druthers, they'd prefer no regulation of the sovereign CEO.

He thought about the steel meeting of two weeks before and of Mitch Daniels's blurted comment. Corporate governance, like steel, was an issue where special interests were armed and ready, where there would be pressure to collect transitory political capital. But if you can't do the right thing, and just forget, for a moment, about those calculations, when you're at 85 percent, then when *can* you do the right thing? He made a note to call Mitch and thank him for speaking so forthrightly.

Across town, the phones in the West Wing rang. CEO contributors to the Bush campaign were weighing in. The calls were mostly of a single message: "I know O'Neill's supposed to be one of us . . . but rein him in!"

It made for a dilemma for the White House *strategery* team, meaning Karl Rove and the political operatives. In the late winter and early spring of 2002, as the scandals broke, Rove told numerous administration officials that the poll data was definitive: the scandals were hurting the President, a cloud in an otherwise blue sky for the soaring, post-Afghanistan Bush. What worried Rove was that anger about Enron and other corporate miscreants tapped into sub-merged doubts about Bush and Harken Energy, Cheney and Hal-liburton. The question was, what to do? When Bush had placed O'Neill atop his own committee on such an important issue, the President was unconcerned about downside, political risks. What-ever his uncompromising Treasury Secretary presented, he could push through.

What he hadn't expected was so many angry CEOs writing and calling the White House. "The base" was upset.

. . .

ON FEBRUARY 28, the Commerce Department reported its prelim-inary estimate that GDP grew at a healthy 1.4 percent in the fourth quarter of 2001.

Inside the Treasury Department, O'Neill and his assistant secre-tary, Richard Clarida, celebrated.

Their joy was not simply a reflection of general good cheer about the resilience of the U.S. economy. For the past four months, Clar-ida had been heading up a task force to do something that neither Treasury nor any other department in the U.S. government had ever done: collect—and almost instantly assess—real-time data about the country's economy.

After 9/11, when O'Neill found himself talking to credit card companies about charge volume and to automakers about order books, an idea had taken shape. "I had always been frustrated by how slow the government was at collecting and analyzing economic data. That's why Alan and I were always looking for the fresh stuff—indicators that showed the present and helped guide your analysis toward what the next few weeks, let's say, might look like," O'Neill said. "So, I put Clarida in charge of an effort to find key indices of real-time data and analyze what the data really meant."

The initiative had been born of frustration as much as anything.

At the Monday economic lunches throughout the year, O'Neill had often found himself at odds with Lindsey's bleak prognosis for the U.S. economy. "I thought it was a self-interested opinion, not backed up by the facts," O'Neill said. "Larry wanted tax cuts—deep, continuing tax cuts—and he was marshaling arguments to support that ideology. Obviously, he never marshaled much in the way of evidence."

In a meeting of the economic team in late September 2001, Lindsey—certain that the economy would now sink badly—had advocated a $150 billion annual tax cut to provide a stimulus. Rather than chiding Lindsey for his lack of evidence, O'Neill decided to collect his own. The next day, this became a full-time job for Clarida, a widely respected professor from Columbia who had served a stint under President Reagan.

The real-time system offered weekly reports on economic activity using an analytical process that gathered data from thirty separate categories. The analysis, in essence, showed the economy's trajectory. Part of what it offered was a reckoning of GDP *week to week*, rather than a three-month amalgam released a few weeks *after* each quarter's end by the Commerce Department.

By early December, the real-time data team was ready to make its first estimate of GDP. It would measure fourth-quarter GDP several weeks before the quarter even ended. The figure: 1.1 percent growth, a healthy rate considering the shocks the economy clearly suffered in the month after 9/11. At that point, leading private forecasts varied between a GDP increase of 0.6 percent and a loss of 2.5 percent.

The post-9/11 stimulus package, meanwhile, floated in and then out of favor through the winter. It was simply not clear that the economy had received a consequential blow from the terrorist attack and that it needed a boost. The uncertainty about something that would otherwise have been generally agreed on was, in some part, due to the way O'Neill relied on his real-time data to offer in speeches, interviews, and congressional testimony a counterweight to anecdotal evidence and the fearful prognostications that flowed from it. In his frequent visits to the Hill, O'Neill said repeatedly, "It may not be as bad as you think," and cited some metrics plucked from the real-time pile, such as that day's inventories of autos.

Treasury's efforts helped block passage of a grab bag of proposals, many proffered by Lindsey, that emerged after 9/11. At the growth rate of 1.1 percent predicted by Treasury's model, a much smaller stimulus package would be appropriate as a post-9/11 insurance policy of sorts.

When the Commerce Department released its preliminary fourth-quarter GDP tally of 1.4 percent on February 28, the markets soared; analysts everywhere registered surprise, and the news line for days noted the amazing resiliency of the U.S. economy. Among those shocked were Larry Lindsey and Glenn Hubbard. The loquacious Lindsey said little about the matter to O'Neill—not wanting to give any ground to his foe—while Hubbard, when all three were together, quietly acknowledged Treasury's victory. O'Neill felt he had constructed an analytical tool to help discern reality.

The next day, O'Neill saw an interoffice envelope from Hubbard marked *Personal* on his desk. He opened it and pulled out a handwritten note on a piece of copy paper.

My math on 2001: Q4 is –1.1%.
Officially eating crow.
Glenn

O'Neill turned over the paper and wrote on the back "For framing."

. . .

ON MARCH 5, the President announced he would impose tariffs of up to 30 percent on imported steel in an effort to shore up the long-declining industry. Steel executives praised the President and said that the tariffs might save jobs. Free trade advocates, meanwhile, wondered how other countries would respond and what the effect would be on the cost of a wide array of goods.

On March 6, the GOP House leadership scaled back its plan for large corporate tax cuts in order to win over Senate Democrats. The so-called post-9/11 stimulus package, which included a $43 billion annual cut in business taxes and $8.5 billion in unemployment benefits, was signed into law by the President a few days later. It was roughly one-third the size of a package that Lindsey and other tax cut enthusiasts had been proffering since the previous fall.

On March 7, the President gave a speech at the presentation of the Malcolm Baldrige Awards about corporate responsibility. He unveiled a ten-point program that included just a few key elements of the ideas O'Neill and Greenspan had championed.

A CEO would have to sign his firm's annual financial statement—a personal certification of its accuracy—though it was left unclear what the penalties would be for signing an inaccurate or misleading statement.

If serious corporate misconduct was discovered and legally proven, there should be disgorgement of assets, such as executive bonuses, the President recommended. When officers buy or sell stock, they should report the transaction within two days, rather than the current standard of forty-five days. The rest of Bush's ten points concerned mainly smaller, technical matters. Nine of the ten needed no legislative approval, and many of them were part of an array of initiatives that were already being worked on by Pitt and his staff. That, of course, is the largely nonpublic realm of SEC rule-making, an arcane realm where Pitt—who rarely took public stances on principle the way his predecessor Arthur Levitt had—could be locked in endless discussion with countless lobbyists.

The move from recklessness to negligence was dropped for fear it would invite a wave of lawsuits. Adoption of a best practices standard for accountants and auditors, with publicly available ratings of how companies measure up, was also dropped. There was no change in the reliance on GAAP, as Greenspan had hoped there would be.

Corporate executives, and various lobbying groups that represent them, praised the ten points for not creating any new avenues for litigation.

O'Neill and Greenspan were discouraged.

"A single issue for the corporate crowd—fear of lawsuits—carried the day," O'Neill said, his outrage boiling over. "If people do the right thing, there's no basis for any lawsuit. How the hell can anyone bring a lawsuit unless there's proof or a very clear suspicion of intentional wrongdoing? How the hell could you get in trouble certifying it? All you've got to do is *do the right thing*. And if it's muddy, you go to the SEC and say, 'This is a muddy issue. How do I do it correctly?' The answer, at its core, is very straightforward. It's about building a constituency for doing the right thing. The problem is that it takes real leadership."

CHAPTER 7

A REAL CULT FOLLOWING

O'NEILL HAD A MIGRAINE in Ghana.
A real brain splitter, with pounding temples—his eyeballs bouncing on each thump. He gets one of these every
year or so and lies down for an hour.

But down time was not on the schedule for this morning. The
Treasury Secretary was drum major to a parade of sweaty corre-
spondents from *The New York Times, The Wall Street Journal, The
Washington Post, The Economist, Time, Newsweek, Rolling Stone,* and
plenty of others, ducking with their pads between turreting lenses
from CNN, ABC, BBC, MTV—yes, MTV—and a dozen grim,
brusque Secret Service agents, some walking their first jumpy steps
onto a suspect continent. And those were just the folks in tight—
clustered ahead of Nancy; Paul's daughter Julie Kloo; White House
media guru Mark McKinnon; the U.S. ambassador; Treasury aides;
representatives of NGOs . . . and Bono.

"Where's Bono?"

"I'm back here, Paul."

And then the nimble rock star/AIDS activist and FM Gandhi

wove up to O'Neill's side, where he was staying for better or for worse . . . and, God knows, it could have gone either way.

This, after all, was roiling, restless Africa, and O'Neill and Bono were all but strangers to each other. They'd spent only two hours to-gether—most of it in an encounter during the previous summer, 2001—when Bono had to audition at a pre-meeting with chief of staff Tim Adams before being granted a fifteen-minute audience with O'Neill. It ran past an hour. Bono was serious, knew his stuff about AIDS and debt relief and the World Bank, surprising O'Neill, who incidentally has a collection of leather jackets and soft rock CDs impressive for a man who remembers Franklin Roosevelt. And, yes, he'd heard of U2. They had seen each other again at the World Eco-nomic Forum in New York in February, where Bono was impressed by O'Neill's talk of the perfidy of currency traders and international financiers who profit from the woes of developing countries. All of that was fine and good, it was a start: a Washington-style meeting of common purpose and a few shared ideas.

. . .

BUT, NOW, it would be ten days of performance art with a world-wide hookup.

"*Dating Game* meets *Survivor*"—that was what Aufhauser had dubbed the trip a few weeks before, and it stuck—the Odd Couple on Safari, Felix and Oscar Hit the Savanna, with support staff.

The White House was modestly intrigued by the idea—they'd given up trying to manage O'Neill, anyway—but seriously con-cerned. Themes needed to be set and adhered to.

"We propose that the trip focus on countries that have made sub-stantial commitments to promoting market-led growth and living standards," stated a memo to O'Neill from his undersecretary for international affairs, John Taylor. "Your trip will highlight progress and encourage them [the countries visited] to continue to be models for the region." In March the President had proposed the creation of a Millennium Challenge Account, a new foreign aid program that would favor a select group of low-income countries committed to sound development policies, rewarding good behavior with aid. There was a pile of briefings on Africa that O'Neill read before boarding the plane—memos on global development policy, AIDS transmission, and, care of Powell, the geopolitical landscape, to supplement O'Neill's long-standing belief—often expressed to vigorous nods from Bush—that "we don't really know, in a straight-line way, how to encourage or support development in other countries."

In this area O'Neill had been trying to rethink the *hows*. His "tough love" posture on debt in Argentina and then Brazil—where the international financial institutions, with U.S. support, had granted loans—seemed to have created a good cop/bad cop balance in the ensuing months. If O'Neill—or the threat of O'Neill—was the stick, that was fine. By spring of 2002, Argentina was showing signs of fiscal discipline, looking a bit more seaworthy. O'Neill matched that twist with an unexpected stance, which was drawing surprising international support, that countries should be permitted to reorganize their debt in crisis—a kind of bankruptcy protection for countries heading toward fiscal disaster that would keep creditors and financial institutions at bay while debts were restructured.

Ann Krueger, the progressive number two at the IMF, and O'Neill had become something of an odd couple as well, trumpeting the virtues of extending to troubled nations the same reasonable protections that multinationals enjoy in Chapter 11. Banks and investment houses hated the idea, saying they wouldn't extend credit to the developing nations of Africa, Asia, and South America if those countries were protected from creditors. O'Neill's response was that over the past decade their investments had been risk-free, because they knew the U.S. Treasury would bail them out in a crisis.

Bono, who had worked for months, virtually unnoticed, at an AIDS orphanage in Africa and regularly whistle-stopped Capitol Hill calling for the forgiving of Third World debts, saw O'Neill as an exciting mishap: a supremely successful man, now with genuine power, who liked to collect unfiltered, down-to-the-ground observations and act on them.

So, a dare had been proffered at the end of that first, long meeting in the summer of 2001: If you want U.S. money to flow to Africa, O'Neill said, take me to the green hills and show me what works. Bono, in his blue wraparound shades, smiled. Let's set a date.

• • •

"WE NEED HELP. We need help. We need help!" The large African woman waved wigs—one in each hand—in O'Neill's face and started supplicating about capital to build a wig factory and how she "just received a fax yesterday from Atlanta, in Georgia—yeah!—but, only, we need money. I have to build a factory, but I don't have money. . . ."

O'Neill tried to fix his gaze through the timpani throbs of his temples. "Ummm. How much do you need to build it?"

"The factory?" The woman had wigs on her fingertips, but no figures. "I have to sit down to make an estimate." She shrugged and—having failed the crucial "How much?" question—upped the volume. "We need investors! We need investors!"

O'Neill nodded, turned away, and felt as if his head would explode.

Nearby, Bono took up the slack. "People are jumping up and down—they're glad to see the United States here. But I'm telling you this. If this country doesn't get help, doesn't get a sense of a new beginning . . . you come back here in five years, and they'll be throwing rocks at our van."

It was May 22 in Ghana, near the start of the trip, and the surf of people and cameras and noise seemed to carry them forward, on through the winding, dusty streets of Tamale—a city of about three hundred thousand in Ghana's impoverished northern plain—at a steady clip. O'Neill had to do little but nod earnestly or just look in the right direction. Here he was a symbol of U.S. power and possibility and cash, accentuated by a hint of improvisation. His partner, after all, was a rock star internationalist. His President didn't seem to have set particularly clear parameters as to intentions. And he, a slightly dazed, white-haired man in a blue open-neck shirt, was known to be unpredictable. In all, an interesting mix.

Which is why the cameras stayed poised as the sun rose high overhead and O'Neill lifted children and talked to a lady who ran a cooking oil distributorship—"How do you fund purchase of inventory?"—and held in his hand small, warty tomatoes the size of golf balls.

The migraine started to vanish only when his head became otherwise engaged. He began firing questions at the entourage: What are the figures on economic development? How much money is entering the country from NGOs? What does health care look like?

Then he stopped and looked at the pitiful, warty tomatoes in his hand.

"How much of the country has clean, potable water?" he asked.

"About half," the development official said.

O'Neill looked hard at him.

"Half? Jesus, that mystifies me. Only half the population has clean water? Without good water, people get sick, crops don't grow . . . you can't get started *developing* anything."

And then he began walking faster and talking, unfettered, in full paragraphs, about deeper issues of "what we can do as a country to help, really help."

At a meeting at a vocational center, Bono spoke bleakly about institutions, such as the IMF, which trade money for controlling "how these people run their economy . . . and that's why the anger is there." O'Neill responded: "We can create the basis for real change . . . the potential is there, the potential exists here for a much more productive society that has much better enjoyment of life and life's conditions." Which of them was hopeful? Who was bleak? Who was dreaming? Who was pragmatic? The script notes started to blur.

Meanwhile, reporters scribbled, nosing about for the tension beneath the repartee. Bono made no secret of the fact that he was looking to convince O'Neill that more money should be committed to sub-Saharan Africa—a region with the world's worst poverty and 70 percent of its AIDS victims. The United States annually devoted $10 billion to foreign aid—a total Bush had promised to increase by 50 percent with his Millennium Challenge Account. But that amount, the largest of any country, was still just 0.1 percent of America's GDP, the lowest percentage among the twenty or so richest nations that make up the Organization for Economic Cooperation and Development.

Bono wanted the U.S. percentage to rise—the average was just over 0.2 percent for wealthy nations, still short of a UN-set goal of 0.7 percent—while O'Neill was preaching his now familiar sermon about value: the desire to see results from foreign aid spending, something the United States had failed to do, he asserted, for hundreds of billions it had spent over decades. The UN goal was arbitrary, he said, meaningless, and daunting problems were solvable with resources already available, if someone thought for five minutes about how the dollars could be better spent. Of course, there were people who'd spent more than five minutes on the subject matter—

namely, the foreign aid community of myriad NGOs and program-
matic altruists—but O'Neill had felt those groups had been shielded
from hard questions about how money is spent and how progress
is measured. He was looking for value; he was a strange CEO/policy
wonk hybrid with a proven track record of calling things by their
proper names and cutting through excuses, so let him look.

But then human value—the divine value of each blessed and beleaguered African—started to intrude on O'Neill's calculus. The parade squeezed into the narrow halls of a regional hospital: 380 beds
in an unsanitary, crumbling sprawl that supported itself, and turned
no one away, on $200,000 a year.

"Did you hear that? Two hundred thousand a year!" O'Neill said.

"Okay, right," Bono said, nonplussed. O'Neill didn't notice. He
was factoring how fast *one patient* could run up that total in a Washington hospital. "What's your biggest problem?" he asked the doctors. They huddled. Unsanitary water, lack of medications, but the
worst was electricity. Power would quit during surgeries. Patients
would die on the operating table. They needed a backup generator.

"Good God, the disparities are overwhelming," O'Neill said.
"Just mind-boggling."

The observations were coming too fast. He fell back on his
mantras—every problem is solvable, push past excuses, embrace lim-
itless potential—but they were under siege, the truisms, overcome
by the scale, by the eyes, so many eyes, and the faces of the children.
Bedridden people looked up through the buzzing flies and smiled.

How can they be smiling? he thought.

Come on, Bono said gently, let's get some air.

Outside, O'Neill ate a piece of fried dough from a street vendor,
a hard little item, and said, to no one in particular, that "the President ate one of these pretzels . . ." He thought of Bush choking on
one, and then how shut off he was from unscripted experience, his
circle of White House advisers closed ever more tightly around him.

"I thought of how wonderful it would be for him to walk these streets, how much he could learn—how much he could grow. How good that growth could be for so many people."

. . .

JUST BEFORE HE HAD BOARDED the plane for Africa, O'Neill had received a letter from "41," a thank-you note. He'd received a few of these over the past sixteen months for this and that. It was like the old man was egging him on, saying, Go speak truth to my boy, O'Neill felt, broaden the kid's horizons, keep him thinking big.

This note concerned a speech O'Neill had given in Washington at a conference on globalization sponsored by the George Bush School for International Relations, a part of Texas A&M. O'Neill ended his address with a plea for fearless engagement, saying that "the world economic pie is limited only by our imagination—when we back up our imagination with the necessary social institutions and structures, and human beings and resources are organized to create value. This is an exciting time for those of us who relish the challenge of unleashing human potential around the world. . . . We can create vibrant, self-sustaining local economies and a rising standard of living for people everywhere. We can unleash the human potential—and we will not be satisfied with anything less."

Bush Senior wrote that the conference was wildly successful and "you were the key reason for its success. Many thanks for giving the keynote speech and giving such a good one." Then he invited O'Neill down to Texas.

O'Neill saved the note—as he saved almost everything—and was thinking about it as he gave Bono a pretzel and looked down at the red African dust on his Johnston & Murphy wingtips. The former President Bush loved this sort of thing—mixing in with people in

China, Russia, the Mideast, seeing what they thought and why, picking up keepsakes, sending notes to keep in touch. His eldest son seemed to move in the opposite direction on this score, as on so many others, trying to differentiate himself from Poppy. And that, O'Neill thought, was a shame at a moment like this, with the world on edge and so many people in need. "The war of ideas you win on the ground, walking with the people," he said later, "not with pronouncements from on high looking down." But it was something he himself could help correct over the next few days. The first step, he recalled from his Alcoa days, is to show them you care—and the key to that is *you actually have to care*.

And you do it with water and electricity. The prerequisites of civilization. The United States would step up—make it happen. And do it without strings attached. It would be the start of a new conversation.

The sun was beginning to set behind thatched roofs of the mud huts in impoverished Wamill Village, in Tamale. The afternoon heat had passed, and a choir, dressed in vivid blues and reds, began to sing a song for the occasion. In Africa, songs catch quickly. In an instant, everyone was clapping in rhythm, hundreds of clappers, crowding close to the visitors. Come, the song beckoned, be African. There was a lightness everywhere, a buoyancy. The local tribal chief approached O'Neill and Bono with two long robes and floppy caps. These are ceremonial, worn by those of sacred purpose, he explained. For holy men. "Would you accept from our people the honor of wearing these?"

They were each handed the garments. O'Neill looked at Bono. "If we put this stuff on, this is the picture that will be transmitted across the world—you know that."

"Well, we came to Africa," Bono said sympathetically, "but, God knows, you shouldn't do anything you don't want to do, that's not smart to do."

They both looked up, and a hundred pairs of eyes looked back.

O'Neill looked off for a moment, then bent in close. "What's most important are these people here, and that they know you and I think they are really valued. . . ." Then he started to slip into the robe. And Bono laughed. And O'Neill laughed. "You're now a tribal chief," Bono said, "or a chief's best friend."

"So what if we never live this down," O'Neill said.

Bono's robe fitted; O'Neill's was a few sizes small, and his hat, too, but the singer knew from years onstage how to take a deep breath and seize such moments. With the robe on, he carefully put on his hat—a floppy stocking cap, like the one Ebenezer Scrooge wore to bed—and then, with the flair of a superhero donning his mask, placed his trademark wraparound blue shades back on the bridge of his nose. The crowd hooted as the singer folded his arms up high and beamed—with a nod—like a chief.

O'Neill, his hat flipped forward, giving him the look of a Dr. Seuss character, watched it all with admiration. He put his arm on the singer's shoulder. "Come on, let's step up for a picture." A photo flashed worldwide of the rock star and the leading financial official of the world's greatest power, wearing hats that speak of honor to Africans and of comedy to much of the rest of the world.

. . .

THE DAYS MOVED ON in a swirl of ups and downs, a fever dream in broad daylight. The plan was to leap across South Africa, Uganda, and Ethiopia in eight days, with each country's itinerary having a similar progression—day one, meeting with president, senior ministers, and relief organizations; day two, walk with the people.

After a day spent in government chambers in Pretoria, South Africa, meetings for which O'Neill had even less patience than usual, they arrived on the morning of May 24 in the slums of Soweto, the country's seething doppelgänger to sleek Johannesburg.

O'Neill was glad to be on the ground, collecting fresh data. Bono, for his part, appreciated the access to leaders and presidents and how easily O'Neill worked the big mahogany tables. But he knew that progress, if it was to be made, would happen in the slums, where O'Neill's heart could be engaged. His head, and all that value-added analysis, would follow.

The first stop, though, was a Ford plant on the outskirts of town, where they were carted about and surveyed assembly lines. O'Neill, in full power suit regalia, blue pinstripes, starched white shirt, and red tie, was looking at levels of mechanization, quality-control procedures, and workplace safety to determine whether the plant was at the first rung of global competitiveness. He could do this in his sleep. But it was part of a life that was receding further by the hour.

Disparities awaited. The entourage left the spotless factory floor for the urban core of Soweto and the Chris Hani Baragwanath Hospital, an AIDS clinic for mothers and their babies. Here, mothers were treated with nevirapine, an AIDS drug that could prolong a woman's life and, if she could afford it, that of her baby.

There are as many as 30 million Africans infected with HIV, and anyone in this building would be considered fortunate. They had traded disclosure of their illness, and the stigma it brought, for life-saving medication. It would seem a reasonable transaction, but one that surprisingly few women embrace, with the grip of suspicion still so strong.

The two talked to a mother who had got the nevirapine to her baby, who does not have HIV, but couldn't afford it for herself. The problem: She couldn't risk breast-feeding her daughter, nor could she tell anyone of her plight, so she sneaked over to the clinic a few times a day to feed her baby from a bottle, another taboo. O'Neill listened, not sure what remedy he could offer. Then his daughter, Julie Kloo, asked the woman if her father could hold the baby. She knew he loved babies.

A moment later, the little girl snuggled against O'Neill's lapel and he kissed her pink cap. He wouldn't let go of the baby. As they walked on, he held her, like a talisman. One baby saved.

Outside, they held a press conference. Bono talked about the stigma against HIV, about the courage of the women in the hospital, many of whom had come out in their communities, but could afford the nevirapine to save only their babies, not themselves. "I'm dumbfounded by a world that says that's okay."

O'Neill started to dig in. His head was following up the "digging in," as Bono had hoped. He took the microphone and said that he'd just inquired about how much NGO money came to this city each year. That he'd been told $50 million, and that he'd done some calculations, multiplying the number of those infected by the $1.50-a-day cost, for a total of $2 million. "The obvious question is, if fifty million dollars is coming in, why are not all the women getting treatment?"

Bono grabbed the mike back, all smiles, and talked about O'Neill's "insatiable curiosity for statistics and data" and that "he will get to the bottom of how, the best way, American tax dollars can be spent here." The bond was sealed. The day unfolded like an opera, with singing, more singing, in this case along with dancing, by a youth troupe, to Bono's lyrics: "I have climbed the highest mountains / I have run through the fields / Only to be with you / Only to be with you . . . But I still haven't found what I'm looking for."

George Stephanopoulos from ABC showed up to interview them for the Sunday show *This Week*, and the three huddled in the street as O'Neill, burning with activist passion and punching the air, cited the $2 million for the nevirapine and roared, "We shouldn't accept bureaucratic mumbo jumbo that we can't reprogram the money, we need to use it for prevention. It's a question of people living or dying, and we should not let that happen!" Stephanopoulos stayed with him for a moment, nodding—yes, yes—until a look, a squinting, world-wise skepticism common to journalists, crossed his gaze, that there's nothing new under the sun, and any passion this acute must be reviewed with a cold eye.

Some reporters attacked O'Neill for offering insupportable, or at least unstudied, recommendations for Africa's vast problems, while others, like *The Washington Post*'s Paul Blustein, wrote that "as the trip progresses," it seems possible that something "momentous may result, perhaps an alliance between liberals and conservatives to launch a fresh assault on global poverty using less softheaded approaches than in the past."

The actor Chris Tucker joined the tour as it raced onward to Uganda, toured more slums, and looked at a water-well project in a village near the capital, Kampala. O'Neill's interest in water had been growing since Ghana. This project was dear to Bono's heart: a well dug with $1,000 made available after foreign investors had forgiven much of Uganda's debt. The tap—just a pipe emerging from a bunker of concrete that kept it from attracting animals—served 420 people, and their health had improved. Disease carried by water is one of the great treacheries in developing countries, where 1.5 million children die each year from diarrhea alone. Someone mentioned a local belief that a snake controlled the area's water, that disturbing the supply could result in a snakebite or induce the snake to redirect the flow. Yet the well had been built and no snake had appeared. Superstition, O'Neill said, giving way to progress. But the distances were vast, and as in Ghana, half of Uganda's people had no clean water.

Two days later, O'Neill and Bono sat with Ugandan president

Yoweri Museveni and his staff in a stately white building in Kampala. A warm wind blew through tall open windows as O'Neill described his impressions and Museveni affirmed that, yes, the problems in Uganda were profound. Then the talk turned to water.

O'Neill had been asking questions for a week. In Ghana, he had done some calculations. A good, working well could serve one thousand people, and well digging was priced by each foot dug. Using data on the depth of Ghana's water table, he estimated that the 10 million Ghanaians without clean water—about half the population—could be supplied potable, well-drawn water for $25 million. Ghana's president was delighted and wondered when and how such a project could start.

Now, after a week of seeing hospitals without clean water, stunted crops, and the ravages of waterborne diseases, O'Neill was armed for Uganda, with a population of 24 million. Uganda's water table is even higher than Ghana's—easier and cheaper to drill. He laid it out, with gusto, for Museveni—as if he were offering a gift. All of Uganda with clean water for $25 million.

One of Museveni's aides interjected. Oh yes, they had already done a study of the matter. "It will cost many times your price," he said. O'Neill asked if he had the study. After a moment, it was produced. As Bono and Museveni chatted, O'Neill flipped pages. It had been done by a U.S. consulting firm. It recommended a complex array of treatment plants and heavy metal pipelines. Total cost: $2 billion.

"President Museveni," O'Neill said, shaking his head, "this is recommending you build a water system like in Detroit or Cleveland. You won't need that for a hundred years. You just need to drop wells, and mostly maintain them. Your people can handle the rest. We can do this quickly, maybe a year or two."

. . .

MAY 30 in Ethiopia. One day left. They'd dropped in on an epicenter of crisis. Poverty and neglect had long ago found homes in Africa. What had changed things was the arrival of the plague. The trip would end with a tour of the shadowland: the HIV/AIDS Hospice and Orphanage run by the Sisters of Charity in Addis Ababa.

No cameras in here. Not appropriate. But others came, the reporters, the NGO people, the deputies from Treasury. They walked among the beds—rooms filled with the suffering. O'Neill was quiet. Bono was quiet. All the ravages of earthly hell were on display.

Some rooms were off-limits, and the doctors rushed the entourage by—tuberculosis, highly contagious. And others were just quiet, as people waited for the inevitable, holding on. Then came the room of children with HIV, many of them orphans. They were not quiet. They were kids. They laughed. And ran about, if they could.

A toddler, a little girl, maybe two, hugged O'Neill's leg, and he picked her up and held her as they walked. The child was in a tiny white gown, and he kissed her head, his eyes welling up. "She's so beautiful," he whispered to Nancy, now by his side. And of course, she would die soon. But how could anything so lovely vanish without a trace, as though it had never been?

The entourage was quiet, respectful. This was what they had come for, they knew it now—so that a man who could make a difference would hold a dying baby.

A room was prepared by the sisters, a place where the visitors could sit. During the respite, adults at the hospice, all with HIV, told their stories and sang songs of hope. Paul and Nancy were in the front row, Bono beside them. A radiant young woman named Agnes spoke about a husband who wouldn't tell her he had AIDS, even in the moments before his death; how she discovered she was infected, and told her son, then an eleven-year-old, who ran, wild-eyed, from their house, never to be seen again; and how she had a younger son, for whom she'd prepared a book. She had the book in her hand and offered it to Nancy. Agnes flipped the pages. It was simple, a drawing of her and her husband and some words about when they were together as a family. "This," she whispered, "is so my son will remember us," and Nancy began to weep, and couldn't stop, and Paul did as well as he rubbed her back.

This, of course, is why leaders, people in power, don't spend too much time in dank hospitals and shantytowns. Quick media events are recommended. Seasoned handlers know prolonged exposure can be perilous to certainty. A person could lose his head, forget what's expected of him.

. . .

O'NEILL WALKED into Condoleezza Rice's office on the ground floor of the West Wing at 11 a.m. on June 3, with his chief of staff, Tim Adams.

Rice remarked about how good he looked. "Never better," O'Neill said. He was tan from his ten days in Africa, fit and buoyant. "I should go more often."

He liked Rice and trusted her. She was clearly doing her best to be an honest broker in foreign affairs—a role desperately needed in economic affairs and domestic policy. O'Neill was afire with purpose. He talked of HIV and hunger and moments on the trip that echoed still. He spoke about water.

"We can focus on this and show real results, and that really can help the people of Africa." Rice nodded; she knew about O'Neill's water mission. It had been in several newspaper stories. And on ABC's *This Week*, when George Stephanopoulos had asked O'Neill and Bono: "What can the U.S. government do?" O'Neill responded: "We can insist that our aid money go for tangible results in creating wells and the distribution of water."

Rice had been surprised by that—they'd talked only in passing about water before O'Neill left. But, when Stephanopoulos pressed O'Neill about how he would know whether the trip was a success, O'Neill was emphatic and *specific*: "I think we'll know if we can show quickly and—and in significant magnitude in the next three years, for example, that HIV-positive women are getting treatment in massive numbers and that people are getting clean water. These are tangible, real things, and we should be able to do it in two or three years' time."

This was a breach of message-control protocol in this White House: extemporaneous speech with commitments attached, even if they were modest, nonbinding commitments. Of course, those unmanageable qualities were crucial to the level of media coverage, which had surprised the White House, including the President. The coverage, reaching even the elusive young viewers of MTV, was virtually all favorable, notwithstanding some snide asides by Wall Streeters about the funny hat photo—"How could the markets have confidence in a guy who places himself in that position?"—joined by far right conservatives and, as always, those on Larry Lindsey's call list.

Rice witnessed O'Neill's passion, heard his argument about the positive effects of U.S. engagement on this fundamental issue, and was noncommittal. He might be right, but he was dangerously autonomous—in this case creating a media event with a sort of edgy, anything-might-happen appeal that had few, if any, precedents for a cabinet secretary. She knew the President might not like that.

The next day, O'Neill met with Powell at the State Department, and it was much of the same. He ran though the extraordinary ten days and then dove into the water. "If we bring the water, it's something, Colin, we'll be remembered for—and remembered favorably for—long after the two of us are gone. How many things can you say that about?"

Powell laughed. "You certainly can stir things up, Paul, just like always. . . . I think you're really on to something." But Powell said he'd have to think through the geopolitical logistics. A common refrain at State was that fresh water—growing scarce in many parts of the world—would be the oil of the twenty-first century.

As O'Neill remembered it, "At the core, both Condi and Colin said pretty much the same thing. On one hand, if we say we're going to do this within a certain time frame for a certain amount of money, and then we can't deliver, we'll be attacked and ridiculed as not following through. On the other hand, if we do spend $25 million to create a successful demonstration model in, let's say, Ghana—everyone will want wells. Then what will we do?"

Three hours after meeting with Powell, O'Neill went to a meeting of the National Security Council principals about the Persian Gulf in the White House Situation Room. The plans for regime change in Iraq, spoken of during the first week of the administration, were now, seventeen months on, starting to become public.

With growing talk about a possible attack on Iraq, Bush had given an address at West Point on June 1 in which he described a policy of preemption. "If we wait for threats to fully materialize, we will have waited too long," the President said, speaking at the commencement of the 204th graduating class of West Point. "We must take the battle to the enemy, disrupt his plans, and confront the worst threats before they emerge."

Bush, in a saber-rattling address, said, "The only path to safety is action. And this nation will act." In the speech, meant, it seemed, to prepare the nation for war, he did not mention Iraq but warned that rogue states, weak regimes, or terrorist groups "could attain a catastrophic power to strike great nations."

After the NSC meeting O'Neill composed a memo to the President about Africa. He tried to place his insights in a broader context of foreign policy. "We were never going to dissuade countries from building destructive weapons and maybe aligning against us with just threats and force," O'Neill said later. "We needed a nonmilitary side to our foreign policy, where the U.S. could start treating much of the beleaguered developing world—the source of so many of the threats to our security—in a way that showed we valued and respected them. We needed to do some things that showed measurable good—that the U.S. could be a force for good in people's lives."

A lead sentence in his memo to Bush: "How do we better serve the mutual interest of developed and developing countries in promoting global peace, stability, and prosperity?"

He used the document to reassert foreign policy and development standards that he'd mentioned before to the President—such as "enforcing a rule of law, respect for human rights, and fighting corruption"—and, while not specifically calling for added funding, he wrote that the United Nations' goals of cutting illiteracy in half by 2015 and doubling per capita incomes in the poorest countries "are not ambitious enough."

At the bottom of the second page, he highlighted priorities— "areas where our support could make a visible, measurable difference in a short period of time"—starting with a paragraph on "the plague of HIV/AIDS." "The numbers are rising rapidly, with potentially disastrous consequences for life expectancy, future economic growth and the social fabric," he wrote.

After a section on boosting the availability of primary education, he finished with clean water. "This is an area where we should be able to make the greatest difference in the shortest time."

O'Neill then requested that they get together "regarding my ideas for an action agenda" and copied the memo, dated June 6, to Cheney, Powell, Rice, and Card.

. . .

ON THE AFTERNOON of June 10, O'Neill strolled out the westerly entrance of the Treasury Building and across the drive that separated it from its neighbor, the White House.

It was a warm day—there were blossoms everywhere on the Mall—and he felt a growing sense of mission, with the colors of Africa still fresh in his memory. He'd met that morning with Dr. Anthony Fauci, the National Institutes of Health infectious disease expert, who had been called to the White House while O'Neill was making news in Africa, to talk about AIDS. Bush had committed $500 million to AIDS treatment and prevention and suggested that he might want to do something more ambitious.

Or so Dr. Fauci told O'Neill at breakfast. O'Neill suggested that he, and any others in the White House thinking about AIDS, press the President to the "theoretical limits—that means many billions and a program that will really work."

Fauci said that he'd appreciate it if O'Neill—with his regular access to the President—would be a voice for dramatic action. O'Neill said he would and told Fauci about the $2 billion consultant's study—that he was sure he could do the same thing for $25 million—and how "looking for what will work, and work quickly, based on their level of development, is going to be the key to any AIDS intervention. Think outcomes. Quick outcomes. It's an emergency."

O'Neill crossed through the White House's eastern security gate, a folder under his arm with memos on raising the debt limit. That was the brewing controversy that had prompted today's meeting with the President and an array of economic and budget staffers. Over the past six months, the administration had requested that Congress enact a permanent increase of $750 billion in the statutory debt ceiling—the amount of debt that the federal government was legally permitted to hold. That ceiling, $5.95 trillion, needed to be raised to accommodate revenue shortfalls from recession, the 2001 tax bill, and the post-9/11 stimulus bill that had produced steady increases in federal spending, some of it related to 9/11, during the Bush presidency.

The limit had been reached, in fact, on May 16. O'Neill, Daniels, and the White House legislative team had pushed through a stopgap extension to June 28. The government was nearly out of money and couldn't borrow much more. Monthly tax receipts were significantly lower than projections. At some point this summer, obligations to Social Security beneficiaries, government employees, defense contractors, and the like would not be payable. The situation was much like the deadlock in 1995–96 between President Clinton and Speaker Newt Gingrich's Republican House, when brinkmanship led to the government shutting down.

Democrats in Congress saw the issue as gift, a way to highlight how the administration had been fiscally irresponsible.

After finishing his Africa memo, O'Neill had written an extensive strategic memo to Bush, outlining options and responses to the Democrats. He favored a commitment "to protect the full faith and credit of the United States" as a way, he wrote, "to eliminate/postpone the urgency of raising the debt ceiling. Ends defensive administration posture. Decouples debt ceiling from supplemental budget negotiations"—something the Democrats were eagerly doing. That, of course, could invite legal challenges. A second option was to set "a hard deadline of June 28, but prepare to act if Congress does not." That plan, O'Neill wrote, "risks administration credibility if Congress calls this bluff," and it also "disturbs financial markets."

The third option was a replay of 1995: "Set a genuine hard deadline, and commit to a bad outcome if Congress fails to act."

O'Neill counseled against both the second option and this third one, which some in the White House were considering—with support from conservatives in the House who were still smarting from Clinton's artful maneuvers six years earlier. He laid out the argument succinctly:

Pro: Maximizes chances that Congress will pass debt ceiling increase by deadline.

Con: Opens Administration to charges of recklessness with government finances. Congress may also misread us and fail to act—triggering the bad outcomes.

I would counsel against making this ultimatum because the bad outcomes are too serious to contemplate.

O'Neill was preparing to proofread and send this letter to Bush when he received a memo from his assistant secretary for financial markets, Brian Roseboro, laying out strategy and "state of play" for today's big meeting. Before moving into a sharp-edged assessment of "potential conflicts" with the White House and OMB, Roseboro's memo offered this alert:

Key Development. Your draft memo to the President argued for extending the "debt issuance suspension period" to get past June 28. Based on new information, Treasury Legislative Affairs advised last night that if your proposal leaked out to the Hill, it would upset the Administration's legislative stratagem. We thus advise you not to send paper prior to meeting with President.

So O'Neill had his memo tucked under his arm. Obviously, the President wouldn't be reading it. O'Neill was bringing it now as reference, and he was not happy about that. His memos had been leaked before. It seemed to him that his were some of the few memos leaked up to this point in the administration. A year or so back, after the global warming memo to Bush ended up in Paul Gigot's *Wall Street Journal* column, O'Neill had ranted to Michele Davis, "I'll be goddamned if I'm going to stop writing memos to the President because some bastard at the White House is trying to leak me into extinction." So he kept writing them. The President might not read what he sent, but, O'Neill felt, "he should have the opportunity to see coherent thoughts on paper."

What troubled him most about this current incident was that some leaker in the White House would want to get him so badly that they'd "upset the Administration's legislative stratagem."

He cut through the portico beneath the First Family's residence on his way to the Oval Office. He hadn't seen the President since he'd got back from Africa. He wondered if Bush, who often picks out some feature or garment to note in convivial greeting, would notice his tan.

Lindsey, Hubbard, Daniels, Rove, and the political and communications team, the legislative staff, Andy Card, Josh Bolten, and assorted others were already in the crowded office.

Bush was huddled in conversation as people milled about. He saw O'Neill cross the threshold.

"Hey, there, Big O. You know something? You're getting quite a reputation as a truth-teller. You've got yourself a real cult following, don't ya?"

Bush wasn't smiling, and everyone knew not to laugh. It wasn't a joke.

The room got quiet, and people hustled to find seats.

That night, O'Neill left for home on the early side—five forty-five—and was happy to see Nancy at the apartment, preparing dinner.

She poured him a glass of white wine, and one for herself, and sat beside him on the couch.

She was conditioned, after four decades, to expect he'd be home late, so when he arrived before sundown she considered it a treat. They'd been talking a lot about Africa, about what it would be like to adopt some of the kids they'd met there, give them a better life. But it was mostly talk that made them feel young and ready to start again.

"Hey, you okay?"

He mumbled. "Something the President said today . . ."

And he relayed the moment, in full detail.

Of course, she had worried from the start about how he'd fare in the blood sport of Washington, and how he'd get along with Bush. They were so different.

But he knew her feelings—so she moved gingerly. "Are you saying that this is not a good thing?"

"No," O'Neill said. "It's a bad sign."

CHAPTER 8

STICK TO PRINCIPLE

O'NEILL ARRIVED at the Waco Hilton on the night of August 12, musing on how far East Texas is from Ghana. Unfathomably far, he decided. A world, a lifetime, away.

The President's Economic Forum was the next morning. He'd have to get up at 4 a.m. to start his round of interviews with the East Coast–based morning shows. It was barely worth going to bed.

He decided to go for a walk in the night air and wandered past the Texas Ranger Museum and a few fast-food joints before he returned to the hotel to look over his thick dossier: briefing materials for a media event.

For the first time, he wondered if being Treasury Secretary was the best way to spend his time. It had been an awful two months— and this was a low ebb. Nothing had come of his grand plans for Africa, or the sense of moment and high purpose. A story filed from Africa by Paul Blustein in *The Washington Post* had noted, "O'Neill is using words that could haunt the administration if not followed by action, vowing that problems such as the lack of clean water will be addressed promptly."

But no one seemed haunted by anything. Officials at aid or development groups such as Oxfam, or the World Bank, told reporters that the water issues were more complex than O'Neill understood—they'd been at it for years, after all. "It's not enough just to drop a well down in the middle of a community," said an official from Save the Children, the charitable organization. "It's been done lots in Africa before. You have to think of the maintenance of the wells. That's always the biggest factor, skilled people to maintain the wells. What usually happens, and this happens all over Africa, is that there are no spare parts and the well falls apart."

In the United States, O'Neill had told everyone who would listen the same thing he had told NGOs in Africa: "The way to make really great progress, more quickly than people think is possible, is by taking away the excuses."

He said those exact words to Bush in a meeting they had in the Oval Office at 4:15 on June 12, two days after President's arch "truth-teller" comment.

He still had his one-on-ones with Bush—a golden opportunity even for a Treasury Secretary—but they had become less frequent, occurring, at most, every few weeks. So he didn't waste a minute—heading right into an ardent appeal for an action plan on water "that would be a real demonstration model, Mr. President, for what America can do to make life better for real people with real struggles."

Bush asked a few perfunctory questions—about how the water situation was now on the continent, what groups were engaged in this area—but seemed more focused on how O'Neill's thoughts might help with the reordering of international financial institutions, like the World Bank and IMF.

O'Neill said, yes, there would be structural issues to deal with, but those were to be taken up once a "courageous, unifying commitment" was made, a commitment that would bring groups together.

It was no use. If the President didn't connect in the first minute or two, it was a lost cause. There seemed to be nowhere to go. He had already been to Rice and Powell. He gave it one last shot: "For just twenty-five million," he said, "we should establish a project, with goals of twenty-four to thirty-six months at the outside, to help provide clean water to everyone in Ghana as a *demonstration model*, demonstrating our values as Americans, and our ingenuity, and that this can be done for a reasonable cost and it can be done fast. You don't have to leave another generation to the vagaries of whether it rains or not, for chrissake!"

As Bush looked blankly at him, O'Neill's mind raced through all the excuses he'd heard over the past few weeks: "That, you know, 'Oh God, we can't establish goals like that, because what if it failed, we'll be held up to ridicule for not being able to organize it.' But that's what leadership is all about. This is just an engineering problem. Then they said, 'Well, there aren't enough drill rigs.' I said, 'Bullshit.' There are all kinds of drill rigs you could put together for multiple thousands of dollars, but it's not a huge amount of money to do the kind of drilling that needs to be done." The other argument was, "Oh my God, what if we succeed? Then everyone will want this and expect us to do the same thing." When he had gone around Africa, he had been thinking about the hundreds of billions of dollars spent in economic assistance since the 1950s. What the hell was so important that water didn't make the cut?

But there was no way to relay any of these frustrations to the President. So, O'Neill had taken a deep breath—said he'd keep the President updated on his efforts to create an "action plan" for water—and switched quickly to AIDS. He told Bush that "a historic effort should be undertaken" to fight the disease in Africa and laid out some plans for how it might be done. He recounted his meeting with Dr. Fauci.

"I'm on the case," Bush told O'Neill, and mentioned he had met with Fauci and others who were looking at what the United States could do about AIDS in Africa. "I think we need to do something important there. The question is what, and how big."

"I'd push to the theoretical limits of the possible," O'Neill answered.

Bush nodded and changed the subject. Whenever O'Neill visited, there was a presumption that'd they talk a bit about the economy—but just a bit.

"The economy is improving, just not as fast as we might like," O'Neill told him. "I don't think we need to do anything dramatic, but it would be worthwhile to have a real discussion about economic conditions—where we've been, where we are now, and where the economy seems to be headed. We went from the first tax cut to 9/11 and we haven't really created an 'economic policy.' Tax cuts alone aren't an economic policy."

The President seemed attentive and said they had a few more minutes. O'Neill described the conference he'd helped organize in 1974 for President Gerald Ford. The economy then was roiled by steep inflation and high unemployment. Leading economists, CEOs, and labor leaders with competing philosophies had gathered around a giant felt-covered table in the East Room, and—with TV cameras running—Ford and his team, which included O'Neill and Greenspan, then head of the Council of Economic Advisers, hashed out the theory and practice of fiscal policy, what ailed the economy, and what must be done.

The conference, meant to build bipartisan support, contributed to the "grand plan" Ford soon presented to Congress, which included social programs for the unemployed, tax relief for middle- and lower-income Americans, and fiscal austerity. That last element had been pushed by Greenspan and O'Neill, who believed, then as now, that inflation was driven by fiscal profligacy and deficits. "Ford was really good at the meeting," O'Neill said to Bush. "He showed that he was attentive and really knowledgeable about all competing positions, and how able and insightful and grounded he was in solving the nation's problems . . . which was important. Remember, this was right after Watergate. People needed their confidence restored. And to see a President, with complete mastery of the issues, looking for solutions, is the key."

Bush sat for a moment and then said, "I think I can do that."

. . .

O'NEILL HAD THOUGHT no more about the idea of a major economic conference until a few weeks later, when he read a memo from the White House.

It was like a blow to the chest. The conference would be in Waco—not the White House—and the President's Economic Forum was now Lindsey's show, helped along by Karl Rove, Karen Hughes, and the political/communications team. A carefully vetted group of more than 240 executives, economists, and even a few labor leaders was being assembled. They'd seem diverse and independent to the untrained eye: in fact, nearly every one would be a Bush supporter, and many were major fund-raisers. Attendance was, in a way, a reward for support.

O'Neill was not asked to suggest names. He was assigned to run a small morning seminar—one of eight taking place simultaneously. His assigned topic was economic recovery and job creation.

Bush, accompanied by the core White House circle of Hughes, Rove, Card, and Bolten, would move, like a senior delegate with his entourage, among the meetings.

O'Neill's staff had been incensed. In mid-July, Tim Adams had called Michele Davis into his office. "It's a second-tier role," he told her. "It's not where a Treasury Secretary should be. It's an affront."

Davis nodded. "You're right. That's why our Treasury Secretary may decide not to show."

Adams closed the door. "You're kidding." Such an act was a step away from resignation.

A few minutes later, they were both in O'Neill's office. "I don't know if I can do this," he told them quietly. "It's stupid to fly out there and back to be a prop. There are important things we can be talking about, like fixing Social Security, or Medicare, or really simplifying the tax code; none of those things are on the agenda. It'll just be a lot of people reading from a script that says, 'I love the President.' Where, exactly, does that fit in the grand American ideal of free and honest inquiry?"

O'Neill seemed to be building a case for an exit. Davis, desperation rising, pulled together threads of several arguments: "The President will follow an agenda that you help craft," and "This is the way he gets the public's attention for whatever you ultimately decide," and "Part of being President is having to feed the beast; you are a part of a team that will help him do that."

O'Neill looked at her, unmoved.

She pulled out the meet-Americans-wherever-they-are pitch: "Fine, I agree it's mostly imagery, but more people read *USA Today* than *The Wall Street Journal*, and you may look at your Bloomberg screen twenty times a day and read the *Post* and the *Times*, but that's not where most people get their news. This is about a husband and wife trying to get the kids off to school so they can go to work, and they're pouring the cereal while the TV is going—*and there's no time for lots of numbers and complex concepts*—so if one simple idea and a picture breaks through, and becomes part of their day, that's a huge victory."

O'Neill's brows went up. Not bad.

"And, if we were doing water in Africa," he then responded, "we'd be saving hundreds of thousands of lives."

Adams and Davis left to work on plan B. They began sifting through the piles of invitations O'Neill received every month, looking for dates in the Southwest or West for mid-August. Then they hit the phones. There was the "Rural Economy" breakfast sponsored by the Farm Bureau in Portland, Oregon, on August 14—perfect, an open invitation to see the high-tech Kenworth Truck Plant near Seattle, O'Neill loves plant tours—then to an Asia-Pacific Economic Cooperation roundtable at the Bell Harbor International Conference Center in Seattle. He could be the keynote. Next day, the 15th, a meeting with the editorial board of *The Denver Post*—sure, they said, if the Treasury Secretary is passing through town—and a tour of the U.S. Mint in Denver.

A few days later, they were back in his office to make the sell: Treasury Secretary Paul O'Neill will stop in Waco on a four-day tour of the western United States.

O'Neill nodded. Very clever. Just before leaving for Texas, he saw Dan Bartlett in the White House. Bartlett had been promoted to communications director when Karen Hughes unexpectedly resigned in April to return to Austin.

"Hey, Mr. Secretary," Bartlett said with a smile. "We're doing your idea."

"Give me a break, Dan—nothing could be further from my idea," said O'Neill impatiently. "I ordered a blue sedan, you're giving me a green skateboard."

. . .

ON THE MORNING of August 13, in a conference room at Baylor University, with fourteen thousand undergraduates the largest Baptist university in the world, just forty-five minutes from Crawford, where the President was on his mid-August break at his ranch, O'Neill began his panel discussion on economic recovery and job creation.

He had blotted Ford out of his mind—the way he and Greenspan had prepped him and then cut him loose at the table of leading economists, liberal John Kenneth Galbraith on one side, conservative Milton Friedman on the other—and then watched, expectantly, the way you watch a world-class sprinter you'd been hired to train or a heavyweight with a killer left hook.

No, he had to blot that out, because he wouldn't have been able to proceed through his prepared opening remarks about how "the recession would have been much longer and deeper" if it were not for the tax cuts and rebates, how, in corporate suites, "those with high responsibility have to have high accountability," and then on through a list of initiatives ahead, such as providing terrorist risk insurance, because developers and construction companies couldn't get financing for projects after 9/11 and pension protection after the corporate scandals.

Michele Davis watched from across the room. This was the rah-rah part of his presentation to the horseshoe table of about thirty executives, economists, Chamber of Commerce members, industry representatives, and three labor leaders. But her boss could barely break a monotone. Until the end, when he spoke of the "need to control federal spending . . . we need to put ourselves on a path that even under modest economic circumstances we're not running a deficit."

After a few short, prepared speeches by other panelists, the door opened and the President strolled in with his phalanx of selected advisers—Rove, Hughes, Bolten, and Card—and sat at the middle of the horseshoe in front of a sign: ECONOMIC RECOVERY, JOB CREATION. There was an empty waiting chair between a black businessman and a striking lady who looked as if she could be a model in a Talbots catalog.

The woman—a restaurant owner from North Carolina named Van Eure, who'd contributed $1,000 to the Bush-Cheney campaign—was cued by O'Neill, sitting just to her right. She began: "First of all, I run a restaurant in Raleigh, North Carolina. We employ two hundred and forty people. The restaurant will seat seven hundred to one thousand people a night. And we—I want to thank you for the tax relief and the stimulus package. That really has helped and we did see a difference. One thing that would really help restaurants, small, independent restaurants and, really, all restaurants, is the one hundred percent business deductibility. Because when you are out of town and you are traveling, your travel—you know, your airfare and your hotel and everything else—is one hundred percent, but where you're going to do your business, you do have to do it in a restaurant. So we would like to see that restored.

"And one thing that I was personally affected by was the death tax—twice—because my father died first and then my mother died fourteen years later. And had we not had life insurance plans and the ability to liquidate other assets, we probably would have lost the restaurant. And I feel—what worries me is that people that can't do, you know, what I was able to do and do lose their businesses. But overall, I have employees that feel great about their jobs. They are so happy to have jobs, and they are very much behind our country right now, and they're just very proud—my staff is very proud of what you've done. . . ."

Davis watched O'Neill carefully, fearful that he would offer some unscripted aside that would reveal his disdain. He looked nauseated. Virtually every utterance to Bush had been scripted. Participants who were to speak in his presence had sat in advance with a White House communications staffer to review how long they would speak and what they would say.

But, then, Ms. Eure's own enthusiasms seemed to prompt one of the few unscripted exchanges of the day.

She turned to Bush. "I'm just honored to be sitting next to one of my heroes."

The President smirked. "Who, O'Neill?"

Eure turned, flustered—no, course not—as Bush reached around her to tap O'Neill on the shoulder.

"We found one, O'Neill!"

The Treasury Secretary forced a smile as everyone threw back their heads and laughed.

. . .

BY NOON, the conference was shutting down. The newsline was already a few hours old. At another of the morning's sessions, this one entitled "Small Investors and Pension Security," the brokerage firm CEO Charles Schwab mentioned raising the limit for the write-off of investment losses from $3,000 to $20,000 and eliminating the so-called double taxation of dividends, referring to the way dividends are taxed once as corporate profits and, again, as they reach the shareholder.

Hearing that, the President said to Schwab, "I love your ideas about how to account for loss and/or double-taxation dividends. That makes a lot of sense."

That comment—like the conference—was meant to display an impromptu, unmanaged acuity, as though Bush were in Waco to learn what animated some of America's most accomplished economic thinkers and businesspeople and decide—in full view of the cameras—which ideas were of value.

At least that was the concept. Not only did most reporters find Bush's performance unconvincing on that score—he had seemed barely attentive during some of the morning's conversations—but the ideas presented were mostly Republican evergreens.

The dividend idea, for one, had made its first major public appearance in the early 1980s. It was a favorite of Reagan's Treasury Secretary Don Regan and was in a mix of favored proposals, again, during the first Bush presidency. The idea that dividends are doubly taxed refers to the taxation of a corporation's gross profits—from which dividends are drawn—followed by a second tax paid by the recipient of the dividend, the shareholder. There are various economic discussions about how this taxation may unnaturally encumber capital or alter corporate behavior and whether it was putting a drag on the economy, but by the summer of 2002—more than two years into the market's slump—there was general agreement on Wall Street that eliminating, or even halving, the tax on dividends would boost stock values.

This idea was loudly trumpeted in the lead-up to Waco. On CNBC, talk-show host Lawrence Kudlow, a close friend of Dick Cheney, had been pushing for elimination of the double taxation throughout the summer; and *The Wall Street Journal* had written an editorial the week before Waco about eliminating the double tax. Test-ballooning the double tax proposal was—like everything at Waco—the stuff of scripting.

O'Neill and Davis, of course, knew that to be the case. The reduction or elimination of the dividend tax was simply the lead item of a preordained list of proposals that were expected to emerge from Waco. Right behind it was another item mentioned by Schwab—an increase in the deduction for investment losses—and then a proposal to reduce the rate at which capital gains are taxed. A related proposal focused on indexing capital gains for inflation, which meant subtracting inflation from a capital gain in determining the amount available for taxation. And, finally, there was a proposal to raise the contribution limits for IRAs and 401(k)s, or to accelerate the phase-in of increased limits that were part of the 2001 tax cut legislation.

. . .

BACK IN WASHINGTON after his tour through Portland, Seattle, and Denver, O'Neill set his staff to work on the basket of proposals—looking to clearly assess the benefit and cost of each.

Though the debt limit stalemate had ended on June 27—when House Republicans, anxious to avert a potentially damaging crisis and move on, approved an increase of $450 billion, to $6.4 trillion, exactly what Senate Democrats had decided a month before—the material issue remained: the federal budget deficit for the fiscal year ending in September was estimated to be north of $150 billion.

O'Neill was certain it would be even larger than that. Monthly memos that crossed his desk showed a troubling decline in government tax collections throughout the year, and it seemed to be worsening. In June 2002, the government had collected $20.3 billion less than in the same month of 2001. The next month, collections, though exceeding those of July 2001, were $4.3 billion less than government forecasts. The tax receipt memo on O'Neill's desk when he returned from Waco showed that August receipts had come in at $5.7 billion below forecast.

While federal revenues sagged, economic indicators in August provided a mixed picture that could prompt a wide range of conclusions. A Labor Department report showed unemployment at 5.9 percent, with employers cutting hours and limiting new hiring. Wage levels, according to the Commerce Department, had stagnated. Commerce also reported that factory orders had fallen sharply in June. Together, the numbers from Labor and Commerce prompted analysts to doubt whether there would be a quick recovery. In the wake of the reports, according to *The New York Times*, "A number of economists moved from expecting a strong recovery in the second half of the year to concern that the economy might face a longer period of weak growth."

These were the figures and assessments that Lindsey seemed to rely on most—the ones bespeaking disaster. It had been that way for much of the year. On various pads, with jottings from long flights or long meetings, O'Neill wrote: "What is our Economic Policy?" He didn't feel that tax cuts qualified as policy.

During the spring and summer, the weekly economic meetings had become bloodbaths.

On one side was Lindsey—ideologically pure, but, as one of his friends and former aides puts it, these days "the only calculations Larry does are on the back of an envelope." Lindsey is a man with models and rigidly fixed positions.

O'Neill, meanwhile, was attentively checking in with his custom-designed information bank—assistant secretary Richard Clarida and the real-time data shop.

After its near bull's-eye prediction for the fourth quarter of 2001, the real-time system continued to prove surprisingly accurate for the first quarter—predicting 5.1 percent GDP growth in mid-March, close to the 6.1 percent final figure (and the 5 percent revised figure that appeared a few months later). For the second quarter, it over-shot; tracking what seemed to be a 2.6 percent GDP growth—a bit higher than the 2.1 percent predicted by the leading private fore-caster, Macroeconomic Advisers. Then the Commerce number, re-leased a few months hence, showed growth of 1.3 percent.

After Africa, O'Neill had huddled with Clarida to fine-tune the system. Clarida's weekly offerings in mid- and late July showed third-quarter GDP growth at nearly 4 percent.

Coming off his Waco victory—and busily working the permu-tations of the four different tax cut proposals that were unveiled—Lindsey was dismissive of O'Neill's qualified optimism on the third quarter. For much of the year, Lindsey had been predicting a ruinous economic slide. He recommended to Bush that there be an almost immediate tax cut of $300 billion *to occur in a single fiscal year*. For the most part, he still stuck to that position.

Hubbard, meanwhile, hedged. He thought that moderate tax cuts should rely largely on the double-taxation-of-dividends proposal; it would provide some short-term stimulus but improve the tax code to allow for a gradual, long-term boost to the economy.

Neither seemed to be particularly concerned about the Treasury Secretary. As the President passed late August in Crawford, and O'Neill disappeared for a week to his sweeping, four-story summer house in Bethany Beach, Delaware, it seemed as though Lindsey, with Hubbard offering sober support, had leverage, proximity to the President, and plenty of allies.

. . .

ON SEPTEMBER 4, O'Neill arrived at his office before dawn, full of purpose. He got his coffee and checked the quartet of Bloomberg screens, stacked two on two against the wall behind his chair, beside an elegant eighteenth-century rolltop desk that dates to Alexander Hamilton.

He dug into the overnight numbers on commodities futures and early trading on the London Metals Exchange, the glowing screens pulsing with symbols—the numerology of an exploding world economy—that he tried to look beneath, to steel beams and bushels of wheat and pears from Pakistan, ripening on a distant dock. For decades, he'd been telling colleagues to be precise—to separate fact, analysis, and opinion—and these were facts, the starting point.

Five morning newspapers were neatly laid out on his desk, all filled with news about Iraq. The administration's rhetoric had sharpened dramatically during August, closing the gap between what had long been clear inside the White House and what was being revealed to the public. The stated position—that the President hadn't made any decisions—was eroded with each news cycle by the administration's desire to start making its case for war.

Cheney and Rumsfeld spoke to Iraqi dissidents in exile in mid-August, promising that the United States would depose Saddam Hussein. The President said the same day that Saddam was an "enemy until proven otherwise." A few days later, Condi Rice made the humanitarian case, telling a BBC interviewer, "We just have to look back and ask how many dictators who ended up being a tremendous global threat and killing thousands and, indeed, millions of people should we have stopped in their tracks. . . . We certainly do not have the luxury of doing nothing."

What the argument needed, of course, was better discovery, a case supported by key facts. O'Neill, from attendance at NSC meetings, or reports from deputies who attended in his stead, knew that such desired facts, like a provable link between Saddam and al-Qaeda, might not exist—an absence that was truly a material issue. What was known seemed to make any such link unlikely. Saddam Hussein had been slaughtering Islamic fundamentalists for years—al-Qaeda hated him as much as they did the United States. Saddam was no fool—he'd been tamping down fundamentalists in his country for two decades; the last thing he'd do was arm them, if he had any arms to give.

O'Neill had read the late August papers at his beach house with growing consternation. Two weeks earlier, *The Washington Post* had reported leaked allegations from anonymous administration officials that al-Qaeda members, including "names you'd recognize," had found refuge in Iraq. Then, on August 26, a two-pronged message flowed forth. That morning, major newspapers carried front-page stories that White House lawyers had ruled international law allowed the U.S. administration to topple Saddam, based on his violations of the accords ending Operation Desert Storm, the 1991 Gulf War. And later that day, Cheney gave a speech to a Veterans of Foreign Wars convention in Nashville, Tennessee, where he raised the specter of Pearl Harbor and said the United States could find itself at the mercy of a nuclear-armed Saddam if it failed to act soon. The next day, August 27, in *The New York Times*, Cheney's speech was seen as a definitive statement of policy. "When Cheney talks, it's Bush," William Kristol, the prominent neoconservative pundit, told the *Times*. "I think the debate in the administration is over, and this is the beginning of the serious public campaign."

"There were two prominent ideologies at work," O'Neill said later. "One was the sweeping idea of preemption, which was the thing that drove the Iraq policy, and the other was the idea that tax cuts were always good, the deeper the better. I focused on the one I could do something about."

A lesson O'Neill had learned in his days running OMB, and never forgot, was that the budget is often the only place where there is a true competition of disparate ideas—a competition over who will get the money and who won't. And the only way for that competition to work is for the budget to be finite. A ballooning deficit—he'd often tell cabinet secretaries or department heads, who feared his visits—is a sign of casual thinking and tough choices not made. Balancing a budget, thereby, is not just a matter of fiscal good sense. It compels companion virtues—such as intellectual rigor and honest assessment of the intentions that underlie action. Do you know what you're doing—and do you know why?

Today, September 4, was a day to ask such questions again. A black sedan was waiting outside, idling with air conditioner on in Washington's early morning humidity. Within a few minutes O'Neill and Ken Dam were in Greenspan's dining room, eating fresh fruit.

The talk was intense and strategic, quiet and serious. They could speak in half-sentences. There was a history at this point, reference points stretching across almost two years of effort and outcome. They had been right on triggers, more right than either could have imagined at the time. The $5.6 trillion surplus was a distant memory. The federal books were beginning to bleed red, with significant deficits expected for this year and a $1.6 trillion tax cut—the deepest cuts still ahead—now locked into law. Dysfunctions of the political system, where it is often more effective to wield illusion than reality, would make attempts to repeal the cuts a suicide mission.

The view that the triggers would undercut investment "was a credible argument, a correct argument," Greenspan remarked, reviewing the terrain. "It is an issue of weighing the advantages of one desired goal, and another desired goal, when they are effectively partially contradicting each other. In my judgment I think that triggers are a better balance. Would I prefer that taxes were cut and stayed that way? Of course I would—that's not the choice that the real world is confronting us with."

Now, the "real world" would make them pay for ignoring its dictates. The baby boomers were coming fast—the money to bridge from Social Security to some form of altered, or successor, program was gone. Kent Smetters, a University of Pennsylvania assistant professor and a Martin Feldstein protégé, had been recruited by O'Neill and Greenspan to crunch the numbers on Social Security in spring 2001. O'Neill filled in Greenspan on Smetters's progress. The shortfall was $44 trillion over the life of the program, far more than previous estimates. Recommendations of the Social Security Commission were all but tabled by Bush. It was a bomb locked in a drawer.

"What's your plan?" Greenspan asked. "Is there any way to get control of this situation?" Expectations of annual budget shortfalls for the coming years supported a projected ten-year budget deficit of around $3 trillion.

"Deficits at that level will cripple the government," O'Neill said. "It has to be stopped."

He told Greenspan that Lindsey was busy "spotlighting" selective economic data that supported his case for more tax cuts, that Waco had been just a media event to support that position. Hubbard, meanwhile, had a special affection for killing the double taxation of dividends, an idea he had initially embraced when he worked in the Treasury Department for the first President Bush.

Both men respected Hubbard—even if he often came to different conclusions. But there was a shared language. The three, O'Neill included, appreciated the possibilities of the supply side—the idea that tax cuts could provide stimulus, and growth, and some lifting of tax receipts. It was a matter of degree, of where you fell on the spectrum between the pure concept, on one end, and hard, complex data about how tax cuts actually affect the economy, on the other. Hubbard tended to see the potential boost in receipts as greater than either Greenspan or O'Neill felt the data supported. Nonetheless, they both felt the dividend tax reduction was a fine idea, in a perfect world. "Eliminating the double taxation is a very important project. The issue isn't that. . . ." Greenspan said. "The issue is whether you can finance it appropriately by cribbing expenditures."

O'Neill agreed. The economy didn't need dramatic stimulus at this point—GDP growth estimates were solid to strong for the third quarter, and it looked as if they had come in right on the 4 percent growth predicted by the real-time model, and the stimulus effects of the dividend plan would be modest, in any event. The problem was the cost. IRS figures showed that individuals declared $126 billion in dividend income on their 1999 returns. To cut the dividend tax in half would cause more than a $20 billion shortfall in 2003.

And that was the key point of differentiation: people could quibble about the stimulatory effects of tax cuts, but O'Neill and Greenspan agreed utterly about the perils of deficits. There, they had twenty years of good data. O'Neill had just finished the messy business of raising the debt ceiling. Those were real dollars. Not theories.

Greenspan raised his caterpillar brows. "So?"

"I'm going to make a stand on principle—a principle actually supported by fact," O'Neill said. "Call it a human sacrifice."

. . .

O'NEILL STROLLED into the Oval Office on September 4.

"Hey there, Big O."

The nickname had changed. "Pablo" was out. "Big O" was in, just in the last month or two. The nicknaming always unsettled O'Neill—it was a bully technique: I've given you a name, now you wear it. And, after the change, O'Neill had bumped into Dan Bartlett. "Is that a good thing, Dan?" O'Neill asked. Bartlett frowned. "Don't think so." He said he thought "Big O" might be an appliance dealer in Austin.

O'Neill told the President that he looked tan and fit, coming off his vacation, and he thanked him for moving quickly to set up this meeting.

The meeting had been called, after all, at O'Neill's request. After Waco, O'Neill had pressed Card—"Andy, I need to see the President." The others had adjusted their schedules to be there.

It was called "Principals Only Policy Meeting with POTUS" on O'Neill's schedule, "Principals" meaning the economic policy principals, namely, Lindsey, Hubbard, Mitch Daniels, and himself.

Everyone settled in. There was some perfunctory talk about the condition of the economy and the reaction to Waco.

Then O'Neill took charge.

He looked directly at the President.

"It's a time when we have to think clearly about being fiscally responsible—about looking at the real facts, and not theories of what might or might not happen."

No one spoke.

"All right, then," Bush said finally. "Give me the facts."

O'Neill laid them out in an order that he felt showed the irrefutable logic of a closing trap.

He started with the various tax reduction proposals. Their stimulatory effects would be modest—or simply unpredictable—and the economy doesn't need "as much stimulus as you might think." He went through the real-time modeling data of a strong third quarter, mixing it with some private forecasts that corresponded. "In a word," he said, "we may need stimulus in the future—but the facts don't support stimulus now."

Second major point: Tax cuts were going to be expensive. He laid out the costs, stretching over ten years—they would cost nearly $400 billion and would take a huge bite out of the budget, all of it deficit spending.

"This is a fine structural change to make to the tax system if you have sufficient funds to manage it. Right now, you don't."

Lindsey and Hubbard were visibly discomforted. Bush looked around the room—he hates open conflict of this sort, a death struggle over complex ideas.

O'Neill was sitting bolt upright.

"So, what are you suggesting, Paul?"

"Let me be perfectly blunt, Mr. President. Tax receipts are sluggish. And costs are rising. You have bills for Homeland Security. We're spending money for reconstruction in Afghanistan—which is important to do right, not on the cheap. There may be other terrorist incidents on U.S. soil that could depress economic activity. And, clearly, we may end up in Iraq. And that could cost a fortune."

Bush seemed to be nodding. O'Neill felt he was getting through. He softened it, just a bit.

"Mr. President, if you start pushing through a second, major stimulus plan, you run out of money. You won't have any money to do anything you want to do, such as changing Social Security or fundamental tax reform, for the rest of your term. Now's the time to keep your powder dry. Any other path is not responsible."

Then the two men simply looked at each other. And, it was crystal clear, O'Neill was telling the President this: If you want to move forward down this road, you'll have to fire me first.

Bush took a deep breath. "Got it. Okay, then."

. . .

O'NEILL TOOK some trips in September and October to Phoenix and Portland, Maine, to Kentucky and Mexico, to Cedar Rapids and Lima, Ohio. He worked on passage of terrorist risk insurance and on getting more cooperation from the Saudis.

The President vanished into a cloud of international engagements—starting with a UN speech on September 12. There was the Iraq resolution in Congress, the Bali bombing, and the crisis of North Korea's admission that it had an active nuclear weapons program.

And, of course, there were the midterm elections. Going into autumn, the Democrats seemed to have a strong hand. Polls showed voters trusted Democrats more than Republicans on economic issues. On September 1—the day before the traditional Labor Day kickoff to the campaign season—the *Los Angeles Times* reported that Democrats led 47 percent to 39 percent on a generic ballot.

The advantage was short-lived. Democrats were betting they could ride generalized economic worries all the way to victory. Their campaign strategy focused almost entirely on criticizing the President's economic policies. Events intervened. North Korea, Iraq, and the sniper shootings in the Washington area dominated the headlines in the fall, pushing economic news off the agenda. The race narrowed when the Democratic message failed to gain traction. As elections approached, the Democrats began to see the writing on the wall. On October 28, the *Los Angeles Times* reported "fading hopes" among Democrats of retaking the House.

The White House seized the opportunity. Bush spent nine days in October on the campaign trail, attacking Democratic incumbents in closely contested states like Missouri and South Dakota and even venturing into Democratic strongholds like Massachusetts.

A newsline emerged: gutsy Bush puts his reputation on the line in the midterms. It would be a referendum on the President. But it was less risky than it might seem; Rove saw things tipping toward Republicans. Bush could make it a rout.

When the votes were counted, the result was worse than the Democrats had feared. Not only did the GOP retain the House, but Republicans retook the Senate. Incumbent presidents usually lose seats in midterm elections, and Bush's victory was almost unprecedented. It was widely read as a reflection of the strength of the GOP and the weakness and indecision of the Democratic leadership.

Bush and his political team, headed by Karl Rove, were praised for engineering a historic victory. *Time* magazine put Bush and Rove on its cover, under the headline HOW THEY ACED THEIR MIDTERMS. *Newsweek* showed Bush in his jeans and bomber jacket, under the words TOP GUN.

The White House tried to keep congressional Republicans from overreaching. The day after the election, Bush ordered them not to gloat in public—they should remain businesslike and nonpartisan and not give in to boastfulness. GOP leaders in Congress were restrained by the White House from moving immediately on a new round of tax cuts, which, according to *The Washington Post*, the White House said would alienate voters by giving the appearance of overstepping their mandate.

Still, the Republicans wasted no time in pushing through a few delayed bills. On November 12, Democrats gave up their fight against the labor provisions of Bush's Homeland Security bill, allowing the administration to ignore civil service hiring and promotion rules in staffing the new Homeland Security Department.

At that moment, O'Neill was making final preparations for a two-week foreign tour. The key stops would be Afghanistan and Pakistan. He was already being briefed on security arrangements—he'd be visiting some high-risk areas on this long, rigorous trip. He'd be meeting with Pakistani president Pervez Musharraf and others in the troubled region, who were looking for clarity and consistency from the United States. He'd be one of the highest-ranking U.S. officials to go to some of the most dangerous places on the globe.

So, before he left, he decided he should make a phone call—just to be sure. A latest round of rumors was swirling about the possibility of his departure from Treasury, with a few names floated as potential replacements. This game had been going on for more than a year: a name floated every few months, from Donald Marron of UBS America—an initiative traced to Marron's public relations man—to Charles Schwab, because of his strong performance at Waco.

O'Neill called Josh Bolten, deputy chief of staff and someone he trusted, to ask whether "there was any possibility that the President was looking to make a change." If Bush was, O'Neill told Bolten, then "maybe I should reconsider going on this trip. Not just because there are some dangers. It's not a good idea to send a Treasury Secretary to build relationships in this part of the world if he's not going to be around very long." O'Neill asked Bolten to check with the President in the next day or two.

Soon, Bolten was back on the phone. He'd checked with Bush. " You should definitely go on the trip " he said emphatically.

O'Neill had a meeting with Bush at 1:40 p.m. on November 14, the day before he was due to leave. It was a short meeting, about a half hour. The President could talk to O'Neill about his hopes for the upcoming trip. It was an opportunity for O'Neill as well.

They talked very generally about Musharraf and about the difficulty of building the "K-to-K road"—Kandahar-to-Kabul—because of the sniping at the construction workers.

Then O'Neill asked his question. "Are you satisfied with the way things are going, Mr. President? Because if you're not and are thinking of making a change, I probably shouldn't go on this trip."

Bush paused for a moment. "No, there's not a problem. You should go."

. . .

ON THE MORNING of November 15, O'Neill went to an NSC meeting on Middle East policy in the situation room. The President and NSC principals were there. Now, nearly two years since Bush's first NSC meeting, in which he had said the United States should withdraw from the Israeli-Palestinian conflict and focus on Iraq, matters had, in a way, come full circle.

The unleashing of Ariel Sharon, as Powell warned in January 2001, had torn the thin fabric of self-interest that was to have brought the Palestinians and the Israelis to the table. Rather than "getting things back in balance"—as Bush had said, noting that Clinton had agreed to too much at the bargaining table with Yasir Arafat—Sharon's show of strength had prompted violent reactions by Palestinians. The post-9/11 idea that Israeli retaliation against Hamas or Islamic Jihad was an adjunct, of sorts, to the United States' war on terrorism had encouraged the use of force over diplomacy.

Now, in the fall of 2002, the situation in the West Bank and Gaza was bloodied and raw.

As the meeting convened, O'Neill quietly reread his briefing materials. The discussions at many NSC meetings with the President were so formal and scripted, both procedurally and intellectually, that he increasingly found himself turning to the well-crafted analysis in his packet. He understood now why Nixon and Ford were so particular about their Brandeis briefs and how important they were in preparation for informed debate. Those exchanges were the conclusion of a complex process.

The principals began to offer their reports, as the President listened impassively and O'Neill glanced down at the "sensitive" memorandum that his undersecretary for international affairs, John Taylor, had prepared. The goal today, the memo stated, was "to discuss options for advancing the President's agenda on the Israeli-Palestinian conflict over the next three months." They'd also discuss the "desirability of convening a peace conference or sending a special envoy to the region" and various operational issues, including one that O'Neill would head up implementing a U.S.-proposed plan to encourage transfer of Palestinian Authority revenues held by Israel back to the Palestinians. Israeli authorities collect Palestinian customs revenues on behalf of the PA but had suspended transfer of those revenues after the start of the intifada in September 2000. They were a significant sum—$850 million—and a sore spot.

The central issue, today, was what to do about the so-called road map that was the centerpiece of Bush's reengagement in the conflict.

In June, the President had laid down his hand, endorsing a two-state solution by broadly discussing a three-year plan—a road map—to achieve peace, but saying the United States would not negotiate with Arafat, that the Palestinians needed to select a new leader to represent their interests. Not much had occurred since then that could be called progress. Five months later, Arafat was still in power, and the Mideast, like the rest of the world, was fixated on the U.S. justifications and preparations for an invasion of Iraq. Everywhere, a new Clausewitzian axiom—of war as diplomacy by other means—was guiding events, whether it was the U.S. invasion plans that had developed into a blueprint by mid-October or Sharon's long-held idea that the only time to arrive at the bargaining table is when an opponent is bloodied and desperate.

The State Department, at this point, was "in the process of finalizing the 'road map' by incorporating comments from key allies"—Russia, the European Union, and the United Nations—as well as the Israelis and Palestinians. The question, for Bush and the principals, was what to do: put the road map on hold; finalize the road map and exert pressure on Israel and the Palestinians to implement it quickly; or finalize the road map but "don't insist on immediate action given domestic political uncertainties in Israel."

New Israeli elections had just been announced. Maybe it was a time to wait, to see if Sharon survived. The question, as was often the case, came down to an issue of the President's credibility.

Taylor noted an NSC deputies meeting, where issues were often hashed out. In this case, as his document articulated for O'Neill, the "deputies felt that putting the road map on hold could undermine the President's credibility with key allies (all of whom are looking to the U.S. for leadership on this issue) and is therefore not a desirable option." Finalizing the road map and exerting pressure to implement it would help maintain momentum on the initiative but could also lead to the road map's failure if the parties involved refused to respond positively. And the last option—"Finalizing the road map but taking a 'wait and see' approach on implementation would also help maintain momentum and would preserve our options when parties in the region signal a willingness to reengage on the road map."

After a half hour, the room seemed to settle on a hedged wait-and-see strategy—option three—whereby the United States could exert some pressure on the parties involved but would not be judged by whether there was material progress.

O'Neill said little as this predictable path was sketched out. He talked a bit about the transfer-of-payments issue—one that was resolvable and should be resolved—but felt, once again, that an opportunity for leadership was being missed.

At 11 a.m., O'Neill ducked his head into the Vice President's office in the West Wing.

The meeting—titled "Economic Growth"—brought together the senior economic team with the White House staff.

Over the past few months, Cheney had shown up at a few of the regular meetings of the economic team. He didn't say much—he never said much—but his presence seemed to quiet the combatants, especially O'Neill and Lindsey.

Now, the group was meeting on the Vice President's turf. As the meeting in Dick's office progressed, it became clear that the Vice President was ready to weigh in on economic policy.

The package of post-Waco tax proposals, led by a 50 percent cut in the individual tax on dividends, had been all but buried since O'Neill took his stand in early September. It came up infrequently, and always in the past tense—what we were thinking of doing but couldn't afford.

After the midterms, though, O'Neill could sense a change inside the White House, from Rove, Lindsey, and others. A smugness, a sureness. No one mentioned to O'Neill that the proposals were back on the launchpad. They knew better.

Now Cheney mentioned them again, how altering the double taxation of dividends would provide some positive stimulus. . . .

O'Neill jumped in, arguing sharply that the government "is moving toward a fiscal crisis" and then pointing out "what rising deficits will mean to our economic and fiscal soundness."

Dick cut him off.

"Reagan proved deficits don't matter," he said.

O'Neill shook his head, hardly believing that Cheney—whom he and Greenspan had known since Dick was a kid—would say such a thing.

He was speechless. Cheney moved to fill the void. "We won the midterms. This is our due."

. . .

O'NEILL LEFT Cheney's office in a state of mild shock. Yes, he knew Lindsey believed this brazen ideology. And Rove, and others. But to hear it from the Vice President seemed to stop the world turning. The inscrutable Dick had finally shown himself.

As he walked back to his office, to prepare for that evening's flight to Rome and then Pakistan, O'Neill took Cheney's statement and started to pull it apart. Of course, one of the most significant things Ronald Reagan had proved was that *deficits do matter*—a fact that defined nearly twenty years of fiscal policy.

"I thought that, clearly, there's no coherent philosophy that could support such a claim"; and then O'Neill pondered the difference between philosophy and ideology. . . .

He started to deconstruct.

"I think an ideology comes out of feelings and it tends to be non-thinking. A philosophy, on the other hand, can have a structured thought base. One would hope that a philosophy, which is always a work in progress, is influenced by facts. So there is a constant interplay between *what do I think* and *why do I think it.* . . .

"Now, if you gather more facts and have more experience, especially with things that have gone wrong—those are especially good learning tools—then you reshape your philosophy, because the facts tell you you've got to. It doesn't change what you wish for. I mean, it's okay to wish for something that's, you know, outside of your fact realm. But it's not okay to confuse all that. . . .

"Ideology is a lot easier, because you don't have to know anything or search for anything. You already know the answer to everything. It's not penetrable by facts. It's absolutism."

. . .

CHENEY AND O'NEILL had had more conversations on process in the preceding months, until O'Neill gave up.

They talked about everything that was apparent. The President was caught in an echo chamber of his own making, cut off from everyone other than a circle around him that's tiny and getting smaller and in concert on everything—a circle that conceals him from public view and keeps him away from the one thing he needs most: honest, disinterested perspectives about what's real and what the hell he might do about it. But then "I realized why Dick just nodded along when I said all this, over and over, and nothing ever changed . . . *because this is the way Dick likes it.*"

But O'Neill had stopped trying to discern where Cheney ended and the President began. Not only was it not clear—it might not be pertinent.

In the end, it was Bush's White House—his administration. Finally, O'Neill connected his long study of process to a President he now knew quite well.

"I realized that it's very hard for an organization or an institution to achieve more than the leader can imagine," he said. "If you determine to run a five-minute mile, you'll never run a four-minute mile. The leader sets the conditions as to what it is we aspire to. It's not clear to me that you can create a process that will impact whatever the leader brings with him, in terms of his instinct of imagining what could be. I'd like to think that maybe that's not right and think that someone can be a leader and see or smell a new idea and then own it. But there has to be an openness of wanting to do that. There has to be a market there, otherwise you can just spin your wheels all you want to. You can have a lot of great ideas, and if the store is closed, it's not going to make any difference. . . ."

It was clear to O'Neill that Cheney and a handful of others had become "a praetorian guard" that encircled the President. In terms of bringing new, transforming ideas to the Oval Office, "that store is closed."

. . .

THE SMALL military transport plane took a sharp turn over Kabul
and began to dive almost straight down. O'Neill, Tim Adams, and
the Treasury's press secretary, Rob Nichols, held tight to their seats.
They'd been told this would happen—that this would be the maneuver to protect the plane against antiaircraft fire—but that was no
preparation for the vertiginous fall.

In Kabul, they took a Chinook helicopter to a spot a few miles
from the city to see the end of the road—the Kabul-to-Kandahar
road. "The most important thing we can do right now is this road—
finishing it would demonstrate that we're not about occupation, but
about progress, about helping the people here," O'Neill said to Tim
Adams and a delegation of Afghans as they all clustered on the black-
top. The road was only 20 percent finished—construction workers
had been attacked. Men with automatic weapons stood on all sides of
the group. No one could leave the paved area. O'Neill asked one of
the Afghan officials why. "Mines," he said. "On all sides of us, mines."

The next day in Islamabad, O'Neill's desire to see the state of the
real Pakistan, rather than just to meet Musharraf and jump aboard
the plane, meant that the itinerary included a visit to a school about
twenty miles outside of the town. As the heavily fortified military
convoy roared out of Islamabad, O'Neill could see clearly the tension between destruction and progress—and his own strange role in
its midst. Every thousand feet for twenty miles were heavily armed
Pakistani soldiers, staring out on the country's rutted terrain, automatic weapons poised. This was so the U.S. Secretary of the Treasury could go and see a school for girls.

"I watched the soldiers with their backs to me—thousands of
them—ready for an attack, and thought this is a world gone mad,
that this is what absolutism does," O'Neill remembered. "And that

makes the most important institution in the country a school. A place where kids can ask questions and get real answers."

. . .

ON NOVEMBER 26, O'Neill arrived at his office jet-lagged from the two-week tour. He had his list of "deliverables"—he'd met with Musharraf, tried to work out logistics for building the K-to-K road across Afghanistan, dined with the sultan of Oman, and toured various European cities.

It was good to get away from Washington, away from the day-to-day routine of internecine combat and public posturing with little to show.

But as he walked into the Roosevelt Room on the first floor of the White House on November 26, it was clear he had stumbled back into the main arena of U.S. domestic policy.

It was a big crowd for a working session—a rare coming together of the economic and political/communications staff. Even Hughes was here—and her presence, ever since she'd left the White House, indicated a special occasion.

Everyone arrived at 11 a.m. and stood at their assigned places at the long mahogany table: O'Neill at the center, with Hubbard and Keith Hennessey, Lindsey's deputy director at the NEC, to his right; on his left was Lindsey, then Evans and Daniels. Directly across the table from O'Neill was a chair for the President, with Bolten, Rove, and Bartlett to his left; Card, Hughes, and Fleischer to his right. At the end of the table was a video screen. O'Neill looked over and squinted. Dick Cheney was gazing at them from an undisclosed location.

The President entered from the northwest door, in a blue pinstriped suit, blue shirt, red tie, American flag lapel pin; he was looking a bit tired. He sat down, cueing the rest of them to sit, and put on his reading glasses.

"All right, how are we doing?"

Lindsey began. "I'm reminded, looking at the table, of a joke I heard from Prime Minister Koizumi of Japan, that he gets two opinions from each economist, and since, Mr. President, you have five economic advisers—"

"What are you talking about?" snapped Bush.

"Yes, sir. Your economic team agrees on the key elements of an economic growth and jobs package: reduce the double taxation of dividends, accelerate the rate cuts, and provide more expensing of investment losses. Let me now turn to Secretary O'Neill."

O'Neill shuffled some papers—thinking maybe Larry and the President weren't getting on so well after all. But now that he knew about Cheney's posture, it didn't much matter where Larry was.

"I'm just back last night from my trip to India, Pakistan, and the United Kingdom," O'Neill began, giving Bush a thirty-second summary, and then described his view of the current conditions. "On balance, I am more optimistic about the U.S. economy than the group, and I remind you that I was right last year, and we've mostly been right this year in our real-time forecasts. And that leads me to believe we don't need a major, expensive stimulus package. But this is all beside the point. I think you have made up your mind, so we should get on with discussing the package. I am concerned that what we do now not tie our hands on major tax reform or on creating Social Security private accounts. And when I look at what we have got here, in this package of proposals, I am dubious that we can get anything enacted in time to do much good."

Bush looked at him quizzically. "What is your point about Social Security private accounts?"

"There will be a transition cost, Mr. President," O'Neill explained, surprised. "Perhaps a trillion dollars over many years. This will be more difficult to do with large budget deficits. It will also be difficult to keep Congress in check."

"We have had some success on the spending side, but also some setbacks," Bush said.

Gazing down the row, Bush now looked at Hubbard, a cue that it was his turn.

"I don't think of this as a stimulus package, but a growth package," Hubbard said. "The economy is facing headwinds from increased risk aversion. The third-quarter numbers were strong, but they borrowed from the fourth quarter. . . ."

"Do we have to give it back?" Bush quipped, getting off a good one to big laughs.

Then to Keith Hennessey: "The priority should be eliminating double taxation of dividends. I think that the revenue loss will be much smaller than the static estimate," Hennessey said, referring to the supply-side methodology of using growth projections to boost estimates of tax revenues. "We should also include more expensing of investments and accelerating the rate cuts. I think of this as an insurance policy, not against a double dip back into recession, but against 1 percent slower growth in each of the next two years, when there could be a rise in unemployment to 6.5 percent. I am not saying this is likely, but it certainly is a downside scenario."

The President nodded and looked at Evans. This was the way most meetings went. The President looks at you. You deliver. He moves on.

The Commerce Secretary echoed much of what had been said. "I think we need an insurance policy. Accelerating the rate cuts and eliminating double taxation of dividends is good policy. I think expensing of capital losses is less important. We should also consider an investor package, where capital losses can offset ordinary income, and expanded tax breaks on IRAs. . . ."

As usual, not a real discussion, O'Neill thought as he looked over at Daniels, next up. He'd had many discussions with the OMB chief; O'Neill knew that terrain intimately—he'd been trying to talk Daniels through the ideals of fiscal probity. He knew Daniels was focused on the perils of rising deficits, but it would take gumption to air those concerns in a room full of tax cut ideologues.

"I think we need to balance concerns," Daniels said, sounding as if he'd rehearsed his opening. "You need to be out front on the economy, but I am concerned that this package may not do it. The budget hole is getting deeper, it will be at least $225 billion next year, and we are projecting deficits all the way to the end of your second term."

From across the table came glares from the entire Bush political team.

Daniels paused, as though he'd been struck. "Umm. On balance, then, I think we need to do a package that makes"—he paused—"long-run sense: accelerate the rate cuts and the double taxation of dividends. You need to occupy the space and propose a complete package before State of the Union."

O'Neill looked with astonishment at Daniels. He had seemed to turn 180 degrees in midsentence.

Lindsey jumped in. "Mr. President, *this is* an insurance policy, and it's a bad time to go uninsured. With the world economy as it is, the United States is the only game in town."

Bush looked with disdain at Lindsey and went in another direction. "We are slowing from third to fourth quarter, but O'Neill hasn't been wrong yet. Why have nominal wages stopped growing?"

The answer was complex—about the underside of the continuing productivity miracle, that GDP growth could occur without traditional pressure to lift wages—the kind of academic discussion the President generally abhorred.

But maybe not today. Bush seemed to be encouraging unscripted exchanges, prepared to search for an answer on his own, in a crowded room. For O'Neill, that was both exciting and unsettling.

This discussion could go in a lot of directions. Maybe, in fact, Bush hadn't decided on this second huge tax cut package, and he was finally asking a few pointed, now-hold-on-one-minute questions. Or, O'Neill mused, it could be a devil's advocate exercise such as he'd seen the President attempt a few times—a way for him to collect succinct responses to anticipated attacks. Either way, it was enough to make O'Neill snap to attention.

Same for Lindsey. "What we are proposing is good long-run tax policy," Lindsey said in a non sequitur, trying to get the President back on track.

Bush acted as if he hadn't heard him. "Are you proposing that we accelerate all the tax cuts, or just for those in the middle? Won't the top-rate people benefit the most from eliminating the double taxation of dividends? Didn't we already give them a break at the top?"

The 2001 tax cut had been criticized for the disproportionate boost it gave to the top 5 percent of earners; it wasn't literally regressive, but it surely departed from progressive ideals that had long defined the tax policies of both parties. The White House's response, that those who pay the most in taxes get the largest reductions, was now echoed by Hubbard. "Mr. President, remember the high earners are where the entrepreneurs are." This was the mantra that had guided much of the administration's stimulus-through-tax-cuts policy. Giving incentives to those with money would drive investment, and that would drive job growth, and newly salaried employees would buy and boost demand. Some economists contended that that is a long way to travel to reach stimulus.

Bush seized on it. "This is about demand," he said. "I want this to work."

"It's also about the supply side," Lindsey said.

"Eliminating the double taxation of dividends is a game changer," Hubbard added. "Game changer" is one of Bush's favorite phrases.

Rove finally spoke up, a rare event in a meeting of this size. "You should be basing the package on principle—if double taxation of dividends is wrong, why do we want to settle for just eliminating 50 percent of the tax for individuals?" "Stick to principle" is another phrase that has a tonic effect on Bush.

A 50 percent cut was the consensus recommendation, owing to steep revenue shortfalls brought about by the dividend change. Rove was pushing for 100 percent.

Josh Bolten leapt into the fray. "This burns a big hole in the budget."

Rove seemed surprised. The ramparts of conservative economic theology—reduce taxes as far as possible, starve the beast of the federal government—were under siege.

Daniels, having changed direction only a few minutes back, now spoke as an ardent supply-sider. "Yes, but we get a lot back."

Without cues from Bush as to when to speak, it had become a free-for-all. They were all on the edges of their seats. Hubbard pushed to protect his prize proposal. "It has to be permanent to work," he said emphatically.

Lindsey also went on the offensive, answering unasked questions. "To get the votes we need, Mr. President, we shouldn't peel back things that work, but add other items as necessary."

"But this is a harder problem, Mr. President . . . ," O'Neill began.

Bush waved him silent. Something was on his mind. It was the class issue again. "I am not in favor of excluding people," he said, almost to himself.

O'Neill picked up his unfinished sentence. ". . . The trouble with the double taxation is that it could have near-term effects, boosting the market and providing some stimulus, but there's a strong chance it will all be dissipated by the middle of next year. With the economy already improving, this could cause an unnecessary boost—that's how you get a bubble—and it could pop in '03 and '04." He put forward an alternative: the permanent expensing of capital expenditures, which lightens the tax burden for small businesses (and is a step toward abolishing corporate taxes, an O'Neill favorite) and prompts expenditures on capital goods that benefit the wider economy. He looked across the table and saw the President was befuddled. He quickly moved to hold the floor by reviving the earlier political argument that the double dividend cut could create a bubble. "We don't want to slam the door on our toes in the fourth quarter of 2004 after the current provisions expire."

Bush picked up on that last dangling reference to the date: "Just as long as we don't slam the door in the third quarter of 2004."

But Rove seemed intrigued by O'Neill's idea of expensing capital expenditures. "On the Hill, there is talk of a plan to change all the depreciable lives," he said, and then ticked off the newly proposed intervals of thirty years, ten years, five years, and three years—in an I-know-this-stuff-too reference to the way businesses depreciate capital equipment based on its useful life. House Republicans wanted to make the useful life shorter, effectively raising the amount you could write off.

The President was now thoroughly lost. "What are you talking about?" he barked at Rove.

Hubbard moved to smooth things: "This should wait for a time when we do major tax reform."

"Glenn thinks that a deficit of $200 billion pushes up interest rates by just three basis points [or .03 percent]," Josh Bolten interjected, bringing things back to the key issue of whether the dividend tax cut was affordable.

"That's right," Hubbard said. Sitting next to him, O'Neill shook his head. Greenspan and he had been running tables on the effects of deficits for years; that figure was wildly low.

Bush waved his arm dismissively.

"Hold on. We're betting that revenue streams come back with

growth and that we can hold the line on spending," he said, edging toward the core issue of supply-side growth versus deep deficits. Then he stopped and went in a new direction. "This focus on the top rate, is it a high priority? Again, won't the high end benefit most from the double-taxation elimination?"

No one seemed to want to reply. Eliminating the double taxation is a benefit heavily weighted to those who hold stock; the more stock held, the greater the benefit. A total elimination of the dividend tax was already being estimated to cost nearly $400 billion over ten years.

Of course, the "high end" was the "base"—the income distribution of the proposed cuts was largely a political calculation searching for an economic rationale. Those justifications had already been offered.

After a noticeable, pregnant pause, Dan Bartlett moved back to politics. "We are hearing from governors about state budgets."

Andy Card said, "We need a quick payoff, Mr. President."

Hubbard was intent that they not forget what had brought them here: "Elimination of the double taxation will boost stock prices and repair balance sheets."

Card jerked things back: "There is excess capacity, so why do we want to boost investment?"

O'Neill was pleasantly surprised. "Mr. President, the Business Round Table of the country's leading CEOs says the focus should be on boosting consumption demand. Their warehouses are full. They need a boost in demand to clear away inventories. I'm not sure that a tax cut that benefits mostly wealthy investors, many of whom will just push these gains into savings, will do much for demand."

Bush nodded. He was in a cul-de-sac. The ideology of ongoing tax cuts seemed to make less sense when certain economic realities were considered. Finally he spoke, haltingly. "The dividend tax cut could repair corporate balance sheets," he said, feeling his way, "and that's a kind of growth package, isn't it?" O'Neill was thinking that this is true only if you believe that companies will increase their spending on capital goods, even if demand remains sluggish, because their stock has risen. You also have to be certain the proposal would have that effect on the markets, a very long string of imponderables.

Hubbard rushed to the President's aid. "Households who desire to save more can do so through higher stock prices."

Bolten attempted closure: "I think we have agreement on the components. Now, how big should the package be? How much extra should we allow for so we have something to give back in the legislative process?"

The President didn't seem quite ready to close. "Didn't we do the investment package already? What would you rather have? We went through this last year, are you telling me we did it wrong?" The "investment package" was what they often called the 2001 tax cut, which had investment incentives for small business and rate cuts for the high-end "investment class."

"There are headwinds," Hubbard said.

"Not additional headwinds," Bush countered. "They can say, 'They did it twice and it didn't work.' Why do we play our hand now, negotiate against ourselves? I want to stay with principle."

This seemed to be a cue to Rove. Trying to discuss the basics of fiscal policy had left the room in tatters. Karl moved to tactics. "We want to dictate the debate, Mr. President. Not be too specific out of the box. That is a prescription for piling on; we have to have something to trade."

Daniels, still looking to redeem himself for his earlier deficit hawk comments, jumped to support Rove: "I suggest a $50 billion package—$50 billion a year—and that we go on the offensive, including accelerating the rate cuts, and expensing, and dividends."

The President seemed relieved, as though the key issues had been considered. "Thank you for all the briefing materials, this was good research. So when do we roll this out?"

"You are speaking in Chicago on December 10," Lindsey said. Bush looked surprised. "That's news to me."

Rove leaned toward the President. "Sir, that's not scheduled yet, but it is important to move earlier rather than later. The Democrats are coming out with a plan."

Then Ari Fleischer, seeing that matters had moved safely from the *whys* to the *hows*, summoned an overall precept, one of the administration's guiding principles. "Perception lags reality," he said importantly.

O'Neill looked on astonished. Rove and Fleischer and the others rarely spoke this way around the centrist Treasury Secretary. Maybe this meant they didn't care anymore what he heard. Not a great sign.

"Democrats will say we don't care about the middle and bottom, but these class arguments work less and less," Fleischer added. "We should do the right package and roll out in early December."

Throughout the meeting, Hughes had sat back, observing. She was now a consultant, traveling every few weeks from Austin to Washington, and not in on the White House's day-to-day workings. But she still carried clout, as the only one with weight equal to Rove's. She eased in: "Will the announcement of a package boost Christmas spending?"

"Yes, this could be important for consumer confidence," Hubbard said.

O'Neill shook his head. "The truth is nobody knows."

The President was absently watching the back-and-forth. He was thinking of something else.

"What are we doing on compassion?" Bush asked.

No one answered.

The President seemed to get agitated. "Well, you know . . . do you know what the unemployment rate is?" he said, raising his voice. "It is 5.7 percent! There are a lot of presidents who have had to confront much higher unemployment. This argument that the economy is bad does not resonate with voters. This is all posturing . . . that is why we did so well in the midterm elections. . . ."

Rove laughed. It was coming together—it was as if the President had caught a strong wind, his sails now filled. Another massive tax cut proposal was ahead. "So, we should accelerate the rate cuts and not tax dividends twice? . . ." Rove said.

Then, it was just the two of them, talking to each other. Bush was emboldened. "I can figure this out! We did well in the elections because the economy isn't so bad. What are the optics of this? How specific do we need to be on this proposal?"

Hughes, whose July departure to spend more time with her family was also due to exhaustion from her role as pragmatic counterweight to the ideological Rove, stopped the proceedings. "But there is uncertainty in this economy," she said with her usual bull's-eye candor. "Real uncertainty that this won't solve."

She didn't even have to say the word: Iraq. The administration's drive to justify a war in Iraq had cast a pall over the economy since the previous summer. The lines had crossed. It was something no one wanted to talk about. Businesses were frozen, capital investments had flatlined, people were tightening belts and storing their cash like canned goods in the bomb shelter. The two cherished ideologies of the administration—ongoing tax cuts on the domestic front, and the doctrine of "preemption" in foreign affairs—"were both big, sweeping ideas that were in collision with reality," O'Neill recalled thinking. Now they were also in collision with each other.

Bush stopped in midstride and looked hard at Hughes. He was silent for a moment. "The economic uncertainty is because of SEC overreach," he said pointedly. Directly across the table. O'Neill couldn't quite believe what he was hearing—SEC overreach? No wonder the White House had backed off from the toughest medicine for crooked executives and eventually ceded the corporate governance debate to Congress. How, though, could the President believe that the largely overwhelmed SEC had any significant effect on the vast U.S. economy?

But Bush wasn't finished.

"And look," he said after a moment. "Until we get rid of Saddam Hussein, we won't get rid of uncertainty."

Everyone was quiet. The President looked up and down the table, and then at Cheney, gazing at them from the screen in the breakfront from an undisclosed location.

"Good, what I am hearing is that we roll out in mid-December," President Bush said as he began to stand.

Rove looked at the President with pride. "Stick to principle," he said.

On O'Neill's left, Daniels was still of two minds. "Not a typical Republican package," he muttered. "Definitely not."

. . .

OVER THE COMING WEEK, O'Neill thought often of that extraordinary meeting in the Roosevelt Room, its haphazard, improvised quality, the way portentous issues had been raised and spun and tossed about, untethered from the weight of their consequences. "That's what you get without Brandeis briefs," he thought, "without the hard factual analysis that allows you to make informed judgments about the worth of various proposals, about what you can reasonably expect, about what is known. You just can't balance the competing ideas of how to govern a country this size without that. Do we need stimulus, and will this provide it? How much does it cost? How much can we afford? What are our goals? What are the best-case— and worst-case—scenarios? I think of a meeting like that, with so much at stake. . . . It's like June bugs hopping around on a lake."

CHAPTER 9

A TOUGH TOWN

BY EARLY DECEMBER, construction of the next tax cut proposal was well under way—a proposal to eliminate the dividend tax and accelerate provisions of the 2001 tax cut. The cost of those two items would be more than $600 billion over ten years, even using dynamic "supply-side" scoring of the costs. Preparations for an invasion of Iraq had already been reviewed by the President and were well honed. Both preemptive war and deep tax cuts were proving to be ideologies that, as O'Neill often said, "were impenetrable by facts." One fact O'Neill monitored with great care was the deficit, now estimated at more than $200 billion for 2003, even without a full reckoning of the cost of war or the occupation of a vast foreign land. "If we go to war," O'Neill told Richard Clarida, "tack on another $200 billion, at least."

. . .

O'NEILL ENTERED the cabinet room on the snowy morning of December 5 with a big smile. Smiling back was the Ethiopian prime minister, Meles Zenawi.

"How are you, my friend?" Meles said.

The man is a potentate—the ruler of Ethiopia, with a sometimes spotty human rights record—but he and O'Neill had spent four hours together in May on the odd couple tour and made a productive connection. Meles understood water, the politics of water, what fresh water could do for his population, and much more. But during their winding discourse, Meles had talked of power being too concentrated at the top of his regime, and wanting to distribute it to the Ethiopian people. O'Neill had mentioned his favorite though somewhat obscure text, *Beyond Human Scale*, by Eli Ginzberg and George Votja. Meles said he had read it, even citing some passages. The two men had talked about management process late into the night.

Now, six months later, they met in a world far away from the African night. Clustered with the President in a tight little trio, O'Neill recounted the story to Bush about Ginzberg and Votja's book.

Bush, in offering some opening remarks for the group of African leaders seated around the cabinet table, singled out Meles, "who, I understand from my Treasury Secretary, is an extraordinarily well-read man." Meles beamed.

During the meeting, O'Neill offered memories of Africa and talked about what providing water and electricity would do for the continent; then he returned to his office.

His schedule was full, but he felt an odd detachment, as though he'd stepped off a train and were watching the cars speed by. At 1:30 p.m. he went into a meeting with David Aufhauser and Peter Fisher, the President's working group on financial markets. The issues were arcane—assessing Treasury's position in complex negotiations with the SEC over new rule-writing—with half the town's lobbyists, representing every Fortune 100 company with an issue, yammering on all sides. An opportunity had been missed on corporate governance, O'Neill felt. That was the top line of this discussion.

Annabella Mejia ducked her head in. "The Vice President's on the phone."

O'Neill left Aufhauser and Fisher on the couch at the far end of his office and picked up the phone at his desk.

"Yes, sir?"

"Hey, Paul."

"What can I do for you?"

"Paul, the President has decided to make some changes in the economic team."

Pause.

"And you're part of the change."

O'Neill sat down. "I'm perfectly okay with that, Dick. If the President wants to make a change, I'm okay with that." O'Neill looked up at his two trusted lieutenants on the sofa. "Dick, I've got some people in my office. Let me call you back."

He finished up with Aufhauser and Fisher. And called Cheney back.

"We'd really like to do this in an amicable and gracious way. The President thinks you should say you decided to return to private life, and you can decide whatever timing is good for you."

Something about Cheney's voice—his bloodless description of what would now happen, as though the Vice President had merely been an observer of events over the past two years rather than a central actor—compelled O'Neill to stop and think: "There are moments when everything becomes very clear to you, and this was one of them."

O'Neill paused and gathered himself. "You know, Dick, this is fine. The President is entitled to have people around him who he wants around him. What I'd like to do is announce it tomorrow morning. I will submit a letter, indicating my intention to resign and, for transition purposes, that I should stay until the last day of December."

Suddenly he felt very much like himself again. "I'm not willing to say I want to return to private life, because I'm too old to begin telling lies now.

"If I took that course, people who know me well would say that it wasn't true. And people who don't know me well would say, 'O'Neill was a coward—things aren't going so well and he bailed out on the President.'

"I'm perfectly okay with people knowing the truth that the President wants to make a change. That's his prerogative."

There was silence on the other end. Ten seconds passed.

"Okay," Cheney said, and hung up.

O'Neill called Tim Adams into his office and said, somewhat cryptically, that "the President is going to make some changes" and that Tim should be on alert over the coming day.

At 4:15 p.m., the Ethiopian prime minister stopped by.

For a half hour, they talked of Africa. "You are a hero in Africa— you must come back," Meles said.

"Maybe someday I will."

. . .

NANCY WAS SITTING on the couch in the living room when the phone rang.

"Hello?"

"Hi, babe, how was your day?"

It was the first thing he'd said in every phone call since they were kids.

"Oh, just the usual. Went out to see Mother."

"How is she?"

"Oh, she's fine. It breaks my heart how she's losing her short-term memory . . . she's still playing bridge every night until ten."

She was surprised that he was calling so early, just after 5 p.m. He usually waited until about quarter to nine, before her shows, *Frasier, The West Wing*—"which is a complete joke, I know it's not really like that"—and *Everybody Loves Raymond*, got started.

"So, what did you do today?"

"I'm coming home."

"Great. When?"

"No, I mean it. I'm bringing everything. I'm done."

She just sat, speechless. It was something she'd dreamed about, but not this way.

"Did you quit?"

"No, they told me the President wants a new team."

"The President told you?"

"No, Cheney called me. He told me the President said I should say publicly that I wanted to return to private life. Well, I haven't lied in all this time, and I'm not going to lie now. The President can have whoever he wants in there, but if he wants to choose a new team, that's fine with me."

He paused.

"But I'm not going to say 1 quit."

A few times over the fall, O'Neill had expressed his frustrations to Nancy, his doubts about the President and Vice President and where the administration was heading. She had told him not to quit— "especially when your press is bad"—and reminded him that they'd taught the children and grandchildren never to retreat from a challenge.

"I never wanted you to be a quitter, you know that."

He knew that. And he hadn't quit.

Then they just sat there for a moment on the phone, hearing each other breathe.

"Do you want me to come down to Washington?"

"There's no point in that. I'm going to make an announcement in the morning, and then I'm coming home. I'll just drive up in the morning."

Nancy thought for a moment. The logistics, here, were a little puzzling.

"What about all the stuff at Treasury?"

"They'll send it to me."

Then . . . nothing.

"What?" he said. She didn't want to ask—but what the hell.

"What are you doing with the chair?" Of course, she meant the official cabinet chair, with Paul's name and "Secretary of the Treasury" on a brass plate along the back. It's a nice chair, the cabinet chair. Joyce and Don Rumsfeld had one. Lots of their friends did.

"You don't want that damn thing!"

"It's a memento, Paul, a piece of history. For the grandchildren!"

Sitting alone in his Watergate apartment, O'Neill couldn't help but laugh.

"By now, I bet it's sitting in the snow on the White House driveway."

• • •

THERE WERE THINGS to pack, but just for the weekend and, maybe, a few days next week . . . then again, there were closets full of clothes in Pittsburgh. The Watergate apartment—a showcase of gadgets and fine art, a drop-down wall screen, a sound system that could pump up a nightclub, a gourmet's kitchen—felt like an airlock between past and future, a place where light bends. He had never been fired. It was an odd, abrupt sensation—a weightlessness—like being pushed off the high dive. He'd hit the water come morning. And, after two years of noisy, raucous, round-the-clock engagement, the room was silent, all cool, whispery surfaces.

He tapped across the marble floor into the kitchen. There was a Stouffer's frozen dinner, Salisbury steak. He put it in the microwave.

The phone rang. It was Andy Card.

"The Vice President tells me the President would like to meet with you at four p.m. or four-thirty tomorrow. How does that sound?"

O'Neill thought that through—it took only a second. "Andy, I don't think he needs another meeting, and, for sure, I don't need another meeting with him. I think it's too late for that."

Card doubled back. He filled in O'Neill on the broader media strategy. They were getting rid of Lindsey, too, though Larry didn't know it yet. Card said that they'd like to wait, and "we can announce you and Larry together" early the next week. "We don't want to have to do this twice," Card said.

Appearing with Lindsey anywhere, much less at a glorified firing, was about the last thing on earth O'Neill wanted to do. He figured Andy should know that. "Look, Andy, first thing in the morning, I'll have somebody bring over my resignation letter. My intention is that at eight-thirty in the morning I'll announce it, so it'll be out before the markets open."

He hung up, called Tim Adams, told him that he'd be resigning, not to tell a soul, and to call Michele and make sure she was in early the next morning.

Then he poured himself a glass of red wine and sat down on the couch near the window.

. . .

IT WAS COLD and gray in Washington. There were ice floes on the Potomac. It's a tough town, he thought, but more these days about power—its preservation and expansion—than it is about principles or the transforming idea. "Sitting there, I thought about how I expected to find a bigger market for the truth, but it didn't turn out to be right," he remembered. "Even friends in the media were more interested in small conflicts than in what was right or wrong, more interested in the push and shove of personalities rather than in the real conflict over ideologies that was going on inside the administration."

He thought of the "whole notion of preemption versus retaliation. It's a threshold issue. This is a changed world, there's a fork in the road . . . it's profoundly important. It's not my view that says preemption is all wrong . . . it just gives to the appropriator such a weight of responsibility to really be right. And that's where it breaks down, because politics, as it's now played, is not about being right. It's about doing whatever's necessary to win. They're not the same."

And around he went, rethinking and rehashing, as he ate the Salisbury steak, caught a little TV, thought about his resignation letter, and turned in early. He set the alarm for 4:30 a.m. Tomorrow would be a long day.

. . .

MICHELE DAVIS and Tim Adams were in O'Neill's office by 6:30 a.m. He told Michele, his trusted companion throughout, always at his side.

"This is so unfair," she said, her eyes welling up, and she wept as they hugged. Then Ken Dam joined them. O'Neill filled him in. Dam had relocated from Chicago to be deputy and bought a $2.2 million house in Georgetown. His wife was no fan of Bush. He wondered aloud how long the White House would want him to stay. He shook the hand of his old friend. You're better than this, Paul, he said. But, now that the team was assembled, they got to work.

O'Neill gave Davis his resignation letter. "I hereby resign the office of Secretary of the Treasury." One sentence.

"You can't do this," she said, getting over her tears from a moment before. "It's an affront. There is a way this is done. There are certain things you have to say, or their absence will create news."

"I refuse to say I'm leaving to spend more time with my family," O'Neill said, "or any of that bullshit."

She drafted a resignation letter. It was filled with standard resignation prose—about what an honor it has been to serve this President, and how hopeful he was about the country's future, what a great team he'd been a part of—four paragraphs of the stuff. "I'm not doing that," O'Neill said. "Makes me gag."

They compromised.

> Dear Mr. President,
> I hereby resign my position as Secretary of the Treasury.
> It has been a privilege to serve the nation during these challenging times. I thank you for that opportunity.
> I wish you every success as you provide leadership and inspiration for America and for the world.
>
> Respectfully,
> Paul H. O'Neill

The letter was printed and signed, and Tim Adams left to take it over to the White House.

It was 8:20 a.m. The plan was to get the announcement on the wires before the Treasury Market—the exchange for the trading of Treasury bills, bonds, and notes—opened in New York at 8:30.

Precisely as the market opened in New York, Treasury's senior staff gathered in a large conference room often used for press conferences. It was a long-ago-scheduled meeting to plan for the coming year. O'Neill was due to preside, so he did.

He entered the room and went to the podium. Before him was an enormous horseshoe table, with forty or so of the department's top staffers sitting around it, drinking coffee in paper cups, shuffling papers, unaware. Just another morning.

"I know you're assembled for another reason this morning, but there's something I want to tell you. I have the privilege of telling you this news before you get it some other way.

"The President decided he wanted to make a change in the economic team, and I'm part of that change. We're making the announcement right now that I'm resigning from being Secretary of the Treasury and that I'm going to be here until the thirty-first of December to help with transition."

No one seemed to breathe.

"So," he continued, "I wanted to take this opportunity to thank you all for your service and support and for granting me the privilege of working with all of you. I know that this team is the best team that's ever been assembled at the department."

He paused. People were crying. He needed to finish up and get out of the room. "You're a wonderful group that has been trying to do the right thing, and it's important that you keep working to do the right thing for the new Secretary, and also for the people."

Then he slipped down to his office to grab his jacket and briefcase.

Fifteen minutes later, he was at the Watergate, changing into a pair of jeans, as CNBC blared. "President Bush fired Treasury Secretary Paul O'Neill this morning . . ."

O'Neill grabbed his bag and flipped off the TV set—feeling a first, unanticipated wash of freedom. No need to worry anymore about the infernal news cycle and the tyranny of perceptions.

It takes about an hour, really, to get clear of Washington, to hit the gentle hills of western Maryland where tract houses for young families who can't afford to live closer to D.C. give way to fields and not much else.

The Audi TT roadster, a silver two-seater with 230 horsepower and a "governor" to prevent it from stretching out above 156 mph, was revving steady and true, and O'Neill—speeding along without his usual escort of Secret Service sedans—was thinking, oddly, about Christopher Columbus.

There was much to do, up ahead. The Pittsburgh Regional Healthcare Initiative, which he had helped start, was growing in renown—gathering, for the first time, evidence that might drive changes in American health care. And there were wells to dig in Ghana. He thought about how these crusades "could leverage how governments think about what their potential is . . . because someone's efforts have put them to shame."

And that was what brought him to Christopher Columbus.

"If you can imagine Columbus sailing off and coming back with a brown-skinned person and three species that no one ever saw before, people who think the world is flat have to begin reexamining their notions. So, what have you got to do? You've got to go out, search far and wide, and bring back evidence.

"Evidence of what is real—that's what changes everything."

EPILOGUE

THE CITY IS ASLEEP, if fitfully so.

Jets hum through the darkness, invisible. Antiaircraft batteries near the Lincoln Memorial scan the sky. It is March 17, 2003, St. Patrick's Day, and Washington is tense with rumors of a terrorist attack. A wild-eyed farmer slowly chugs toward the Reflecting Pool for a midmorning plunge. National Guard reservists sit in their vehicles, wondering what a terrorist might look like. And bound newspapers, thrown like hay bales across the town, report that the President will give a speech that night about the plan for war in Iraq.

Paul O'Neill is up as early as when he was the Secretary of the Treasury, a job he officially left three months ago. He's trying to sleep a bit more now, but not making much headway.

The clock reads 5:32 a.m. He hears Nancy breathing in deep sleep as he tiptoes to the bureau, grabs a handful of quarters, crosses the marble floor of their apartment at the Watergate, flips on the coffeemaker, and pulls the door shut.

A moment later, his black BMW 740 is on an empty Pennsylvania Avenue.

This is his favorite time of the day—a pleasure he relishes every early morning as he sets off in darkness to buy the papers. He's been doing it since he first came here in the sixties, and at every stop since. At his early-bird news vendor in Pittsburgh, the woman who sells him his papers welcomed him back to town and then asked if she could use him as a reference. She said she was looking for a better gig. He loved that. "Sure," he said. "I'd be honored."

The only time this four-decade ritual had been disrupted was during the past two years. As Treasury Secretary, he lived in a bubble of Secret Service and sealed limousines that rubbed against his go-it-alone style. I'll be just fine on my own, thank you. They'd have none of it. The stack of papers was next to the silver coffee service when he arrived at his office. It felt wasteful to go out and buy his own.

The BMW turns off Pennsylvania onto I Street and then Lafayette Square, across from the White House and its neighbor, the Treasury. He knows too much to wonder about what they're thinking in there. He knows what they're thinking and, for the most part, who is thinking what. He doesn't miss it, and he's not really angry—people ask him that all the time. Disappointed, sure, and troubled about the way the business of governance is being conducted. But, the way he sees it, it's nothing personal.

On Vermont Avenue, he pulls over. There are homeless huddled on the sidewalk. He puts his quarters into vending boxes for *The New York Times, The Washington Post, The Wall Street Journal,* and *Financial Times,* his morning companions. He hasn't seen any homeless people in the past two years, he thinks. Part of the isolation that separates you from what you ought to be seeing. Now he's starting to feel reconnected.

It takes a few weeks to quit a job as complicated as Treasury Secretary, and during that time there were hundreds of calls. Not Bush, Cheney, or Karl Rove, but almost everyone in the cabinet—some who commiserated or confessed unhappiness, others who offered perfunctory farewells; congressional leaders, corporate chiefs, and Republican stalwarts, like Gerald Ford and George Shultz; and then Brent Scowcroft and the men around "41," and they mostly expressed outrage. David Broder of the *Post,* the Washington press corps dean, said the town would miss his straight talk. Bono called. "You're not a politician, that was always your strength," he said, and that O'Neill had "tried to make a real difference but found out it was about winning." The conservative columnist Robert Novak slashed at him—said he was wrong for the job from the start and suggested that the President should have checked O'Neill's ideological credentials before he hired him. *The New York Times* and others said the problem was mostly that O'Neill was hard to keep on message and hadn't effectively communicated the President's economic policy.

Larry Lindsey called in mid-December and asked if O'Neill would "walk with him on the beach"—parlance for a stroll on the long, rounded drive in front of the White House—so the news programs "could get shots of us looking okay, like, we're okay with each other and this whole thing is just fine with us." O'Neill declined politely.

At the American Enterprise Institute annual meeting just before Christmas, its chairman, Christopher DeMuth, looked out on those assembled, including the guest of honor, Dick Cheney, and scolded the administration for "the clumsy and backstabbing manner in which the departures" of both O'Neill and Lindsey were handled. Later, in an interview, DeMuth said the White House was now largely bereft of what he called rigorous "O'Neillian analysis" and that the "circle around this President is smaller and tighter than any we've seen in recent times . . . and I was in Nixon's White House."

On his last official day at Treasury—Friday, December 20—there had been a lot of sneaking around. O'Neill's a tough man to surprise, always checking under rocks and noticing small changes, but they tried anyway. And when he left from the side entrance, he saw them all—hundreds of people lining the drive, there in the dead of winter, clapping like lunatics. Jesus, why did they have to do that? He got in the car and drove slowly through them, waving, his eyes filled with tears.

All that felt fine, comforting, and restorative: the people who knew him still knew who he was and didn't think less of him, even if for the first time he was wondering how he should act in public, what he should or shouldn't say.

In late December, he fretted over an invitation he'd accepted six months earlier. It was for a speech at the Sulgrave Club, an elegant Washington club for women, redolent with the ease and decor of a time when the wives of powerful men didn't work but kept the town lit with graceful energies. He told the ladies that he'd still come. He hadn't died. He'd just got fired.

My wife, Cornelia, is a member of the club, one of the younger ones. Just after New Year's Day she slid a pale blue flyer across the dining room table—"You might be interested in this." I spun it around and read skeptically. "O'Neill? That's impossible," I said. "I thought he was in the witness relocation program."

In fact, the next night, January 7, he was in a cluster of gray-haired men in Brooks Brothers blues on the second floor of the club. The place was jammed. I wedged into the circle and asked O'Neill whether "creating an economic policy was actually in your job description." He laughed at that. "I probably should have checked—they didn't seem to want one of those."

I introduced myself, and we began talking about a story on the White House I'd recently published in *Esquire* magazine that featured John DiIulio, former head of the administration's Faith-based Initiative. A centerpiece of the story was a three-thousand-word memo that DiIulio had sent me, articulating his concerns that the administration lacked even the most basic policy apparatus and was being run by the "Mayberry Machiavellis," his description of the political operation directed by Karl Rove.

O'Neill had heard about the story, it had gotten some coverage, and he was interested, as was a lot of Washington, in what happened on the day of publication in early December. DiIulio received calls from the White House, and using the exact words Ari Fleischer had spoken in that day's press conference, he said his observations for the story—including the sober, carefully worded eight-page memo describing his personal experiences inside the White House—were "groundless and baseless." This prompted a swirl of follow-up coverage about the nature of the White House's calls to DiIulio, a celebrated University of Pennsylvania professor and longtime ideas man for Republicans. *The Washington Post* wondered about "bloodcurdling conversations with former colleagues" at the White House that drove DiIulio into his bout of remorse; commentators opined that the professor would soon be sent to Guantánamo Bay for interrogation as an enemy combatant. It was months before CIA officer Valerie Plame would be outed by the White House as retaliation for the public disclosures by her husband, former ambassador Joseph Wilson, that the administration had misrepresented facts about Saddam Hussein's plans to buy uranium in Africa. People, at this point, weren't sure what to make of this brand of intimidation, of making an *example* of anyone who had the temerity to speak truth to power.

O'Neill became engaged as we talked about DiIulio. "You know, I thought a lot about this guy, about why he would do something as absurd as say that a few thousand words of 'my deep thoughts' are baseless and groundless, and I thought about how it must look from inside his shoes. He's a young man, that's one thing. And these people are nasty, and they have a very long memory. And I guess he had to make a calculation of, you know, what it's worth to be in a fifty-year battle with this gang. What's the price of that? Personally and professionally, can he really afford that?" He looked off in midsentence, as though he'd spotted a pattern in the ornate wallpaper.

He turned back and looked at me intently.

"But here's the difference. I'm an old guy, and I'm rich. And there's nothing they can do to hurt me."

So that brings me to the question I was often asked over the past year as it became known what O'Neill and I were doing. *Does he know what he's getting into?* My response: "Better than any of us."

. . .

THE FARMER in the Reflecting Pool has snarled traffic for hours. He says he's not moving. He has grievances and explosives. Rush hour is a nightmare, and it takes the O'Neills an hour to go three miles from the Watergate to the National Building Museum, where much of the city's ruling class is gathering for the America-Ireland Fund's annual dinner, tonight honoring the world-famous humanitarian Bono.

In the noisy, black-tie scrum, it's hard to say who is getting more attention—the Outcast or the Rock Star. O'Neill moves in a throng of well-wishers—Republican senator Orrin Hatch, Democratic senators Chris Dodd and Pat Leahy. "If you're going to get shot, at least it was for telling the truth," Leahy says. Please call with any good ideas, they say.

Bono and he hug. O'Neill had left a pair of purple glasses Bono had sent him in the car, killing a gag he'd planned for the evening. They talk about someday digging wells in Africa.

They are seated for dinner in a vast room of two hundred tables, as they pick at beef tenderloin and wait for the speeches by Irishmen, like HHS commissioner Tommy Thompson, about other Irishmen, like Ted Kennedy and, of course, Bono.

The chatter dims, and on a big screen up front, the President's face appears. Rather than cancel the evening, the hosts had made audiovisual provision; at 8:00, Bush begins what is, essentially, a declaration of war.

". . . Intelligence gathered by this and other governments leaves no doubt that the Iraq regime continues to possess and conceal some of the most lethal weapons ever devised. This regime has already used weapons of mass destruction against Iraq's neighbors and against Iraq's people. The regime has a history of reckless aggression in the Middle East. It has a deep hatred of America and our friends. And it has aided, trained and harbored terrorists, including operatives of al-Qaeda.

"The danger is clear. Using chemical, biological or, one day, nuclear weapons, obtained with the help of Iraq, the terrorists could fulfill their stated ambitions and kill thousands or hundreds of thousands of innocent people in our country or any other. The United States and other nations did nothing to deserve or invite this threat, but we will do everything to defeat it. Instead of drifting along toward tragedy, we will set a course toward safety. Before the day of horror can come, before it is too late to act, this danger will be removed. The United States of America has the sovereign authority to use force in assuring its own national security."

O'Neill listens to the speech and feels disembodied, as though the world he'd long known was untethered from its moorings. The President is showing conviction, but from what source? A little later, he attempted to make sense of it.

"Conviction is something you need in order to act," he said to me. "But your action needs to be proportional to the depth of evidence that underlies your conviction. I marvel at the conviction that the President has in terms of this war. Amazing. I don't think he has the personal experience . . ." His voice trails off as he distills it one last time. "With his level of experience, I would not be able to support his level of conviction."

. . .

IN THE DAYS and months that followed, O'Neill and I talked often about the war, about what creates conviction, and about the nature of loyalty. He said, "Loyalty and inquiry are inseparable to me," and that may be where he and the President most fundamentally diverged. Bush demands a standard of loyalty—loyalty to an individual, no matter what—that O'Neill could never swallow.

"That's a false kind of loyalty, loyalty to a person and whatever they say or do, that's the opposite of real loyalty, which is loyalty based on inquiry, and telling someone what you really think and feel—your best estimation of the truth instead of what they want to hear."

There's no doubt that this stance—known to those in the White House familiar with the two-year dialogue between Bush and O'Neill—gave the ousted Treasury Secretary a bloodied-but-unbowed luster evident when the two men met again. That was in July 2003, when Gerald Ford was honored with a White House celebration to mark his birthday. O'Neill, one of the trustees of the Gerald Ford Foundation, attended with his wife.

Bush saw him and seemed surprised. "You know, you look great—you really do," the President said as the two men and their wives crowded behind the Fords for a picture. Later in the evening, after Powell and others greeted O'Neill like a lost brother, Bush did it again, snapping around as though startled. "God, you look good," he said.

"How do you expect me to look?" O'Neill responded.

The President may not have been aware that several of his top aides had sought O'Neill's advice over the past year. Rumsfeld called him to the Defense Department to devise ways to restructure the Pentagon and the armed forces. George Tenet called, and O'Neill visited him several times in the year to discuss reorganization of the CIA and how to restore intelligence assets. In late spring, defense officials called O'Neill to ask if he would take a four-month stint in Iraq to help guide the rebuilding of the country.

That last request, O'Neill declined. He was busy with the Pittsburgh Regional Healthcare Initiative, various boards, investment banks, the RAND Corporation, and plans to return to Africa. He is looking to fulfill his promise to bring the water.

Throughout the fall, he watched the federal deficits grow—needlessly, he felt—and the United States become increasingly mired in Iraq. And wondered about the fortunes of his friends in the administration. He felt special affinities for Whitman and Powell, both of whom, he felt, had found themselves in a position much like the one he had encountered. O'Neill describes it as "being in a boat with twenty people, all rowing in one direction, except you." If, he adds, that "boat moves far downstream and you're still in it, you have to ask yourself a hard question about the value of your presence, or about whether your presence in the boat, no matter which way you're rowing, constitutes a compromise of your moral soundness. At some point, all that's left for you to do is jump out."

O'Neill had said he'd never quit. But whether he acted, especially in the fall of 2002, in a way that would force Bush to oust him—whether, in short, his distaste for where he saw the boat heading in both fiscal matters and foreign affairs drove him to confrontation—is a matter that remains unclear to O'Neill himself. He felt, to the end, that it was his duty to ask hard questions, even as he watched some in the administration construe that as a faintness of conviction or even disloyalty.

One day in November, as questions swirled about the justifications for the costly U.S. occupation of Iraq—what they may have been and what Americans were told—he recalled a conversation he and I had on a Sunday afternoon in the spring, a few weeks before the invasion. We sat on the porch at the Watergate, high above the Potomac, which was bursting with the flows of early spring. O'Neill, who had sat through scores of NSC meetings, was deeply fearful about the United States "grabbing a python by the tail, by dropping a hundred thousand troops into the middle of twenty-four million Iraqis and an Arab world of one billion Muslims. Trust me, they haven't thought this through," he said. He was still hoping there would be "a real evidentiary hearing and a genuine debate" before troops were committed. He knew that wasn't likely. "When you get this far down the path," he said after a long silence, "you want to have a heavy weight of evidence supporting you. If the action is reversible, or if a generation can erase its effects, it's different than if you bring the world to the edge of a chasm. You can't go back."

Now, sitting in his kitchen in Pittsburgh in the late fall of 2003, we thought about that statement, about being well past the point where "you can't go back." What, at this point, is the worthwhile position?

There were no easy answers. That day, news stories cited the troubles of O'Neill's old friend Don Rumsfeld, and rumors were growing that he would be the next one out. Nancy picked up the phone to call Don's wife, Joyce, to offer her sympathies.

And O'Neill, again, returned to process. There was a notion he'd embraced in February when he agreed to do this book. It was that the unfinished American experiment in democracy is, brilliantly, a self-correcting process but that some of those self-correcting mechanisms may not be functioning particularly well these days.

I asked him what contribution, at this point, he felt he could make to that self-correction.

"Truth," he said, mostly to himself. "Just truth."

ACKNOWLEDGMENTS

This book, with its grand designs and tight schedule, required the effort of a team.

At Simon & Schuster my editor, Alice Mayhew, the provocateur behind countless notable books, was the driving force behind this project. Her guidance as to both the *whys* and *hows* of this narrative—everything from reporting strategy to prose pacing—was principled and ingenious. Roger Labrie, her artful deputy editor, held everything together, kept us focused on the prize—a finished manuscript in eight months—and showed depth and sensitivity in some tough times, which I will always appreciate.

David Rosenthal, the head of Simon & Schuster, backed the book from birth and arrived on cue to offer insight and wisdom to keep us on target. Beneath him, the promotion, marketing, and artistic teams pulled disparate elements into coherence with inspiring zeal. In all, a harmonic convergence.

And Andrew Wylie, my agent, did what he does so well—everything. He was integral to each turn and twist of this project from inception to publication.

Who can ever fix a starting point?—so much serves as prologue—but a seed for this book was undeniably planted two years ago. That's when my lifelong friend, David Granger, *Esquire*'s brilliant, obstreperous editor, convinced me to write some stories about the Bush White House. I did two of them for *Esquire* with guidance from David and Mark Warren, the magazine's senior editor. When the

White House launched counterattacks, they were at my side, ready to take the hit, ardent and true.

Along with the scores of sources who cooperated—many of them still working at Treasury or leading other parts of the U.S. government—a special thanks is due to Paul's level-headed wife, Nancy, and his faithful assistant for so many years, Linda Murray. They ably reconstituted key moments over the past three years. Nancy, especially, is a match for her husband in honesty and insight and good cheer. Her support was invaluable.

Year to year there is a collection of folks whom I've communed with, laughed with, and relied on. There are too many to mention here. But I'll note a few—Tony Horwitz, Jack Hitt, Marc Silverstein, Dave Murphy, Dan Morris, Tom Green, and Russ Allen were especially helpful in the past months. Friends from my days at *The Wall Street Journal*—the *Journal*'s deputy Washington bureau chief, David Wessel, and Tom Ricks, now at *The Washington Post*—were ready with their reliably rapier insights.

This year, as in the previous three, Dartmouth provided me a summertime refuge, and folks at the college's Nelson A. Rockefeller Center—ably led by my scholarly friend Linda Fowler—offered nourishment and support at a crucial time.

Always in my corner egging me on is an extended crowd of Suskinds—my ever faithful brother, Lenny, his wife, Laurie, and my mother, Shirl; my close kin, the Klines, led by the wise Rob, and Fran, and Irene—and my in-laws, the Kennedys. The latter clan has had an especially challenging year, when they drew upon reserves of faith and humor and legendary toughness to carry on. Their life force has inspired me and shrunk the challenge of writing this book to its appropriately modest size.

Finally, but foremost, there is my partner in all things, my wife Cornelia. Friends will laugh that this project started when she pushed me O'Neill's way and then nod knowingly. It fits with long-standing lore. She does so many things well, is clear-eyed and insightful in ways I'm not, and from time to time casually proffers that I try this or that. Those quiet encouragements—starting with the suggestion two decades back that I might think about becoming a writer—have made all the difference. She is the source of everything lovely and true that has occurred. This book, like everything else, is the product of her trust.

As for my sons, Walter, 15, and Owen, 12—this book is dedicated to them and their faith in inquiry.

INDEX

ABC, 158, 207, 241, 252, 256
Abraham, Spencer, 89, 127, 146, 148,
  154
accounting, 203, 210–11, 223, 231
Adams, Tim, 91, 150, 172, 242, 256,
  269–70, 294, 310, 313, 314
Addis Ababa, 255
Aetna, 65
Afghanistan, 184–85, 186, 187, 189,
  206, 284
  O'Neill in, 286–87, 294, 296
  war in, 191, 198, 204
Africa, 263, 265
  AIDS in, 200, 242, 243, 244, 246,
    251–52, 255, 256–57, 259, 260,
    267–68
  O'Neill and Bono's trip to, 241–56
  O'Neill's memo to GWB on, 258–59
  water in, 245, 253–54, 256, 257–58,
    265–66, 267, 308, 317, 327
African National Congress (ANC), 200
Agnes (Ethiopian woman), 255–56
Agriculture Department, U.S., 89, 148,
  153
AIDS, in Africa, 200, 242, 243, 244,
  246, 251–52, 255, 256–57, 259,
  260, 267–68
Al Barakaat, 198–99
Alcoa, 12, 17–23, 58, 115, 116
  board of directors of, 30, 38, 138
  Governmental Affairs Office of,
    17–18, 21, 23
  Hair's accusations made against,
    18–20
  health care financing at, 16

labor relations at, 22
number of employees of, 20
O'Neill appointed as CEO of, 29
O'Neill's retirement from, 5–6
O'Neill's turnaround of, 6, 19, 20–21
Pittsburgh headquarters of, 2
political action committee of, 17
sale of O'Neill's stock in, 157–59
Alexander, Lamar, 12
Alliance of Automobile Manufacturers,
  147
al-Qaeda, 184–85, 186, 187, 279, 325
Al Taqwa, 198
aluminum, Russia's dumping of, 22
America-Ireland Fund, 324
American Enterprise Institute, 82, 321
American Indians, 146
American Stock Exchange, 191
Anderson, Martin, 34
*Annual Report on Social Security and
  Medicare*, 141
AOL Time Warner, 151, 224–25
Arab-Israeli conflict:
  Clinton administration and, 70–71
  GWB administration and, 70–72, 74,
    76, 288–90
Arafat, Yasir, 70–71, 288–89
Arctic National Wildlife Refuge
  (ANWR), 144, 154
Argentina, 172–75, 243
Armey, Dick, 11, 89, 131–32
Armitage, Richard, 104
Arthur Andersen, 203
Ash, Roy, 169
Ashcroft, Janet, 190

Chris Hani Baragwanath Hospital, 251
Clarida, Richard, 235–37, 277, 307
Clinton, Bill, 23, 25, 35, 58, 70–71,
    107, 126, 175, 217, 261, 288
  economic policy and, 11, 13–14, 37
  military's relationship with, 79
Clinton administration, 12, 22, 34–35,
    57, 82, 104, 107, 115, 132, 145,
    173, 206
  Arab-Israeli conflict and, 70–71, 74
  military reluctance of, 75
CNBC, 29, 64, 91, 193, 207, 275, 316
CNN, 102, 118, 176, 207, 241
coal, 125, 148
Coal-Based Generation Stakeholders,
    146
Coats, Dan, 78
Cogan, John, 34, 43
Cohen, Jared, 105–6
Cohen, William, 77, 82
Collins, Susan, 133
Columbus, Christopher, 317
Commerce Department, U.S., 3, 89,
    104, 153, 203, 235, 236, 276, 277,
    297
Committee for Responsible Budgets,
    65
"compassionate conservatism," 170
Concord Coalition, 13
Congress, U.S., 11, 16, 55, 126, 168,
    268, 285, 305
  GWB's tax cuts and, 131–37, 149–50,
    162
  see also House of Representatives,
    U.S.; Senate, U.S.
Congressional Budget Office, 53,
    132
Conrad, Kent, 60–62, 64, 111, 131
Constitution, U.S., 192
corporate governance, 203–11, 221–34,
    238–39, 305, 308
corporate taxes, 41, 195, 238, 301
Council of Economic Advisors, 29, 33,
    35, 110, 268
Craig, Larry, 118
Crawford, Tex., 271, 278
Crossfire, 102

Cuba, 192
Cutter, W. Bowman, 22

Dam, Ken, 111, 137–41, 197, 204, 224,
    280, 314
Daniels, Mitch, 68, 69, 110–11, 131,
    169, 218–20, 234, 261, 263, 283,
    295, 298, 300, 303, 306
Darman, Richard, 12
Daschle, Tom, 8, 156–57
Davis, Michele, 89–90, 91–93, 95, 106,
    134, 150, 161, 193–94, 232, 234,
    262, 269–70, 272, 273, 275, 313,
    314–15
"days inventory," 38
debt, long-term, 14
  see also federal debt
Defense Department, U.S., 3, 12, 81,
    83, 84, 160, 187, 326
  Office of Net Assessment of, 79
  Rumsfeld's deputies at, 75
  State Department's power struggle
    with, 96–98
  stature of, 4
Defense Intelligence Agency, 96
Defense Policy Advisory Group, 81
Defense Policy Guidance, 78–79
defense spending, 39, 79
  Rumsfeld's memo on, 76–78, 81–82
de la Rua, Fernando, 175
DeLay, Tom, 131
Democratic National Committee, 158
Democratic Party, 3, 11, 13, 16, 40,
    100, 131, 136, 144, 261, 276, 304
  GWB's tax cuts and, 111
  O'Neill's comments on, 90
  Senate balance of power and, 9,
    162
  in 2002 elections, 285–86
DeMuth, Christopher, 321
Denver Post, 271
DiIulio, John J., Jr., 170–71, 322–23
directors, boards of, 222
disaggregation, 59
dividends, double taxation of, 274–75,
    277–78, 281–82, 291, 296, 298,
    300–301, 302, 307

Stephanopoulos, George, 252–53,
  256–57
Stevenson, Richard, 107
stock market, 46, 138, 193–94, 210
suicide bombers, 74
Sulgrave Club, 322
Summers, Lawrence, 171–72, 173
supply-side economics, 13, 33, 43, 51,
  55, 282, 298, 299–300, 307
Supreme Court, U.S., 2000 election
  and, 3, 7
Syria, 74, 84, 160

Taliban, 184–85, 204
Tamale, 245, 249
tariffs, 22
task forces, reporting requirements for,
  145–46
tax code, 49–50, 54
tax credits, 54, 90, 131, 155–56, 163
tax cuts, of GWB, 98, 107–8, 129, 268,
  280
  as campaign promise, 15–16, 27–28
  conditionality and, 111–12, 117
  Democrats and, 111, 131
  as economic stimulus, 49–50, 66–68,
    111, 136–37, 194, 236, 277,
    283–84, 300
  Greenspan's position on, 40–42,
    45–46, 48–49, 51, 60–64, 65,
    66–67, 68–69, 93, 112, 118, 131,
    133, 135, 136, 162
  Lindsey's OTA memo and, 67–70
  as loyalty issue, 28, 48–49, 53,
    67–70
  O'Neill's compromise with centrist
    coalition on, 130–37, 149–50
  O'Neill's position on, 28, 40–47,
    49–52, 53–58, 64–66, 67, 68–69,
    90, 111, 117–18
  priority of, 28, 45–46, 47
  second round of, 194, 277, 286, 291,
    299–306, 307
  signing of bill for, 162
  size of, 28, 34–35, 39, 41, 49, 111,
    131–34, 161
  tactical importance of, 117–18

wealthy as beneficiaries of, 55, 90,
  112, 299
  see also triggers, GWB's tax cuts and
tax cuts, of Reagan, 10–11, 13, 41,
  51
taxes:
  level of, 41
  revenues from, 138, 261, 276,
    282
  see also specific taxes
tax hike, of GHWB, 12–13, 17, 21
tax rebate, 137, 139, 149–50, 161,
  163–64
Taylor, John, 34, 243, 288, 290
Temple Mount, 71
Tenet, George, 186, 187, 189, 190, 191,
  326
  in NSC meetings, 70, 72–75, 76, 85,
    160–61, 185
terror, war on, 288
  declaration of, 196
  financial investigations in, 180–81,
    186, 189, 191–93, 196–97, 198–99,
    204
  planning of, 186–91
Texas, 80
  Cheney and GWB as residents of,
    192
  GWB as governor of, 16, 34,
    100–101
Texas A&M, 248
Thompson, Tommy, 324
Tokyo, 176
Torricelli, Robert, 133
toxic waste, 98
trade:
  global liberalization of, 77
  steel tariffs, 58, 213, 216–21, 238
  wars, 22, 57
Trade Promotion Authority, 217,
  219
Transportation Department, U.S., 89,
  153
Treasury Department, U.S., 35, 83, 84,
  92, 108, 138, 145, 154, 173, 224,
  244, 281
  chief departments of, 64

ABOUT THE AUTHOR

RON SUSKIND was *The Wall Street Journal*'s senior national affairs reporter from 1993 to 2000 and won the Pulitzer Prize for Feature Writing while working there. He has recently attracted national attention with his groundbreaking articles about the Bush White House. Suskind, who writes for *Esquire*, *The New York Times Magazine*, and other national publications, appears frequently as a correspondent on PBS and network news. He is the author of the best-selling and critically acclaimed *A Hope in the Unseen* and is a distinguished visiting scholar at Dartmouth College. He lives in Washington, D.C., with his wife and two sons.